At the Threshold of Liberty

THE JOHN HOPE FRANKLIN SERIES IN
AFRICAN AMERICAN HISTORY AND CULTURE
Waldo E. Martin Jr. and Patricia Sullivan, *editors*

TAMIKA Y. NUNLEY

At the Threshold of Liberty

Women, Slavery, and Shifting Identities
in Washington, D.C.

The University of North Carolina Press *Chapel Hill*

This book was published with the support of a grant from Oberlin College.

© 2021 The University of North Carolina Press
All rights reserved
Set in Arno Pro by Westchester Publishing Services
Manufactured in the United States of America

The University of North Carolina Press has been a member
of the Green Press Initiative since 2003.

Library of Congress Cataloging-in-Publication Data
Names: Nunley, Tamika, author.
Title: At the threshold of liberty : women, slavery, and shifting identities
    in Washington, D.C. / Tamika Y. Nunley.
Other titles: John Hope Franklin series in African American history and culture.
Description: Chapel Hill : University of North Carolina Press, [2021] | Series:
    The John Hope Franklin series in African American history and culture |
    Includes bibliographical references and index.
Identifiers: LCCN 2020022824 | ISBN 9781469662213 (cloth ; alk. paper) |
    ISBN 9781469662220 (pbk. ; alk. paper) | ISBN 9781469662237 (ebook)
Subjects: LCSH: African American women—Washington (D.C.)—Social
    conditions—19th century. | African Americans—Legal status, laws, etc.—
    Washington (D.C.) | Social stratification—Washington (D.C.)—History—
    19th century. | Washington (D.C.)—Race relations—History—19th century.
Classification: LCC E185.93.D6 N86 2021 | DDC 305.8009753—dc23
LC record available at https://lccn.loc.gov/2020022824

Cover illustrations: Portrait of Elizabeth Keckly (courtesy of the Moorland-Spingarn Research Center, Howard University Archives, Howard University, Washington, D.C.); map of Washington, D.C. (courtesy of the Library of Congress Geography and Map Division and Wikimedia Commons); vintage wallpaper pattern © iStock.com/Surovtseva.

Portions of chapter 6 were published in a different form as "'By Stealth' or Dispute: Freedwomen and the Contestation of American Citizenship," in *The Civil War and the Transformation of American Citizenship*, ed. Paul D. Quigley (Baton Rouge: Louisiana State University Press, 2018).

For Barbara Spiga, Lewis Nunley Sr.,
and Kim Micha

Contents

Illustrations and Map

Acknowledgments

Many generous people and institutions made this book possible. The American Association of University Women and the Oberlin Faculty Research Grant funded a yearlong fellowship that awarded me the resources and time to complete this project. At the National Archives, Robert Ellis and the library staff were particularly helpful during the early stages of my research. I also enjoyed many trips to Moorland-Spingarn at Howard University, the Historical Society of Washington, D.C., and the Library of Congress. These institutions do the important work of preserving and making available the documents that support this book, and I'm so glad I discovered these stories at such wonderful libraries.

At Miami University, Rodney Coates became a mentor who helped me discover my passion for research. After Miami, I had the privilege of working with the late Manning Marable, who convinced me to study history. These two scholars gave of their time and energy to mentor and encourage me to pursue a career in the academy.

Many scholars paved the way for the study of race in early Washington. For their work on African Americans in D.C., I'm indebted to Letitia Woods Brown, Constance McLaughlin Green, Kate Masur, Derek Musgrove, Chris Myers Asch, Robert Harrison, James O. Horton, Lois Horton, Mary Beth Corrigan, Stanley Harrold, William Thomas III, Kwame Holmes, and Treva Lindsey. I had the good fortune to cross paths with scholars who offered helpful feedback at conferences or generously took time to discuss my work. These scholars include William Thomas III, Kate Masur, Jennifer Morgan, Annette Gordon-Reed, Corinne Field, Pier Gabrielle Foreman, Martha Jones, Adrienne Davis, Alan Taylor, Cheryl Finley, Christina Sharpe, Laura Edwards, Stephen Kantrowitz, Tera Hunter, Dylan Penningroth, Marisa Fuentes, and Leslie Harris. For reading different chapters and offering their insights, I'd especially like to thank Gregory Downs, Lori Ginzberg, and Carol Lasser. They made themselves available at a critical point of revision, and I will forever be grateful for the time they took to seriously consider my work.

The Scholars Workshop at the Omohundro Institute of Early American History and Culture gave me an opportunity to share earlier versions of the book. Karin Wulf, Joshua Piker, Nick Popper, and Nadine Zimmerli gave expert advice and their generous support of the manuscript. They encouraged me to reframe the chronology of the project and helped me with the development of the first chapter. The Bright Institute at Knox College gave me the space and resources to strengthen my research and pedagogy. In addition to providing support for the completion of this book, they have become a vital source of scholarly community. Thank you, Catherine Denial, for your vision, brilliance, and humanity.

I'd also like to thank David Kamitsuka, the dean of the College of Arts and Sciences at Oberlin, for the resources to finish the book and my Oberlin colleagues for their sustained support. My colleagues in the History Department at Oberlin model a commitment to excellence in scholarship and teaching that I hope to emulate. Renee Romano, Leonard Smith, and Annemarie Sammartino served as chairs of the History Department and graciously entertained many panicked and spontaneous questions about the publication process and academia more generally. Pablo Mitchell, A. G. Miller, Ann Sherif, Gina Perez, Wendy Kozol, Shelley Lee, Cindy Chapman, Clayton Koppes, and Meredith Gadsby have been wonderful mentors throughout my time at Oberlin.

Writing a book about African American women can be an isolating enterprise. I'd like to thank the following scholars for their body of work and collegiality: Christian Crouch, Courtney Joseph, Catherine Adams, Kellie Carter Jackson, Vanessa Holden, Erica Ball, Jessica Marie Johnson, Elizabeth Pryor Stordeur, Patricia Lott, Cynthia Greenlee, Deirdre Cooper Owens, Yveline Alexis, Pam Brooks, RaShelle Peck, Fredara Hadley, and Stephanie Jones-Rogers. Christian Crouch, Courtney Joseph, and Catherine Adams became not only cherished colleagues over the years but dear sisters. Danielle Terrazas Williams has been a treasured source of friendship, good humor, and wisdom at an early, yet pivotal, moment in our careers in the professoriate. I can't imagine the past five years without Danielle, someone who has been both a lovely colleague and an inspiring scholar.

Thavolia Glymph, Gary Gallagher, and Elizabeth Varon are what I call a dream team of mentors. They've read numerous versions of the manuscript and generously given of their time to provide feedback that strengthened this book. Every time I received comments and critiques, I gained new insights and learned important lessons about the work we are privileged to do. They are exceptional scholars and mentors, and words inadequately capture how much their support has meant to me.

Chuck Grench is a superb editor, and working with him has been a highlight of my career. At the University of North Carolina Press, Mr. Grench and

Dylan White persevered through various phases of review and revision, and I appreciate their unwavering support of the project. Thank you to the readers who painstakingly read through the manuscript and offered detailed feedback and corrections. The book is a better one because of the outstanding editorial staff at the University of North Carolina Press and readers who devoted time to make suggestions.

I experienced the highs and lows of academic life with my dear friend and sister, Tanya Nichols. She provided encouragement and support both personally and professionally in the years it took to write this book. Tim and Daisy Lovelace provided a safe haven during graduate school, and I'm so glad that we've been in each other's lives ever since. Their support and friendship have sustained me through many difficult and exciting moments. Daisy has become a sister to me, and I can't imagine life without our friendship. Connie Chipp, Jocelynn Hubbard, Christina Hagenbaugh, Daniel May, and Lydia Osborne have anchored me in ways I never knew I needed. Thank you. Your friendship is a gift.

Family means everything, and for their patience and willingness to listen to me rant about black women and self-making in the nineteenth century, I am grateful to mine. Marques, Ronald, and Colleen started this academic journey with me and sowed fervent prayers, love, and encouragement in my life for the past two decades. Thank you to Grandma Virginia, who was always willing to share stories about her life in the Commonwealth over the most delicious apple pie and percolated coffee. She will always be my favorite librarian. I lost my grandma Connie as I revised this book, and her good humor and pride in my work kept me motivated at various stages of writing. My siblings, Angela and Lewis, are a wellspring of unconditional love and exceptional humor, and they kept me well fed with their delicious cooking. I feel the strongest sense of place and belonging when I'm spending time with them and my five nieces and nephews.

Nari arrived in my life when the book was just an idea. Eight years later, and I remain forever in awe of her and I'm so very glad to be her mom. She graciously put up with long bouts of writing and waited for me to wrap up so we could build a small village of wuzzies and collect worm specimens for her homemade lab. Ambrose lovingly supported me through the most challenging phases of revision. I am grateful for his expert selection of the perfect snacks, for showing a genuine interest in my research, and for always seeing the bright side when I struggled. Ambrose, thank you for being my partner in life and for lovingly stepping in when I needed to immerse myself in writing. No one is more relieved that this book is finished than Ambrose and Nari.

My godmother, Barbara, inspired a love of writing, and our regular break-fasts, outings at the art museum, and concerts at Severance Hall gave me a much-needed respite from work. My father filled my world with black history books at a young age, and his unwavering support made my journey through academia possible. My mother, and the story of her life, inspired the work ethic and perseverance that writing a book demands. My parents are my foundation, and this book is for them.

At the Threshold of Liberty

Introduction

Nobody forced me away; nobody pulled me, and nobody led me; I went away of my own free will; I always wished to be free and meant to be free.
—Jane Johnson

I have thought though men enslaved the body they cannot enslave the mind and prevent it from thinking.
—Mary Brent, student at the Miner School

Rightful liberty is unobstructed action according to our will within its limits drawn around us by the equal rights of others. I do not add "within the limits of the law" because law is often but the tyrant's will, and always so when it violates the rights of the individual.
—Thomas Jefferson

On August 16, 1821, Thomas Tingey, commandant of the Washington Navy Yard, placed a notice in the *Daily National Intelligencer* of a slave's escape in Washington, D.C. Earlier that week, Surrey, an enslaved woman he owned, walked out of the kitchen in his residence and beyond the wharf into the residential area of the District and did not return. By the time the advertisement appeared, Surrey had become Sukey Dean—a fugitive within the nation's capital and a free black woman available for hire. Tingey explained in the notice that Surrey had changed her name to Sukey Dean and that she most likely continued to seek employment as a domestic with a local family after having fled the home of one employer when she learned Tingey had discovered her whereabouts. At this point, Sukey Dean disappeared from the available historical record. And yet Surrey was henceforth Sukey—the person she had envisioned, fashioned, and named before her escape that summer of 1821.[1]

According to census records, Sukey had been with the Tingey household at least since 1790 when the family resided in Philadelphia. By the time of her escape, she was one of six enslaved people forced to serve the Tingey household. Sukey's frequent appearance in family correspondence reveals a history of everyday defiance and, more specifically, her plans to wield her own authority over her life. Her escape was the culmination of that history. Tingey's wife, Margaret, had threatened to sell her just before they moved to

Washington, D.C. According to Margaret, Sukey declared her opposition to the move. "I won't go anywhere but where I chose a master, and you cannot oblige me," she reportedly told her mistress. Sukey stayed with the family for twenty more years before she decided to leave.[2] Perhaps she decided to remain for twenty years because she was also raising children? We know that Sukey bore children within the Tingey household. We know very little, however, about their lives, the conditions of life and work in the household, their social networks within the District, or whether they remained with the Tingeys after Sukey left. What is clear is that their mother maintained very specific ideas about her desired life, identity, and work environment. Sukey's own assertions about her choices and obligations developed decades before she escaped.

At the Threshold of Liberty tells the story of women like Sukey—African American women who made extraordinary claims to liberty in the nation's capital in ways that reveal how they dared to imagine different lives. Self-making as it appears in the actions of African American women helps us to consider the possibilities of self-definition, even if black women never acted on these visions in the form of resistance. For instance, Sukey's decisions allow us to recognize the manner in which enslaved women plotted, dreamed, imagined, and created ideas about themselves, as well as the people they knew, and the places in which they lived decades before any evidence of resistance. In other words, Sukey confirms for us the very existence and palpability of black women's sense of self in ways that make this less a story about resistance and more a story about what it means to assign meaning to, and understand the possibilities of, their worlds. This is not to undermine the power of resistance; indeed, this entire book rests on the evidence of resistance to explore the possibilities of self-definition. But what if our conversation is about how women of African descent navigated life in the face of a society built on the bondage and exploitation of black women? Do continuities of survival exist to help us understand how African American women survived and survive the exigencies and "afterlives" of slavery, to use the term of Saidiya Hartman? If so, what does it mean to define and preserve a sense of self in a society that supported a narrow definition of what it meant to be a black woman? This process of self-definition or invention required strategic navigation of the District of Columbia, its institutions, local labor economy, laws, communities, and neighboring counties.

Here, I use the term *navigation* to describe the ways African American women responded to the conditions of slavery, fugitivity, freedom, and refuge. Both the physical and figurative navigation of the capital required an understanding of its laws, its customs, and the people who shaped black women's everyday encounters and experiences. Even in instances in which women strategically and carefully navigated life in the capital, they faced a significant degree of unpredictability. In other words, this is not a journey to or through a promised land or a triumphal narrative. The conditions they experienced were rooted in what Cedric Robinson terms "racial capitalism" and the historiographical conversation about the relationship between slavery and capitalism and the persistent subjugation of black people in American labor economies.[3] The strategies of navigation and invention that African American women employed manifested under conditions of bondage, freedom, and legal emancipation. Acknowledging the presence of racial capitalism underscores the unfinished work of liberty in and out of slavery. Similarly, Hartman complicates our national discourses about the egalitarian possibilities of self-making to help us think through the ways individual autonomy leaves the work of addressing inequality to African Americans.[4] A constant thread in the story of these women who experienced various degrees of freedom and unfreedom, from the formation of the capital to the American Civil War, is the premise that the struggle for liberty remained incomplete. The efforts of these women to search for work, freedom, education, income, and citizenship expose a persistent tension between the racial and gendered underpinnings of capitalism and the limits of liberalism. *Liberty*, then, is a term conceptualized and reconstituted again and again by African American women in ways that push against the limits of Western liberal democracy.

In this collection of stories, the knowledge, actions, and ideas of these women are uncovered, not with the intention to assign agency, but to explore what African American women's strategies of self-making and navigation tell us about how they envisioned their lives and their identities. They crossed geographic borders to live free, litigated freedom suits, made entreaties of the federal government to retrieve family members, developed informal leisure economies to earn a living, and performed the tireless work of uplift to improve black life in Washington. Navigation required an understanding of black women's own proximity to race, law, and gender and could be best described as a process of traversing the dynamic pathways between their social position and the lives they desired to create beyond that position. Their experiences reveal diversions and unanticipated circumstances that required improvisation. The ability to improvise in their navigation of Washington shed light on the different strategies that shaped the contours of self-making. Thus, navigation was also about how African American women gave the capital its shape as a possible site of liberty and identity formation. Self-definition coincided with navigation; they were critical processes and strategies that black women employed in their quest for liberty.

Black women's early nineteenth-century experiences of invention and navigation reveal how they created and sustained a constant tension between bondage and the possibilities for liberty. This tension reflected the ways black women actively exposed the contradictions between slavery and the governing ideals of the nation. The realities of race- and gender-based repression were at odds with black women's desires for the freedom to decide how and with whom they lived their lives. These clashes confounded the symbolism of Washington, D.C., as the young country took center stage as an emblem of liberty.[5] The conflicts waged by black women occurred anywhere from the intimate realms of households and schools to the very public realms of the courts, streets, and government in ways that intensified over the course of the Civil War era.[6] By the beginning of the Civil War, black women appealed to local government agencies to verify the reach and application of new emancipation laws. Moreover, black women's actions during the war were novel to the degree that emancipation legislation positioned them to appeal directly to the federal government. Wartime emancipation, however, did not mark the beginning of black women's liberty claims.

From the founding of the capital to the American Civil War, a history emerges of black women and girls, enslaved and free, who developed their own ideas about liberty and, accordingly, traditions of self-definition that help us understand how they survived and lived in a slaveholding republic. They were driven by the ideals of their time and expressed their desires to govern their own lives without the oversight, force, and violence administered by others. Sukey not only conveyed her desires to live and labor on her terms, but she also assumed her own name. These pronouncements about where and for whom she'd work and the adoption of a new name echo the rituals of liberty. Evidence of self-making peppered area newspapers and correspondence to put locals on notice that black women in Washington actively confounded ideas locals conveyed about them. Furthermore, women and girls who were legally free navigated social norms organized by black codes and local custom. For instance, learning to read and write was not illegal in Washington, but black girls attended school at the risk of mob violence and public ridicule. "I have thought though men enslaved the body they cannot enslave the mind and prevent it from thinking," declared Mary Brent, a student at Myrtilla Miner's School for Colored Girls. Without any assurance that they'd be protected from physical violence, black girls trained as teachers with a determination to make education available to as many African Americans as possible. When local labor prospects foreclosed opportunities for more income, flexibility, and favorable work conditions, black women developed their own entrepreneurial economies. They rented plots of land and sold their produce at the city market, they sewed for wealthy clientele, and some considered a foray into the sex and leisure economy. Freedom did not always correspond with liberty.[7] Local codes and norms supported by a society organized around race and gender meant that black women's desires to pursue life on their terms, with the ability to exercise certain rights, were constrained by such factors. Even when black women became legally free, avenues toward earning a living, gaining an education, or merely surviving did not always appear within reach for them. Moreover, the experiences that unfold show improvisation as a strategy of self-making, the manner in which black women adapted, responded, and shifted their lives and the lives of others in the face of unpredictability. Thus, struggles for liberty appeared in various forms and under different conditions in the lives of African American women in Washington, D.C.

In the nation's capital, conversations about liberty and bondage abounded in public discourse and debates. The promise of the revolution and Thomas Jefferson's definition of "rightful liberty" saturated the identity of the republic even as the new government fell far short of making liberty available to everyone. The nation's founders looked for ways to develop the capital into a beacon of republican virtues, but instead, the city mirrored all of the troubling paradoxes that plagued a nation rife with unfreedom. With the close of transatlantic commerce in slaves in 1808, Washington became a critical site of the domestic slave trade. Correspondingly, in the first decades of the nineteenth century, enslaved people outnumbered the free black population. Abolitionists organized regional vigilance networks and sent political petitions to Congress with the aim of destroying slavery in Washington. As antislavery and proslavery forces converged in the capital, Congress abolished the local trade with the passage of the Compromise of 1850. The concession did not eradicate the practice in the capital completely, and by the beginning of the war, approximately three thousand enslaved people remained in the city. By the time of the Civil War, the District was the home of primarily free African Americans, but the specter of slavery remained as enslaved women were hired out from neighboring Chesapeake counties. The Civil War placed pressure on the Union government to decide the fate of the millions of African Americans enslaved in the South. In 1862, Washington became the first territory to experiment with emancipation during the war when Congress passed the Emancipation Act and abolished local black codes.[8] Although some residents were relieved that they were no longer implicated in the institution of chattel slavery, they were also vigorously opposed to the idea of African

Americans wielding the rights and privileges associated with liberty. As President Abraham Lincoln did for most of his political career, white locals hoped that black people would leave the country and chart their course elsewhere. But African Americans refused to undo the years of hard work that anchored black life in Washington.

Throughout the first half of the nineteenth century, African Americans worked to elevate their reputation in the capital with their own institutions, organizations, businesses, and lineages of prominent families. At the heart of black Washington were women like Alethia Browning Tanner, who purchased the freedom of several generations of family members, and Elizabeth Keckly, who designed couture gowns for Washington's leading ladies while organizing fund-raisers for refugees. Other prominent women include Jane Johnson, who made national headlines in her escape from slavery, and Harriet Jacobs, who felt called to the capital to help refugees in their transition to freedom. More obscure in the archive, but equally important, are the scores of washerwomen and cooks who worked long hours in the homes of local residents, and the women who wove through the alleys selling sex, leisure pursuits, or simply a room in which to play cards. Their aspirations for a better life become visible through stories of women like Anne Washington, whose mother quietly scraped together enough money from her earnings as a washerwoman to send Anne to Miner's School for Colored Girls. Across class boundaries, women in the District shrewdly assembled their resources to assist fugitives, build businesses, form organizations, and establish schools. In the nation's capital, African American women tried and tested the limits of liberty. They sought to imbue republican ideals of "rightful liberty" with an expansive meaning: not limited to but including legal rights, the freedom to assume a new name, flee bondage and exploitative labor conditions, retrieve kin, or seek an education. They talked about liberty, and thought about it, and formulated plans to see it actuated in their own lives.

Over the course of the first half of the nineteenth century, black women disentangled themselves from bondage using their understanding of the legal, geographic, and social scaffolds that made slavery possible. Yet freedom, black women soon realized, posed its own set of constraints and involved both opportunities and limitations. Indeed, bondwomen, fugitives, refugees, and free women encountered a number of freedoms and unfreedoms shaped by race and gender. The reproductive laws of slavery meant that children inherited the legal status of the mother, further delineating any intimate encounters black women might entertain or be forced into.[9] The gendered organization of labor and compensation created economic constraints for single mothers and limited employment options available to black women regardless of marital status. Additionally, women and girls confronted a society that subjected them to sexualized violence and harassment as they encountered hostile neighborhoods of the District or labored in intimate residential and commercial workspaces without equal protection of the law. The experiences and choices of the women featured in this book varied greatly—yet the weight of race and gender factored into the decisions each of them made. For them, liberty appeared as neither "rightful" nor "unobstructed" in the sense that Jefferson described, and yet they contemplated the possibilities as they initiated their own processes of self-making and navigation.

Through navigation, black women interacted with and created networks that corroborate the presence of a vibrant free African American population. Their experiences emerge in runaway advertisements, abolitionist accounts, and networks of vigilance. These sources uncover individual and broader efforts to realize liberty in a regional frame comprising Virginia and Maryland and, later, Delaware, Pennsylvania, and Canada. William Still's collection of fugitive escapes furnishes the most detailed account of flight by African American women from the District. Still's records center fugitive women as the primary agents in their own liberty and illuminate the interregional and transnational trajectory of their escapes.[10] Additionally, leading free and fugitive African Americans shared their reflections and observations of black life in Washington. The story offered here includes the writings of Paul Jennings, Thomas Smallwood, Elizabeth Keckly, Harriet Jacobs, Henry Highland Garnet, and the pupils of Myrtilla Miner's School for Colored Girls. These individuals appear in histories of Washington, D.C., but this will be the first time that the voices of Miner's students center the stories of black girls in the capital. These African Americans played a vital role in the configuration of Washington as a site of liberty.

In addition to memoirs and letters penned by African Americans in Washington, legal and government documents enrich this study. Court cases and criminal records show instances of enslaved women's legal and extralegal activity. These sources capture some of the ways that the black codes and the court system shaped the legal parameters of black women's claims to liberty. In addition to the court documents in the National Archives, O Say Can You See: Early Washington, D.C., Law & Family, a digital archive of freedom petitions and scholarly analysis of these documents, provides critical insights into black women's legal claims. These women used the courts to petition for their freedom, some faced criminal charges, and others appeared in the records as a result of their attempts to escape. Many court records include reports of women who worked in the sex and leisure economies before and during the Civil War. Studies of Civil War Washington presume the absence of African American women, but I show the ways their lives and labor economies led to regular interaction with soldiers, refugees, and both permanent and transient political residents. Additionally, wartime petitions of refugee and free women show the ways they interacted directly with federal and local government officials to secure their liberty. Black women numbered in the thousands among the overall population of Washington, but given the scope of this study, the sources mined for this book reveal several hundreds of names of African American women, some appearing in lengthy vignettes and others in tantalizingly brief mentions in the documentary record.

The breadth of African American women's experiences in Washington appears in a number of topical and historiographical conversations. To begin, I engage with the robust scholarship that examines race in nineteenth-century Washington, D.C. In *An Example for All the Land*, Kate Masur examines the capital as a laboratory where African Americans made "upstart claims" to test the parameters of equality. These claims became the foundation for recognition of their rights during the Civil War and Reconstruction. In *Washington during Civil War and Reconstruction*, Robert Harrison foregrounds the ways African Americans in Washington participated in their own liberation to understand the reach of federal policies. His "grassroots Reconstruction" approach shows the ways black Washingtonians waged battles to secure their political rights. In *Chocolate City*, Chris Myers Asch and George Derek Musgrove deliver an exhaustive and illuminating study of the ways that race and democracy shaped the social, political, and economic dynamics of the nation's capital. They foreground the city's history of slavery and, building from there, provide a comprehensive examination of the ways that local people wrestled with the momentous shifts that shaped race relations. Stanley Harrold's body of work reveals the numerous instances in which African Americans and white allies worked collectively to mount an assault on slavery. These collaborations fostered a culture of activism that was distinctively interracial. This recent scholarship, and this study, is indebted to the groundbreaking work of Constance McLaughlin Green and Letitia Woods Brown.[11]

In *Secret City: A History of Race Relations in the Nation's Capital*, Green offers one of the first comprehensive studies on race relations in Washington to take seriously the ways that African Americans responded to the dynamics of racism. Not long after Green published *Secret City*, Brown broke new ground with *Free Negroes in the District of Columbia, 1790–1846*, a study that examines the early history of the lives of African Americans and their efforts to build the economic and cultural institutions of black Washington. This critical body of work offers an invaluable compendium from which to explore the ways that race, as well as gender, shaped the lives of African American women in the capital. As the present study shows, an examination of gender helps us understand the contexts in which black women gave meaning and shape to the possibilities of liberty in the nation's capital from its founding to emancipation. It also gives us a sense of the ways that their strategies and experiences disrupt our assumptions about gender norms among enslaved and free black communities. Overall, the scholarship provides a multifaceted foundation from which to build the first study of black women in early Washington.[12] Still, black women's lives in nineteenth-century Washington must be contextualized with an understanding of how slavery worked in the capital.

Slavery shaped the social dynamics of early Washington in important ways. First, the placement of the capital on the Potomac ensured that the culture of Chesapeake slavery formed the legal and social scaffolds of the city. Carved out of the oldest slaveholding states in the country, Washington adopted the laws and customs of Maryland and Virginia at its inception. As the population expanded and the capital became more developed with businesses, residences, industries, and the work of government, the District transitioned from village to southern city. Histories of urban slavery underscore the ways that southern cities were important sites for slave hiring.[13] Hiring or renting slave labor created opportunities for negotiations between the hires and slaveholders unavailable to enslaved people more generally. These negotiations might involve avenues for earning additional income, more flexibility in work hours, time for socializing, and better living quarters that might allow a hire to live independently of white households. For enslaved women, who for the most part performed much of the domestic labor, living quarters primarily kept them in close proximity to white residents. Moreover, the labor of black women remained valuable in the capital. Washington was not only significant for its role in the domestic trade that sold slaves to the Cotton South, but agents took advantage of opportunities to exchange human property within the Chesapeake region.[14] Vulnerability to the slave trade loomed large in the daily lives of African American women in the District. As their labor remained in demand in the midst of these market developments, they were susceptible to sale and abduction.[15] Their experiences allow for a closer examination of the ways that gender, urban slavery, and local economic development intersected in the nation's center.[16]

Critical histories that focus on the lives of enslaved and free African American women have proliferated recently, adding depth and nuance to the rich scholarship about slavery and freedom.[17] Historians have explored enslaved women's responses to slavery, from everyday moments stolen for oneself to violent resistance and flight.[18] Building on scholarship in black women's history, this book explores dimensions of their lives in and out of chattel slavery and what it might look like to center black women's claims to liberty during the transformative events of the nation's capital.[19] Their stories are thematically chronicled in the chapters that follow to trace their experiences in Washington across different social and legal categories and to show how race and gender manifested in the lives of enslaved, free, poor, fugitive, and refugee women. The chapters include a range of shards and some substantive material to begin to understand the worlds of black women in slavery, fugitivity, courts, schools, streets, and the government. Construction of these lives demands the kind of risks associated with filling the gaps of what the sources leave unsaid. Thankfully, scholars before me have offered innovative methodologies from which to take seriously the production of black women's histories in the face of archival scarcity and the violence that such sources produce.[20] The historical record offers glimpses into the world of black women that we may not always anticipate, of lives marked by joy, violence, despair, hope, desire, disappointment, laughter, love, death, and political work. As historian Annette Gordon-Reed explains, the work of writing about enslaved women is an "imaginative enterprise."[21] This book, grounded in a wide range of archival material and secondary literature, is such an enterprise.

From 1800 until 1820, slave traders in Washington capitalized on enslaved women's labor when the Chesapeake tobacco economy declined.[22] Traders were not your typical agents from the antebellum slave market; they were neighbors, tavern owners, widows, farmers, and lawyers. Despite attempts to enshrine the capital as the center of a new country founded on republican tenets of liberty, local commissioners appointed by Congress to advance the economic development of the territory also relied on the labor of enslaved women. The decision to move the seat of the government to the Potomac, and the subsequent imperatives to populate and develop the territory, solidified the continued use of their labor. In chapter 1, I investigate the ways enslaved women were marketed and sold alongside lots of land and frame houses to appeal to potential investors and future residents. Here, we see racial capitalism at work as locals took advantage of the opportunities that came with local commerce in human property. The lives of enslaved women shifted as they were exchanged, rented, and used as currency in an increasingly speculative and expanding market. Black women became attuned to the threats posed by the local slave trade and entertained the prospect of escape.

From the beginning of the capital's existence, enslaved women in Washington and surrounding counties escaped from slaveholders. Historians have argued that enslaved women decided against flight because of their commitments to family and community, and children in particular.[23] Indeed, these women were moved to flee by a number of circumstances and provocations. Their stories, motivations, and modes of self-making appear repeatedly throughout runaway advertisements, vigilance records, and abolitionist literature. Knowledge of their future sale, abusive conditions, their desires to be free, an opportune moment, an encounter with the right networks, or a rebuttal against unmet expectations, among many other reasons, led to escape. Chapter 2 examines the strategies of self-making in the context of fugitivity to show that some women were emboldened rather than inhibited by the obligations of kin in their plans for escape. Enslaved women didn't always have children or husbands to consider, and they set out to shape lives and identities in the free labor market within and beyond the boundaries of Washington. Information gleaned from these escapes shows that black women's navigation of the capital was informed by knowledge of the laws, geography, and interregional networks. As Sukey's story shows us, intraregional flight became a common feature of early national Washington, underscoring the processes of navigation that coincided with the presence of black antislavery networks within the village well before the antebellum abolitionist movement gained momentum. Not all escapes were successful, but the struggles for liberty that black women instigated offer insights about how they envisioned their lives. The ways black women navigated the limits of life within and beyond bondage also materialize in their appearances in the courts.

During these early decades of Washington's history, African American women appeared before the justices of the court to pursue freedom, contest wrongful enslavement, and defend their individual choices. Chapter 3 examines enslaved and free black women's experiences in the courts to explore the opportunities and limits of legal recourse. Brown asserts, "Manumission in the District was always easy, and residence thereafter was allowed."[24] Furthermore, freedom suits based on the status of African American women became increasingly difficult to prove as the courts moved in directions that emphasized the strict interpretation of evidence. No longer willing to accept verbal testimonies that verified the maternal genealogies of deceased women, the courts increasingly foreclosed the possibility of legal freedom inherited through the status of mothers. Both enslaved and free black women appeared before the courts, and to examine the broad legal configurations of their experiences is to see both the emancipatory and restrictive possibilities of the courts. As enslaved women petitioned the courts to challenge their legal status as slaves, nominally free women appeared before the criminal courts for various offenses in ways that underscore the challenges of freedom. The proceedings of these courts reveal the degree to which black women, across a spectrum of legal identities, employed both legal and extralegal measures of self-making. If an enslaved woman won her freedom suit, what kinds of opportunities awaited her in freedom? Free women who appeared before the courts often faced limited economic opportunities, and extralegal activities might yield more viable results. Court proceedings reveal the improvised strategies for survival and self-making that black women employed. The legal institutions of the District, however, did not serve as the only venue in which to explore and defend the possibilities of self-making.

From the founding of the capital, black Washingtonians began the work of building a robust set of religious, civic, and educational institutions. The vibrant African American institutions they created made Washington an attractive place for black migration from other southern states. This was of tremendous importance to black women. As chapter 4 shows, a generation of girls in the capital gained access to education. In antebellum Washington, schools for black girls fostered an ethics of socialization that allowed them to envision themselves in ways that defied the racial and gendered social proscriptions of their time. They formulated ideas about intellectual, spiritual, and political self-fashioning as they voiced convictions that reveal their readiness to assume a position in society not yet carved out for them. But they did not need to propose some radical resolution to the nation's contradictions to draw the ire of locals. Washington residents objected to black girls attending school with violent attacks on them and threats to burn down their schools. White men attempted to intimidate them by forcing them off of sidewalks and calling them "hussies." Even if the law did not explicitly prohibit activities such as reading and writing, the social implications of these activities inspired the violent reactions of a broader white public. For black girls, liberty in the capital came with perilous risk. The mere suggestion of equality was so controversial that the mayor launched a campaign to close their school. Yet black women did not cease using their resources to help create schools and pay the fees to provide an education for their girls. Constrained and limited by economic opportunities, black women and girls labored in enterprising and industrious ways, particularly at the outbreak of war. As refugee women came pouring into the city in search of liberty, the women who helped build Washington's black schools mounted efforts to assist them while others looked for economic opportunities spurred by the war.

The outbreak of war expanded the local demand for black women's labor, but no other line of work made headlines quite like prostitution. Entrepreneurial and extralegal strategies for earning a living made survival possible, and yet they also made black women more vulnerable to violence, arrest, and criminal charges. Chapter 5 examines the bustling streets where black women launched their enterprises and many of them worked in the wartime sex and leisure economy. Prostitution typically appears as both a transgressive and a marginal phenomenon or a theme more suited to disciplines that focus on gender and sexuality. The sex and leisure economy, however, employed thousands of black women during the war, and a history of the nation's capital and African American women's strategies for survival and self-making that did not attend to prostitution would render prostitution generically absent. For women working as prostitutes or proprietors of bawdy houses and gambling dens, the mobilization of soldiers and government workers created a boon of possible patrons. District law did not explicitly ban prostitution, but the acts associated with solicitation and socializing with white men led to a number of arrests and fines. With the world's eyes on wartime Washington, political and military officials regarded black women working in the sex and leisure economy as a nuisance. Indeed, the interracial sex economy plagued the efforts of reformers and military leaders alike to rid the district of the problem. Furthermore, nominally free black women confronted a labor market that bottlenecked them into employment that mirrored servitude. Thus, the wartime sex economy could potentially either undermine or make possible navigation and self-making, depending on the dangers, risks, profitability, and legal dynamics associated with sex and leisure commerce. In addition to anxieties about interracial sex, the war brought changes to the capital that raised concerns about the sheer demographic shifts that came with the influx of soldiers, refugees, and prospects of freedom.

In 1862, Congress passed a measure to emancipate bondpeople in the nation's capital. The "experiment" allowed for the compensation of slaveholders and funds to support the relocation of freedpeople. As Republicans enacted wartime measures that chipped away at slavery, refugee women arrived in the capital and employed their own strategies of navigation as they faced off with obstinate white property owners who made claims to their labors and abducted their children and kin. As scholars have noted, these women responded by looking to the government to affirm their liberty claims.[25] With slaveholders unwilling to relent, even with the possibility of compensation in the District, the experiences of freedwomen showed that it would take much more than the enactment of legislation to release them from the grip of slavery. In chapter 6, I explore the role of the government in the self-making aspirations of refugee women in the era of wartime emancipation. Refugee women pursued legal freedom in their appeals to the Board of Commissioners for Emancipated Slaves, a federal agency that recognized the claims of those freed by the Emancipation Act of the District. Enslaved women also sent letters to federal agents of the Freedmen's Bureau to retrieve kin or possessions and resolve disputes with former slaveholders, revealing the ways they were an important source of advocacy for children and kin. Through their appeals to the commissioners and bureau agents, black women initiated an unprecedented relationship between themselves and the federal government.[26] While this was by no means a conclusive process since, in some instances, petitions were denied or the rights of the women were not always recognized, the wartime moment offers an understanding of how black women acted on visions of liberty.[27] Freedwomen articulated ideas about their rights to liberty and the responsibility of the federal government to guarantee the enforcement of emancipation policies. The geographic proximity of the capital in relation to Virginia, Maryland, and Delaware prompted scores of refugee and fugitive women to come to the capital to seek suitable employment, secure the freedom of kin, claim the military pensions of male relatives, and participate in uplift work. These wartime actions were rooted in a long tradition of making formal and informal claims to a life of liberty in Washington.

The pages that follow constitute a history not only of African American women in early Washington but also of the ways they set in motion the strategies of navigation and self-making to define liberty on their terms. Furthermore, black women's epistemologies of liberty expand our understandings of how the capital became the political experiment that Masur and other historians have described in their work. The claims they made, the women they became, the actions they took, and the lives they created made possible the black Washington that became the incubator of equality and citizenship. This study of African American women is based on a large and diverse source base. Memoirs, pamphlets, runaway advertisements, bills of sale, newspapers, black codes, digital sources, wartime legislation, police records, correspondence with federal officials, and abolitionist literature provide evidence of African American women's claims to liberty and processes of self-definition. Memoirs, papers, and pamphlets written by notable figures such as Margaret Smith, Dolley Madison, Charles Dickens, Charles Torrey, Myrtilla Miner, and others provide both "insider" and "outsider" perspectives on life in the capital. Historians have written about these figures, but they have paid less attention to the African

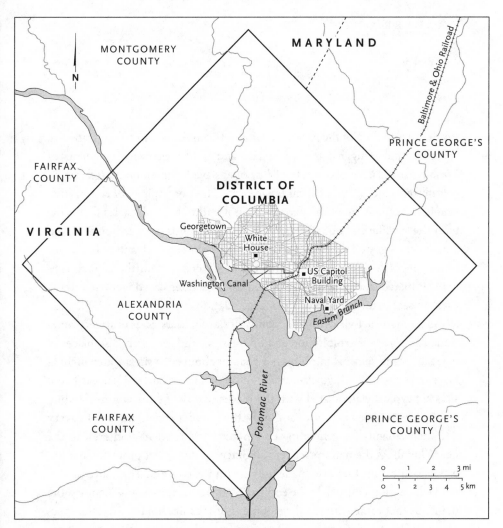

The District of Columbia and neighboring Chesapeake states.

American women and girls they encountered who are at the heart of this book. This book tells the story of ordinary women whose lives were captured in often mundane transactions and notices—newspaper advertisements and bills of sale, arrest records, petitions to government officials, and efforts to educate themselves and their children. It tells, therefore, the story of the nation.

CHAPTER ONE

Slavery

From the founding of the nation's capital, African American women labored, survived, and struggled in its intimate and public environs. Residents of Washington, D.C., employed the labor of enslaved women on local farms, in private residences, and at local businesses. The possibilities of self-making unfolded at the helm of the nation, but not without the obstacles that came with the proliferation of slavery. The labor demands imposed on enslaved women constrained the degree to which they could take advantage of the potential negotiations associated with urban slavery. Within the capital, residents initiated transactions that shifted the lives of enslaved women, forcing them to search for creative ways to forge relationships and engage in personally meaningful activities independently of slaveholders. Sites of slavery functioned as places of exploitation and oppression, and they were also places of navigation and self-making. This is a chapter about such sites, which include taverns, parlors, farms, government buildings, and private residences. These sites are typically associated with the places that define the worlds of white residents and their aspirations and show the interdependent nature of slavery and the demands for generating commercial and residential interest in the new capital. As the nation's leaders embraced politics that protected the liberty of white men, they also made the case for the continued presence of slavery in the nation's capital. In the earlier decades of the nineteenth century, the demands that came with the development of Washington involved the speculation of land, the mortgaging of enslaved people, and the promotion of enslaved women's labor. Washington, D.C., began as a site of slavery.

The challenges of populating, building, and sustaining the local economy of the nation's capital reveal the importance of black women's labor in the early republic. They cooked, cleaned, sewed, washed, nursed, farmed, peddled goods in the local market, and tended to their own families as well.[1] Enslaved women in Washington appeared in local newspapers that advertised slave auctions and hires with particular attention to the skills and services that potential buyers could employ. Newspapers advertised the labor of enslaved women, which allows us to see early patterns of intraregional and interregional economic marketing and transactions of black women's labor. In those same newspapers, as later chapters will show, reports of enslaved women's escapes also reveal early glimpses of self-definition. During the initial years, however, efforts to build the local economy of the District and attract investors exposed the tensions between bondage and the demands of building a nation that mirrored the virtues of republicanism.[2] The degree to which enslaved labor was folded into the project of attracting investors to the capital underscores the ways that national history converged with the history of local African American women.[3]

In 1800, the District had 14,093 inhabitants, of which 4,027 were African American. Only 483 were listed as free people; the remaining 3,544 black inhabitants were enslaved.[4] African American women outnumbered men in the urban South, and this appears to have been the case in Washington as well.[5] Enslaved people lived in the farmsteads of local owners, and some enslaved people were manumitted and permitted to remain in the District. Enslaved and free black residents socialized, married, and forged bonds when their labor and lives permitted. Indeed, membership in local churches allowed for such opportunities, particularly in the Catholic Church, where marriages, births, baptisms, and deaths were formally recognized.[6] Enslaved and free black people participated in Protestant and Catholic services held in biracial congregations, and black parishioners established their own churches in subsequent decades. Catholic churches appeared immediately following the decision to relocate the capital to the Potomac, with the establishment of early congregations such as Holy Trinity and St. Patrick's. These sacred spaces appealed to black residents in the area because they provided a source of community and personal edification. According to historian Mary Beth Corrigan, "Slaves received the same sacraments as did other church members, and marriage and baptism provided spiritual recognition to family ties, which the slave system fundamentally threatened."[7] The recognition of familial relationships and membership in a spiritual community emphasized the personal choices and identities that enslaved people made. While urban slavery afforded opportunities to make meaningful connections, however, those bonds were disrupted or even destroyed in the interest of slaveholders. This was certainly the case among the first presidents who took up residence in the new capital.

Upon learning of his election victory, Thomas Jefferson began the work of assembling his staff for the president's house. The controversy about his relationship with Sarah "Sally" Hemings, an enslaved woman at Monticello, still reverberated in the public criticism of Jefferson by political foes during the election. Subsequently, it was in his best interest to think carefully about the racial and gender makeup of his staff. He assembled a group primarily composed of white workers to staff the residence.[8] There were a few exceptions, including fourteen-year-old Ursula Granger, an expectant mother who came to the president's house to train as a cook.[9] The demands of training in the French culinary tradition, the challenges of motherhood, and Washington's interminable social scene placed incredible demands on her. Not long after the birth of her child, Ursula returned to Jefferson's mountain retreat, Monticello, to perform agricultural work. Two enslaved women, Edith Fossett and Frances Hern, were hired in Ursula's stead to assume the duties associated with entertaining at the president's residence.[10] Washington became the temporary home of countless politicians, their families, and their servants. Relocation, however, uprooted enslaved people away from loved ones and placed them in a new environment with its own set of laws, customs, and people. For instance, Edith's husband, Joseph, worked as a foreman of the nail factory at Monticello.[11] Edith served as a cook for eight years in Washington, meaning that she saw her husband and family infrequently as life in the president's house exacted her ongoing attention and presence. The distance that slavery demanded created such a strain on family life that, in 1806, Joseph left Monticello to find her. He was reprimanded by a slave catcher and spent time in the Washington jail before he returned to Monticello.[12] These stories illuminate the tensions between the principles of liberty that informed the aims of the new government and the realities of bondage that shaped the lives and families of the ones forced to serve the country's leaders at a moment's notice. With distance between themselves and their families at Monticello, these women entered into a world of power and politics at the center of the nation. The early presence of enslaved African Americans formatively shaped life in the president's mansion and the development of the nation's capital.

On the ground, visitors saw a capital that appeared a far cry from a thriving city. A sharper focus on the District reveals a village of small farms with a smattering of taverns and modest buildings peppered along streets comprising muddy pathways and ditches that made inhabitants vulnerable to calamities during carriage rides and promenades. On a visit to Washington, Charles Dickens wrote, "Spacious avenues, that begin in nothing and lead nowhere; streets, mile long, that only want houses, roads, and inhabitants; public buildings that need but a public to be complete; and ornaments of great thoroughfares, which only lack great thoroughfares to ornament—are its leading features."[13] Nevertheless, George Washington and countless others expected an economic boon to come with the placement of the capital on the Potomac. As in many southern cities, commerce and labor stimulated economic development and for Washington, the capital demanded the same toolkit to become a thriving city.[14] Slave labor and, in particular, enslaved women's domestic labor became a staple feature of local property sales. Advertisements of property sales that included land and enslaved women proliferated in the pages of the local news.

Proprietors of the District advertised both developed and undeveloped land and building properties to market the new territory as a suitable place for residence and business development. Advertisements also featured other forms of property to make offers of sale more attractive. James R. Dermott employed slave labor and also worked with free African Americans like the self-taught scientist and mathematician Benjamin Banneker in his role as the city surveyor in Washington. He placed an advertisement in the *National Intelligencer and Washington Advertiser* for "farm territory in the Territory of Columbia improved or Unimproved Property in eligible situations in the City of Washington."[15] One of the many business associates with hopes to profit from the relocation of the capital, Dermott aimed to sweeten the deal, stating, "Also for sale a Negro Wench and two Children, a Boy and Girl." Enslaved women's work and reproductive labor incentivized local sales initiated by development schemes in Washington. Slavery existed in full form in Maryland and Virginia, and efforts to develop the territory into a functioning national capital seamlessly integrated Chesapeake slavery and its customs. Thus, the marketing of the new federal district, and the visions for economic growth and prosperity, reinforced the social and labor customs of the South.

Individuals charged with the construction of the buildings and institutions of the federal government also made use of available enslaved labor. James Hoban, the architect best known for designing the president's residence, regularly employed slave labor. Born in Ireland, Hoban saw great opportunity in the capital, and his aspirations were linked to the local slave economy. For the construction of the president's house, he hired enslaved men from area slaveholders who were paid by the federal government for the use of their labor.[16] The hiring system of exchanging slave labor meant that the relocation of the capital to the Potomac offered lucrative opportunities for local slaveholders.[17] At the beginning of the nineteenth century, enslaved men were trained as blacksmiths, carpenters, and bricklayers, and many of them were hired out for building projects in the city. This iteration of bondage figured more prominently as slavery in the nation's capital evolved throughout the subsequent decades of the nineteenth century. In this case, enslaved people hired to work on government properties most likely possessed the training and experience necessary to construct these buildings, bringing tremendous value to their owners. They primarily worked alongside white laborers, as Hoban also made efforts to hire Irish immigrants.[18] In the capital, both enslaved men and women also cleared and farmed land, and dug ditches. Enslaved women performed the washing, cooking, sewing, cleaning, farming, and childcare associated with everyday domestic labor.[19]

In 1805, Hoban placed an advertisement for the sale of a thirty-three-year-old enslaved woman and her three children.[20] As did Hoban's, the interests of those making their mark on the new capital connected closely to the exchange and consumption of goods and property. A gendered division of labor associated enslaved women with other material goods designed for domestic spaces and a genteel lifestyle. In one notice, the editor included information about a twenty-one-year-old woman "who is a good Cook, and a complete house servant in every other respect," available for purchase.[21] Early advertisements simultaneously promoted the exchange of lands with slaves and goods such as furniture, silver, finery, supplies, and livestock. Along with the woman, a prospective buyer could also pay for a "large well-formed horse, that goes well in a carriage, and pleasant under the saddle." The items featured for sale represent significant investments for the buyer but also reflect the socioeconomic station associated with the consumer. The nature of commerce and property ownership in the District reinforced the racial hierarchies that came with the chattel principle.[22] This manner of exchange normalized the sale of enslaved women alongside fine material goods in the capital, further constituting an important aspect of Washington's social and class formation. Early investment in enslaved women's labor served the purposes of increasing investment in the city and developing social relations in the nation's capital.

The symbolic meanings tied to the capital linked the early republic to ideals of liberty and egalitarianism, but an emerging class structure demonstrated that the aspirations of the privileged relied on the subjugation of others.[23] African American women in early Washington understood that the stratification of society often relegated them to the bottom and that their labor subsequently buoyed the aims of a burgeoning genteel class. Margaret Bayard Smith, wife of the founder and owner of the *National Intelligencer and Washington Advertiser*, Samuel Smith, mingled among the upper crust of Washington society. She was a prominent figure in her own right and authored a number of publications featured in journals that boasted a national readership.[24] Historians rely on the stories and letters that she penned about life in the new capital, but the fact that she charged a number of enslaved people and servants with running her household is less obvious in Washington histories. In a letter to a friend she related, "I have had a fine little girl of five years old bound to me by Dr. Willis." She noted, "While I work, she plays with Julia and keeps her quiet, she is gay, good temper'd and well behaved, Julia is extremely fond of her, and she of Julia; and I hope to have some comfort in her."[25] Enslaved girls learned at an early age how to navigate the expectations of upper-class white families.[26] The demands on black girls, white entitlement to deference, and the expectations of positive dispositions indicate ways that slavery shaped their understandings of labor and power. For the five-year-old girl, her "gay" and "good temper'd" behavior would not always have been a matter of choice but rather a negotiation she learned early on in her socialization. Washington society took shape on the foundations of the racial and gendered power dynamics of slavery as leading women purchased, hired, and sold enslaved women.[27]

Notices of opportunities to purchase enslaved women appeared regularly in the pages of the *Intelligencer*.[28] During the spring of 1802, advertisements like one that featured a thirty-eight-year-old woman, "an excellent Cook, and good washer," available for purchase, appeared throughout the paper.[29] The domestic labor that enslaved women provided ensured the comforts of endless service as lawmakers, investors, and new residents placed their bets on realizing their economic and political aspirations in the new capital. Slave traders, in the form of brokers, executors, lawyers, and ordinary men and women who lived in the capital and in the neighboring Chesapeake states, took advantage of opportunities to appeal to the labor demands that shaped life in the new city. A fifteen-year-old girl appeared in an advertisement in the early years of the capital, with no indication of family or the conditions of her life before her sale.[30] The advertisement, however, indicates that those relationships mattered very little in the calculus of her placement with a buyer. In another instance, the editor posted a notice for a "healthy negro woman under 30 years of age" with two "healthy children" for sale in the District.[31] The domestic market involved a series of decisions and negotiations that determined the manner and configuration of the sale of enslaved people and their families.[32] For those still skeptical about the value of property in the District, the reproductive promise of purchasing enslaved women stoked the hopes of potential investors. These women, as they were marketed, invited consumers to imagine a life in the capital with all of the trappings of success— slave ownership denoted compelling proof of such attainment.

Existing residents looked to the slave trade to resolve personal debts in order to counter the possibilities of financial ruin. One such case appeared in the news offering "a Negro Woman, with her three children," for sale. The notice described the woman as roughly thirty-five years old and a "tolerable" cook and her ten-year-old daughter as "a very pretty, smart girl."[33] The enslaved woman also had two sons aged eight and two and a half with no description. The language about the ten-year-old girl raises questions about the marketing of enslaved girls and what this might tell us about the local market. Was desirability in the Washington market shaped by appearance and intelligence for potential buyers? In the market, these attributes mattered to the degree that they served the interests and status of slaveholder. Furthermore, the seller did make obvious a tone of desperation with the sale of this family. The advertisement confirmed that "they are offered for sale from the necessity of raising a sum of money" and that "they will, therefore, be sold very cheap." Announcements of slave auctions appealed to potential investors and new residents with the mutual incentives between seller and buyer in mind. The local slave trade fostered relationships across county and state lines and stimulated interregional commercial ties from Maryland and Virginia.

Depending on the seller and the motivations for sale, advertisements appeared for larger numbers of slaves available for purchase at multiple locations.[34] Thomas Peter marketed thirty-five enslaved people for sale along with stock and plantation utensils to settle the estate of Robert Peter, a deceased slaveholder and relative. Robert's estate, however, proved much more complicated to liquidate. Another advertisement appeared from Thomas that offered 150 enslaved people for purchase in addition to those listed earlier in the issue.[35] Thomas held the sales on the same date, but at separate locations, one within a mile of the president's house and another in nearby Montgomery County. The larger number of slaves for sale in Montgomery might have appealed to buyers interested in sizeable slaveholdings on rural farms, which would position executors to resolve the estates quickly. A woman who owned twenty-six slaves in Annapolis, Maryland, marketed their sale through an agent that submitted information to the *National Intelligencer*. The information in the notice specified that the sale included "men, women, boys and girls, which will be disposed of separately—one excellent black-smith that had his trade perfect, several handsome boys from 12 to 18 years of age, and girls that can be recommended as good house servants."[36] Why did it matter that the boys were handsome? What do the aesthetics of enslaved people's bodies do for the marketing and sale of enslaved people?[37] These very brief descriptions make clear that within the limited space of the advertisements, the physical appearance of enslaved people, and the range of skills they brought to each household, mattered in the local world of slave ownership.[38] The information in the advertisements also makes clear that any relationship constituted before the sale would not be taken into account in the sale. With few exceptions, sellers typically didn't shy away from selling families apart.[39]

In the absence of an executor or manager of an estate, the orphans' courts submitted notices of public auctions to transact the sale of enslaved people who remained in the event of death.[40] Many advertisements appeared in similar form indicating the name of the deceased, the number of slaves sold, the age ranges and gender of the enslaved, and the appropriate forms of payment. For example, following the death of Mary Lamar of Prince George's County, the orphans' court organized the sale of enslaved people remaining on her estate. An announcement titled "Public Auction" noted that "twelve negroes, among which are women, girls, and boys," were available for purchase.[41] Residents in the area congregated in the various locations advertised in the local news and regularly witnessed public scenes of families sold apart to populate the homes and farms of enterprising slaveholders and to resolve the outstanding debts of the deceased. Such scenes predate the large coffles and multiregional slave markets that lined the national mall in the antebellum decades in the city.[42]

The process of settling estates and building individual interest in the local economy meant that exchanging slaves and developing commerce in the nation's capital made such commercial practices a distinctive feature of nation building. Congress relied on local economic growth in the federal city to finance the majority of the construction and development of the national capital. City commissioners faced challenges in attracting new landowners and potential investors to generate the resources necessary to fund the improvement of the federal city. After legislators agreed to relocate the capital to the Potomac, Maryland and Virginia contributed nearly $200,000 collectively.[43] This sum, while generous, hardly covered the costs of the design and plan for the capital. Congress strongly opposed taxing the public to bankroll the capital, and the commissioners hinged their bets on the rapid sale of lots. By 1800, a decade after Congress approved the new location, promoters of the city still struggled to sell the lots and much of the property in possession of new owners remained undeveloped. The local news marketed slave labor and the sale of slaves as a key feature of property ownership and currency. With unfinished and finished dwellings, commerce in enslaved women helped finance the development of both vacant areas and locations associated with political power.

Federal buildings remained under construction, but the mere promise of locations designated as future sites of national buildings featured prominently in descriptions of private properties on the market. Houses "situated on the Pennsylvania Avenue near the President's house" appeared for sale in the local news. One could find "two brick dwelling houses" that boasted "handsome parlours and passage," as well as several lodging rooms, garrets, kitchens, cellars, and yards "palisaded and set with trees."[44] For the makeshift village, the property included features reserved for the wealthiest buyers. The notice also marketed "walks to the street paved or graveled, which will render the same as comfortable a situation as any in this city for a private family, and will be sold for less than any gentleman can have the same built for." Much of the attempts to make property ownership attractive to potential buyers required the option of finished structures. Additionally, this property might appear to "gentlemen" interested in proximity to the president's residence. Despite the fact that the federal village hardly looked like a completely developed and inhabited city, Pennsylvania Avenue, the unfinished president's house, and the Capitol building already functioned as attractive markers associated with sites of power.

During the winter of 1801, as the Capitol building appeared only partially complete, and Samuel Smith continued to profit from the real estate and property advertisements that filled the columns of the local news, a local seller submitted a notice for two three-story "brick houses" for sale. Both homes, "adjoining each other, 28 feet front each, by forty-feet deep," included a "commodious lot" that stretched back into a deep running alley.[45] The property could accommodate one or two apartments to rent to possible tenants, which further enhanced the commercial potential of the lot. The proximity to the Capitol building, however, underscored the real advantage and appeal of such real estate. Another advertisement, titled "Houses on Pennsylvania Avenue," boasted "Two Houses on the best part of Pennsylvania Avenue for sale."[46] The prominent avenue connected the Executive Mansion to the Capitol building. With twelve rooms and four garrets collectively, the houses sold "low" with "three years credit" available for part of the purchase. The advertisement concluded, "A family of negroes, will be taken in part payment, or Lots will be exchanged for Slaves." Anyone weighing the potential value of these offers needed only to focus on the proximity of the lots to the heart of the federal government. The lives of enslaved people and potential investors converged near these commercial and residential sites of power as enslaved people were used as an acceptable means of payment.

The anatomy of Peter L'Enfant's design of the capital corresponds with the appeal of marketing specific government locations. One scholar notes, "L'Enfant began his work not by laying out streets or by running survey lines, but by the selection of dominating sites. It was from and around these sites that the plan was later developed."[47] Proximity to the nation's political structures appeared in the news as a marker of legitimacy that underscored the projected value of investment in the capital. The exchange of enslaved people figured conspicuously in these potential transactions, but we will later see how enslaved and free African American women also leveraged their proximity to these sites for their own economic and social interests. These early sales of appealing lots entangled individuals and families of enslaved people in local dealings to grow the capital economically.

One strategy to leverage investments in enslaved people involved marketing sales based on the skills that black people possessed. One enslaved girl, approximately sixteen years old, appeared in an advertisement for purchase. The seller noted that she "has been used to house work; she can spin either cotton, flax or wool, and is very handy at the needle."[48] Spinning, sewing, and needlework constituted some of the countless forms of skilled labor that enslaved women and girls possessed in early Washington. Having both a servant and a seamstress to make clothing appealed to those who planned to generate income based on hire. Executors of estates also conducted private auctions that highlighted the assortment of skills that enslaved people performed in the local market. One advertisement indicated that the deceased desired for a family of slaves to be sold together rather than divided, as commonly occurred. The seller described one George as "stout and healthy" and "a very handy negro for every part of field work and good mower, reaper and sacker of grain."[49] Likewise, the seller described George's wife, Grace, as "brought up in a regular family as a house servant to which she is fully equal, and is a remarkable good seamstress, laundress, and a tolerable cook." Another advertisement, titled "For Sale or Exchange, a Middle Aged Negro Woman," noted that she "understands cooking and all kinds of house work, and has an excellent character for honesty and sobriety."[50] Even with her qualifications, she would be sold on "liberal terms" or "exchanged for a girl of 12 or 15 years of age." Again, enslaved women appeared as a form of currency, but this particular advertisement also illuminates the ways age and ideas about skills determined the exchange value of enslaved women. Indeed, teenagers made up the majority of enslaved laborers in the District.[51] These advertisements represent their bodies simultaneously as speculative assets and as indicators of potential revenue from hiring arrangements.

The exchange and sale of enslaved women occurred in various locations throughout the capital and reveal an earlier decentralized market during the formative years of the city. Bulk sales and auctions of enslaved women and families took place in courts, local residences, taverns, and business offices, depending on availability of space and the stipulations of the owner. Historian Bonnie Martin argues for the significance of the financial history of slavery "as an integral part of the social history of ordinary people: the neighbors who lent to neighbors, along with enslaved men, women, and children who were trapped in the credit web of slavery's capitalism."[52] In the early stages of the capital's development, domestic slave markets driven by slave-trading firms and the erection of slave pens did not appear in full form until after the first decade of the nineteenth century.[53] Business transactions and the resolution of estates during the founding of the capital occurred between local residents in the capital and the surrounding Chesapeake counties. These sales involved local business owners of taverns that hosted large sales, arrangements on neighboring farms, or a direct inquiry to the editor of the local news organ. Enslaved women's futures could be transacted between a variety of actors and within a range of public and private spaces in the District.

The different locations of auction sites reflect the diverse interests and connections that shaped local practices of slave trading.[54] After Maryland slaveholder Richard Sprigg died, managers of his estate submitted an advertisement for the public sale of enslaved people at his private residence near Upper Marlboro in Prince George's County. The notice stated that the sale featured "a number of valuable Slaves, Men, Women, and Children."[55] Information about a public sale for "thirty or forty likely NEGROES" in neighboring Loudon County also appeared in the local news.[56] One advertisement confirmed that Semmes's Tavern in Georgetown planned to host a sale of "TWELVE likely NEGROES" consisting of "boys from 8 to 18 years of age, and women and children."[57] Joseph Semmes owned the tavern located on M Street from 1801 to 1832. In addition to the typical offerings of a local tavern, the dining room hosted formal dinners, including a banquet held in honor of President John Adams four years before the sale of the enslaved people advertised.[58] In fact, that same dining hall functioned as an auction venue for the sale of enslaved people. The economic ties to the slave market transcended the practice of slaveholding itself and seeped into homes and businesses connected to the transactions that made the sale of humans possible. Thus, the local traffic in enslaved people involved an interregional network of marketing and sales in which local taverns, municipal buildings, law offices, and private residences all operated as sites of slavery. Such commercial activity occurred across rural and urban spaces that ultimately linked the economic, political, and social ties of people in the geographic vicinity and the futures of enslaved women in the District.

Slavery in the District persisted within an interconnected web of trafficking that showed no signs of diminishing from the vantage point of the enslaved. Black women and girls were keenly aware of the ways that the local trade and labor economy initiated transactions on their lives.[59] They witnessed daily their families and friends unexpectedly sold farther south or within the region. Geographically tracking their sale illustrates the development of a regional slave economy comprising the District, Virginia, and Maryland. Moving from one state, neighborhood, or home to another made for unpredictability in the forced movement of enslaved women and girls. This forced mobility, however, also facilitated the acquisition of geographic literacy and exposure to local networks. They brought with them their own knowledge of the places from which they traveled, and they picked up tips, advice, and possibly material resources along the way. Bills of sale and certificates of ownership constitute the archival receipts of dislocation and surveillance that enslaved women experienced across local and regional geographies. These documents confirm the steady exchange and flow of slave labor in the nation's capital, a dynamic aspect of the local economy that provided financial stability and security to local residents. Such mundane transactions uncover a vigorous regional slave economy that threatened the relationships, sense of place, and identities that enslaved women hoped to preserve.

Slaveholders conveyed enslaved people as gifts, or "chattel" mortgages, in deeds of trust, banking loans, and bills of sale among family members.[60] A man named Addison Belt purchased an enslaved man named Jacob along with three girls named Lucy, Cynthia, and Cate. He attributed this acquisition to an opportune marriage and noted that "they are for his use and not for sale."[61] The District slave codes required a certificate of slavery to confirm the legal status of black women and verify the purpose for bringing them into the city. Bills of sale also recorded the conveyance of enslaved women outside Washington. A man named George Beale, who resided in the District, sold a woman named Kesiah and her two children, a woman named Phillis, and two men to his son for the amount of $1,500.[62] A few days later, Horatio Harbin of Alexandria sold twenty-year-old Charity Jackson for $335 to a slaveholder in Louisiana. The recorder noted that she was married to a man named Elie Jackson.[63] Historian Tera Hunter explores this interjection of the "third flesh," or slave owner, in slave marriages and the impact of the market on relationships and kin in slave communities.[64] Couples like Charity and Elie forged meaningful bonds even with the threat of sale and separation, and yet the sanctity of Charity's marriage mattered very little to the people executing transactions that separated her from her husband. Moreover, the marriages of white women could shift the entire worlds of black women depending on the terms of their sale.

Engaged to John G. Ford of Washington, Rebecca Clements made arrangements to "hold all of her property, real and personal and mixed, so that she may dispose of it for her own sole use and benefit and that of her heirs and legal representatives."[65] She also ensured that her property remained exempt from any liabilities of her husband's debts and legal contracts. Clements sold one lot located in Washington and another lot in Georgetown, in addition to enslaved women Milly and Cely "and their increase," to the Ford family. The bill of sale specified the future status of the enslaved women's potential offspring, a detail that caught the attention of those who hoped to benefit from such transactions. In one case, a man named William Cooper purchased an enslaved woman named Eliza. Thomas Dashiell had only recently purchased Eliza from Prince George's County, Maryland, and now she belonged to Cooper.[66] Cooper stipulated that Eliza serve a term of fifteen years, after which he planned to manumit her. Arrangements like this one underscore a feature of urban slavery that became more frequent over time. Cooper noted that "nothing in the contract 'shall be so construed as [to] affect the children or increase of Eliza should she have any during the [term],' and they shall remain as slaves of William Cooper." This proviso, mentioned almost as an afterthought toward the end of the recorded bond, provided one of many examples of the circumscribed conditions of freedom. Even in the event that Cooper manumitted Eliza, he still held the reins on the lives of any children born during her term, and wielded authority that predetermined any outcomes from Eliza's sexual encounters and relationships during her term of service.[67] Similarly, Edward Diggs sold seventeen-year-old Emma "and all of her future increase" to John Randall Dyer for $350.[68] These transactions tied enslaved women's reproductive labor and relationships to the local slave economy.[69]

The children of enslaved women served as a popular form of credit and economic security for outstanding debts owed by white Washingtonians.[70] The indebted and appropriately named couple William and Ann Gamble mortgaged an enslaved girl named Letitia to Mary Belt until she received the full payment of debts owed. The recorder listed Letitia under the category of "bill of sale [and chattel mortgage]."[71] Letitia returned to the Gambles six months later, but the uncertainty that came with acclimation to a new household and a new set of demands undoubtedly proved jarring. Enslaved children were forced into arrangements that required adaptability and compliance. Countless enslaved people moved from one house to the next depending on the financial interests and obligations of local slaveholders. In over his head with mounting bills, George Walker found himself drowning in his attempts to pay off $2,500 to the Bank of Metropolis, $270 to the Patriotic Bank, $115 to the Bank of the United States, and $150 to the Union Bank of Metropolis.[72] In addition to seven lots of property in the District and two horses, two carts, and a selection of household goods, he sold sixteen-year-old Eliza, ten-year-old Matilda, and seven-year-old Sandy to pay off his debts. Similarly, Charles C. White of Georgetown mortgaged Henny, an enslaved woman, along with her children Kitty, George, and Sarah, to John Barnes, Esq., for debts owed.[73] Thomas Crown signed a contract with George Bomford for the construction of a three-story brick house.[74] He provided Bomford with Mary and Louisa, two enslaved women, as security for fulfilling the contract terms. Thomas Sim paid George Bomford to arrange the sale of Fanny and her twelve-year-old son, Henry, to address a debt of $430.[75] The ability or inability to resolve one's debts or mortgage enslaved people for the acquisition of more property determined the futures of countless enslaved women and their children. This amorphous auctioneering of enslaved women and girls happened outside the purview of the physical slave marketplace and among the private dealings of individuals and banks.

Financial institutions participated in the sale and use of enslaved women as security for debts, placing the lives and destinies of enslaved women in limbo and offering banks a vested interest in the slave trade. This practice, however, was not unique to the District, as countless banks, towns, and cities involved in the slave trade embraced the chattel principle as the framework for using people as collateral.[76] District resident Walter Cox took advantage of such practices when he included Nelly, Charlotte, and John in a deed of trust to secure payment of debts owed to the Bank of the United States.[77] When he proved unable to pay the outstanding balance, the three of them were sold to the highest bidder. In a similar case, J. B. Goddard mortgaged David, Jenny, Jane, and Francis for debts owed to the Union Bank.[78] William Talbott of Georgetown also owed the Union Bank. In arrears to the tune of $2,000, he issued a deed of trust that included Jack, Patrick, Salley, Katey, and Sophia.[79] Richard H. Fitzhugh owed $4,300 to the Bank of Georgetown, $2,850 to the Bank of Columbia, $1,550 to the Union Bank of Georgetown, and $7,000 to the Bank of the United States.[80] To ensure the payment of the debts, Fitzhugh conveyed Maria, Cloe, and Cloe's children Westly, Caroline, John, and Nance. Black women and their children were entangled in the financial maneuvers and speculative ventures of slaveholders heavily indebted to major banking institutions. As a result, children discovered at an early age the realities of sale into unfamiliar homes with strangers who suddenly controlled their every move.[81]

Black girls in the District learned firsthand that the financial transactions of slavery constituted a feature of their socialization into adolescence. John P. Van Ness purchased thirteen-year-old Milly "and her increase" for $300.[82] Her next destination, dictated in one or multiple transactions, informed any aspirations and relationships that Milly might claim for herself. Likewise, James A. Magruder of Georgetown sold Charity to Dr. William Bean for $400.[83] Raphael Thompson of St. Mary County, Maryland, sold Celia and her daughter Sarah Ann to Jonathan Benson of Montgomery County, Maryland, for $197.85.[84] The list also included an enslaved woman, Jemima, sold to Lemuel Townsend of Washington, D.C.[85] Elizabeth Gales and Moses Shelton sold eleven-year-old Fanny to William Doughty of Washington.[86] Charles Conley sold an enslaved girl named Priscilla, aged thirteen or fourteen, to John P. Van Ness for $350 in the District.[87] These brief lists of women and girls show that they were in high demand as domestic laborers in the Chesapeake, even as the agricultural economy of the region declined in staple crop production. At a time when enslaved people from the Upper South were sold farther south, most enslaved women and girls remained in demand for household labor in the region. John Harvey, a resident of Washington, sold forty-year-old Kate along with her children, Hannah, Ann, Alexander, Notley, and Washington, to Cesshan W. Benson of Prince George's County, Maryland.[88] In another transaction, Thomas Crown mortgaged two enslaved girls, Mary and Louisa, along with furniture and household goods, for $3,000 in debt owed to Robert and Edward Lucas of Jefferson County, Virginia.[89] Amelia Dorsett, a resident of the District, sold nine-year-old Polly for $150 to David Stewart.[90] Ownership and guardianship proved at odds, since children could be stripped away from their families at the stroke of a pen.

Children might intermittently remain with their parents after sale, but such instances proved exceptional given the mores of the domestic market. Some buyers, however, purchased enslaved women with their children. William Good of Georgetown paid $600 for Gracy, along with her children Esther, Edwin, and Marshall.[91] As she was sold with her children, and relocated within the same neighborhood that she lived in before the auction, Gracy's case reveals an instance in which the mother was not separated from her children during the sale. Similarly, Molly and her children Sanford and Mary were sold for $750 to Sabret Scott of Washington, D.C.[92] Milly and her children Charity, Henry, and Annette also remained together in the District after they were sold for $400 to Margaret Dashiell.[93] Enslaved women subjected to the horrors of sale didn't always place their hopes in the generosity of slaveholders but spoke up in defense of their families. Historians have interrogated the ways that enslaved people negotiated their sales to include family members in the likely instance that slave buyers showed little interest in keeping the families intact.[94] Keeping families together could, however, benefit slaveholders if the arrangements fostered cooperation from enslaved women. These women went from one set of owners to the next, as the transactions of the local slave trade brought them, and sometimes their families, into the intimate environs of white homes.

The homes of local residents functioned as sites of slavery that formatively shaped the labor and living conditions that enslaved women were relegated to.[95] These dwellings came to shape the early capital and the social and economic ambitions of slave owners, but they also served as sites of intimacy, violence, and surveillance that distinctively shaped the gendered experiences of bondage in the urban South. They arrived from neighboring households, as well as the surrounding Chesapeake counties, bringing with them experiences, ideas, and knowledge that then shaped how they navigated the capital. Even with the decline of the staple crop economy, Chesapeake slaveholders with a surplus of workers appealed to residents in need of domestic and skilled labor for flexible terms. Advertisements such as one that listed "several Likely young Women" for hire "by the year" became a common means for slaveholders to profit from the domestic, skilled, and reproductive labors of enslaved women.[96] Moreover, the local slave trade cemented interregional economic ties as the capital took shape, ties that also constituted customs and laws designed to govern the lives of enslaved women within the region.

In 1801, Congress declared in the Organic Act that "the laws of the State of Maryland, as they now exist, shall be and continue in force, in that part of the said District (of Columbia), which was ceded by that State to the United States, and by them accepted, for the permanent seat of the government of the United States."[97] In other words, Congress integrated the legal customs of Maryland and Virginia (in the case of Alexandria) in order to determine the local rule of law and its application in the lives of African Americans. Slave codes that traditionally appeared in the Chesapeake translated into the daily lives of enslaved women in Washington. These codes included a ten o'clock curfew, outlawed meetings among enslaved people, forbid them from riding ferries, and made slavery inheritable through enslaved women.[98] With slave codes, Congress affirmed existing local laws, a reassurance that Washington resembled the urban cities of the South. While Congress formally incorporated Washington, the local government largely remained subject to the powers of the federal government. Local residents could not vote in presidential elections and did not have congressional representatives. Congress also possessed the authority to veto legislation passed by the municipal government of Washington. The president appointed three commissioners for a limited term to administer the survey of lands and develop property for the federal government. The commissioners were charged with ensuring that Congress, the president, and any additional public offices conducted business in appropriate accommodations. They also directed the sale and construction of plots within the capital.[99] Commissioners encouraged much of the commerce in enslaved women and local real estate that appears earlier in this chapter and subsequently reported their progress to Congress regularly. The governing structure placed the social engineering project of the District directly in the purview of the federal government as black codes remained in place, the slave trade found a foothold, and prominent families began to settle in the city. The legislative decisions of Congress undoubtedly affected the futures of enslaved and free black women in the region as laws based on race and gender solidified the presence of slavery in the capital.[100]

Debates erupted in Congress concerning the nation's involvement in the international slave trade.[101] In 1808, the federal government banned U.S. involvement in the transatlantic exchange of slaves. The prohibition against the direct importation of enslaved people from Africa and the Caribbean changed the character of slavery in the nation's capital. Slave traders saw a lucrative opportunity. The local markets expanded rapidly and set in motion the sale of enslaved women, men, and children farther south, where agricultural economies catalyzed the swelling demand for labor and staple crop production.[102] Slave traders recognized the potential of the region's labor reserves for populating cotton and sugar plantations with surplus slaves from the city. The growth of the domestic slave market particularly affected the experiences of enslaved women, as the appeal of their reproductive capacities became even greater with the prohibition of the global slave trade.[103]

Slave traders and owners alike looked to Chesapeake slaves to avoid the consequences of closing off the international market. Historians have shown that slavery in the District emerged less like slave societies in the Chesapeake and more like urban slavery in cities such as Richmond or Baltimore.[104] Cities in the Upper South typically served as large depots for the domestic slave market, but amid this Second Middle Passage within the interior of the North American continent, the urban slave experience is understood as a transient phenomenon that points toward the Deep South. An examination of nineteenth-century Washington offers insights into what slavery looked like for those vulnerable to sale in the Upper South. Enslaved women appeared in pens and prisons in the District before marching hundreds of miles farther south. Both enslaved and free black women in Washington were vulnerable to the mounting demand of the domestic slave trade, and legally free people were abducted for domestic markets.[105] These stories were published in pamphlets that inspired arguments for colonization.

In his observations about the capital, Jesse Torrey took note of his own assumptions about the "Metropolis of Liberty." Torrey knew that slavery existed in Washington, but nothing quite prepared him for what he witnessed during his time there. He admitted, "I then supposed the instances of the streets of the city consecrated to freedom, being paraded with people led in captivity were rare. But I soon ascertained that they were quite frequent."[106] Coffles appeared more frequently by 1815, and they were composed of "several hundred people, including not legal slaves only, but many kidnapped freemen and youth bound to service for a term of years, and unlawfully sold as slaves for life."[107] Slave traders understood that race functioned in a way that made enslaved and free people fair game. Regarding free African Americans, Dickens observed, "In Washington, in that city which takes its name from the father of American liberty, any justice of the peace may bind with fetters any negro passing down the street, and thrust him into jail; no offence on the black man's part is necessary."[108] Torrey noted that they "are annually collected at Washington, (as if it were an emporium of slavery) for transportation to the slave regions."[109]

Held in chains in a garret in the city, a young widow tried to breastfeed her infant while answering Torrey's questions. She recounted the events that led her to the attic where slave traders kept her in Washington. Originally from Delaware, she explained that her and her husband had been free and dreamed of growing their family and perhaps saving enough money to purchase their own property. These dreams of liberty dissipated when she learned of her husband's death. With her husband, she had imagined a life of liberty in the racialized terrain of Delaware, with the hope of a different reality for her and her family.[110] She didn't know what she would do, especially since she was well advanced in her second pregnancy and now mourning the loss of her spouse. As she prepared for bed in her small quarters, located in the kitchen of a home that she most likely worked in, the owner of the house, along with three other men, burst through the door. They "seized and dragged her out" just before they "fastened a noose round her neck to prevent her from screaming."[111] At nine months pregnant, she was blindfolded, "which she resisted with such violence" that she was able to throw the bandage off. While one of the thieves attempted to adjust the bandage over her eyes, "she seized his cheek with her teeth, and tore a piece of it entirely off." They immediately "struck her head several times with a stick of wood," causing her to bleed profusely. Torrey took note of the large wound on her head as she spoke. She explained that while she struggled to loosen their grip on her, the man for whom she worked "bawled out 'choak the d——d b——h don't' let her halloo—she'll scare my wife!" They forcefully tied her up along with her child, and drove her in a carriage with a rope "fixed to her neck" to a holding pen in the District. " After Torrey's interview, the woman waited in the pen for several weeks, and to her great relief, the men who kidnapped her and her child were indicted once a neighbor verified her free status. The person who gave an account for her freedom described the kidnappers as "numerous, daring—full of money."[112] Free black women and their children were vulnerable to the slave trade, particularly after the close of the international market.[113] The slave trade posed a looming threat to African American women's aims of self-making.

At the close of the transatlantic slave trade, African Americans carefully navigated Washington with the understanding that they were all vulnerable to abduction, exploitation, and the brutality that came with chattel slavery. Historians typically characterize slavery as a relatively lenient labor system in Washington.[114] The work of scholars who focus on cities in the Chesapeake shows how the common practice of hiring out slaves offered opportunities for flexibility in work conditions, mobility, and increased interactions with free people.[115] These observations must be taken together with the reality that free and enslaved black women experienced a tremendous degree of intimacy and vulnerability in their work environments. Work shaped social relations in ways that reinforced divisions of labor based on race and gender.[116] The practice of slavery in the District did not necessitate the same intensity required for producing sugar, but the laws of urban slavery did not prevent the sale, mutilation, rape, or death of enslaved people. Indeed, the conditions of urban slavery did not shield enslaved women from abuse even if they were afforded opportunities to forge ties of kinship and earn additional income in the city.[117] African Americans in the District often found opportunities to interact with free people, family members, and social acquaintances in the city, but the gendered division of labor meant that most enslaved women struggled to disentangle themselves from the intimacy of white households.

Enslaved women in Washington were often hired out or purchased for the purpose of performing the duties required to maintain local households. Their work involved any combination of cooking, cleaning, childcare, nursing, healing, midwifery, washing, ironing, sewing, dressing, and accompanying the people who hired or owned them. In the nation's capital, enslaved women's work provided a vital source of labor for families associated with the political elite. Domestic tasks could take enslaved women's work well into the late hours of the evening, and to strain matters further, the local slave code prohibited enslaved women from going out into the city after ten o'clock at night. Thus, domestic work performed by enslaved and free black women meant long hours and close proximity to white families.[118] Sessions of Congress, inaugural balls, dinners, and levees, along with the formal social season, meant that enslaved women were in high demand, particularly for political hosts and wives. These occasions lasted well after the ten o'clock curfew. No one dazzled early Washington society quite like Dolley Madison, wife of President James Madison.

In the spring of 1809, Dolley took Washington by storm as the glamorous first lady of the early republic.[119] She hosted events in ways that not only contrasted her Quaker upbringing but also challenged the prevailing gender etiquette of her time. Known to work the room and approach male guests with inquiries and pleasantries, Dolley snubbed gender conventions rather than wait for a man to speak to her first. She donned one stunning gown after the next for these official events, at which she offered punch and cake to guests in an impeccably kept mansion. None of this was possible, however, without the enslaved laborers owned by the Madisons. Indeed, no one knew this better than Dolley Madison, who relied on Sukey, an enslaved woman who executed every task involved with maintaining her persona as first lady and Washington socialite.

Dolley and her husband moved to the capital in 1801 when incoming president Thomas Jefferson asked James Madison to serve as secretary of state. The Madisons lived just a few blocks from the president's mansion at F Street NW, but by 1809, it was the Madisons who had moved into the executive residence. Throughout James's term in office, his popularity declined with the War of 1812, but his wife's reputation blossomed in those first decades of the nineteenth century.[120] When the British invaded the capital, some commentators attributed the rescue of the infamous portrait of George Washington to the first lady.[121] Interestingly, if this holds true, Sukey and other enslaved laborers, such as Paul Jennings, were most likely charged with the care of the painting rather than Dolley.[122] But the painting perhaps was the last thing on the minds of enslaved people at the president's house. With the war threatening the stability of the capital, Sukey likely learned of opportunities for escape. Historians estimate that nearly 3,400 enslaved people fled the Chesapeake to outposts throughout the British Empire.[123] The close proximity expected of personal attendants, especially to the president's wife, made this difficult to realize. Anyone who knew the Madisons understood the importance of the enslaved people who worked for them. A number of socialites commented on the precision and quality of the enslaved labor force in their household. Margaret Bayard Smith, Washington insider and socialite, noted that she was specifically assigned her own enslaved girl to wait on her in her visits with the Madisons.[124] She commented on the attentiveness and proficiency of the enslaved girls, attributes that most likely described Sukey as well.

Sukey came to Washington at just twelve years old. Groomed from birth at Montpelier to tend to every vital detail required to ensure that Dolley looked and lived the part of first lady, Sukey was required to wait on her at all times.[125] Indeed, Dolley grew accustomed to such attention and appears to have been chiefly dependent on Sukey. On one occasion, Dolley accused Sukey of stealing from her, writing, "Sucky has made so many depridations on every thing, in every part of the house that, I sent her to black Meadow last week."[126] If Dolley's accusations were true, such depredations might offer insight into the pressures of work demanded of Sukey or her own ideas about redress. Dolley commanded nothing short of seamless obedience or else she'd send enslaved women to labor outside the house. But even Dolley found it "terribly inconvenient to do without her," and she brought Sukey back. She relented, stating, "I feel too old to undertake to bring up another—so I must even let her steal from me, to keep from labour myself."[127] The thought of doing her own dressing, bathing, cleaning, cooking, and serving was simply out of the question, so "stealing" may have functioned as one of the possible negotiations that Sukey employed to navigate her interactions with Dolley. Another woman who possessed the adeptness and experience required to serve in an elite family could cost "as high as 8 & 900$" because the "good ones are rare." Rare indeed. Not only was Sukey one of the "good ones," but she also bore five children while enslaved in the Madison household. There's no evidence to affirm that Sukey did in fact steal, but Dolley's dependence on her and her children underscores her value. Her duties required not only training in the daily execution of domestic tasks but also years of anticipating the demands of the mistress and members and guests of her household. As Sukey was required to be available at a moment's call, her experience with Dolley defies our conceptions of urban slavery. The gendered nature of domestic labor required an intense degree of intimacy and possessiveness that accounted for nearly every minute of the day.

Over the years, Dolley ran into a number of financial obstacles. Her lavish spending and the maintenance of her lifestyle meant that she was an active participant in the local slave trade. She sold scores of slaves and hired out those who resided in Washington with her.[128] Dolley hired out enslaved people such as Paul Jennings to a roster of political leaders that included President James K. Polk.[129] She eventually allowed Jennings to purchase his freedom, and in her dire need she was on the receiving end of his generosity.[130] The experience of enslaved laborers in the Madison household positioned Dolley to market and rent their labor for profitable arrangements in the president's house, as well as the homes of the political elite. With her wealthy and established circle of peers, she could secure steady revenue. As Sukey's experience shows us, enslaved women furnished the skills and acumen necessary to execute the memorable levees, state dinners, and inaugurations, as well as the fashioning of first ladies, that appear in national lore. Indeed, Dolley regarded Sukey as her "most efficient House servant."[131] Sukey performed the tasks required of her miles away from her loved ones, including her five children. The move to the capital required her to reconstitute kinship ties with local enslaved and free African Americans in Washington. The long hours of work, however, imposed limitations to social mingling in the city, as the labor she performed could go well into the late evening hours. Available at any given moment, enslaved women were integral to the local labor economy and configured in the intimate spaces and private organization of Washington households.

In the early national period, hierarchies based on race, class, and gender shaped the social transformations of the capital. Political leaders and their wives did the work of nation building as they articulated political ideologies, economic imperatives, and the social conventions that shaped American society.[132] Labor customs that included both free and slave labor also shaped the racial and gendered contours of white households. White women relied heavily on the labor of enslaved women. Even the wife of Philip Barton Key, Ann Key, placed a runaway notice for forty-four-year-old Barbara, whom she described as "one of the best female cooks in the country."[133] Perhaps learning of Philip's involvement with freedom suits inspired Barbara's pursuit of liberty. Nevertheless, Ann hoped to find her and offered a lucrative reward set at one hundred dollars. The value she brought to the household was clear, and this rang true for many well-known wives of the city. Therefore, the parlor politics of white women was intricately tied to their roles as slave owners. The basis of an emerging political elite hinged on the ways they extracted the labor, skills, and value associated with enslaved women. For white women who did not own slaves, the labor of black domestic servants buttressed the racial and gender hierarchies that made racial subjugation a common and even palatable feature of life among the elite in nineteenth-century Washington.

Just as the international trade came to a formal close, the federal city stood to profit from both the domestic slave trade farther south and the interregional practices of exchanging labor with neighboring states. Another source of revenue from the commerce in slaves came from policies that taxed enslaved people hired to work in Washington. On July 1, 1808, the city council of Washington passed local legislation imposing a tax on slaves owned by nonresidents.[134] The act stipulated specific sums of money, which legislators determined by age and gender. To hire enslaved males under the age of eighteen, slaveholders paid a tax set at eight dollars a year. For enslaved men over the age of eighteen, the capital required a sum of fifteen dollars per year. Enslaved females under the age of eighteen generated an annual tax of four to six dollars annually. The higher sum for men could possibly point to the value assigned to skills based on the gendered ways that slaveholders typically marketed their labor.[135] The potential revenue for the tax applied to the widespread practice of slave hiring encouraged residence within the District. In other words, if one decided to be a slaveholder, why not realize those aspirations in the nation's capital? The work of building a capital worthy of the political project of the new republic required labor, and the city offered the comforts of living and entertaining that slave labor accommodated in an unwieldy and undeveloped village. In his initial plans for the federal village, George Washington showed no signs of abandoning the institution of slavery in the new capital. He regarded the social dynamics and geographical landscape, as they existed in the Chesapeake, perfectly suitable for the new nation and believed that slavery might eventually disappear. The economic and social development of the capital hardly led to innovation, but it reflected the ways that the states of the republic cohered in both the general acceptance of slavery and the eager application of its benefits to the city. The tension between slavery and freedom would have to remain. The scores of transactions that fed the steady commerce in enslaved women and children, however, often inspired resistance in a place like Washington.

One Saturday evening, an enslaved woman named Maria met with three men, also enslaved in Washington, D.C., who collectively plotted an escape from the region. According to one account, "They put their heads together to count up the cost and to fix a time for leaving Egypt."[136] One source noted that Maria, regarded as the "heroine of the party," "found her owners hard to please, and quite often, without the slightest reason, they would threaten to 'sell or make a change.'" The everyday commerce in slaves and the customs of "making a change," cashing in on debts, and putting them up for collateral fueled resentment among enslaved women. The raconteur noted that "these threats only made matters worse, or rather it only served to nerve Maria for the conflict."[137] Maria and her accomplices made it to Harrisburg, Pennsylvania, on foot and proceeded farther north on their journey toward Canada. The biblical reference to Egypt as the site of slavery meant that the "promised land" of the Israelites was the place of imagined liberty, the metaphor for where her life as a free woman could unfold.

Enslaved women's labors and lives were woven into the fabric of the labor economy of the capital, and each transaction that led to their sale or hire involved a variety of actors, including tavern keepers, estate managers, women, men, newspaper editors, lawyers, and people from neighboring Chesapeake counties. Advertisements and bills of sale reveal the vital function of slavery as an engine for the economic growth of the District. Slavery shaped how both enslaved and free African Americans navigated the opportunities and constraints of life in the nation's capital. Washington began as a site of slavery, and enslaved women's lives were a testament to the ways that the nation's capital also functioned as a contested site of liberty.

CHAPTER TWO

Fugitivity

In Washington, enslaved women's experiences and relationships exposed them to information about various avenues for flight. Wherever they went, they navigated the city with an accumulated knowledge of the homes, churches, businesses, and people that populated Washington. Their mobility, albeit circumscribed by slave codes, shaped their comprehension of the advantages and risks associated with escape in the area. If their cards were played just right, enslaved women, traveling with family and loved ones or running alone, made it as far north as Canada. While the exception rather than the rule, these escapes capture women's strategies of navigation and self-making in ways that add complexity to our understandings of the ways gender might have worked in the lives of enslaved women in Washington. William Still explained that "females undertook three times the risk of failure that males are liable to," and yet many of the enslaved women included in his records defied the odds.[1] Moreover, nineteenth-century ideas about gender at times meant that enslaved women remained where they were because of obligations of kin and children. Correspondingly, historians such as Deborah Gray White, Elizabeth Fox-Genovese, and Brenda Stevenson have argued that gender ideals practiced among the enslaved left the responsibility of caring for loved ones and maintaining family ties primarily to women.[2] White offers, "Also important in understanding why females ran away less frequently than men is the fact that women tended to be more concerned with the welfare of their children, and this limited their mobility."[3] According to John Hope Franklin and Loren Schweninger, men constituted 81 percent of people advertised as runaways primarily between the ages of thirteen and twenty-nine.[4] Gender norms factored into the relatively lower rates of female flight in the slaveholding South, particularly in circumstances that involved the care of family members or longer travel distances.[5] This chapter explores the ways that such factors did not inevitably prevent women from attempting escape in the Upper South. Enslaved women in Washington employed strategies of navigation to escape, indicating the ways they planned to shape new identities and lives within and outside the nation's capital.

Enslaved women who lived in Washington deliberated over a number of considerations when contemplating escape, including living a life wrought with the anxieties of being returned or killed, the pain of leaving families and loved ones behind if they decided to run alone, and the sheer uncertainty of surviving and overcoming a lack of resources upon arrival. These factors often caused women to decide to remain where they were. Moreover, enslaved women embraced opportunities for redress in a variety of ways, many of which excluded escape.[6] Existing scholarship emphasizes resistance within the vicinity of plantations to show a broader spectrum of responses to slavery and to explore the rival geographies that enslaved women populated.[7] For instance, enslaved women absconded momentarily by engaging in truancy, and they resisted within the geographical boundaries of the plantation and within the perimeter of the plantation household. Furthermore, enslaved women were not solely motivated by their care for others and were compelled to act for a variety of reasons. Stories of flight offer ways of understanding how enslaved women did not operate within the framework of plantation geographies alone but deployed strategies of navigation beyond white homes. The sources discussed here do not reflect a large number of escapes, nor do they fully capture the complexities of life as an enslaved woman in the Chesapeake region. These cases do show that enslaved women took seriously the possibilities of flight, invention, and their dreams of liberty, even as they were tied to family and kin.

An examination of the shards of information offered in the record illuminates possible motivations, as well as connections and strategies at their disposal throughout the course of their escapes. Information about fugitive women appeared in the most widely circulated medium of human hunting—runway advertisements. Advertisers launched searches of fugitive women that required slave catchers to think more strategically about the antislavery networks that they employed. Runaway advertisements, abolitionist literature, and publicized legal battles foreground enslaved women's escapes amid a booming regional slave market. The growing demand for human property in the southwest and the federal protection of the property rights of slaveholders meant that the District became not just a site of intraregional escape but a "corridor" of flight as the borders of liberty were pushed beyond the North. This dynamic between slave owners and fugitive women highlights the persistent tensions that shaped black life in the city, as well as the ability of black women to adapt to unpredictable and intensifying circumstances. These sources show a multidimensional contest consisting of improvisation, self-making, and strategic navigation among enslaved women. But the actions of these women did not unfold without the threat of reenslavement. Notorious slave-trading firms such as Robey's, William H. Williams's Yellow

House, George Miller's Tavern, Franklin and Armfield's, Price, Birch and Company, and Kephart's Slave Mart, as well as countless local agents, traded thousands of slaves annually, regionally and farther South.[8] The lucrative enterprise of the slave market gave weight to the hostilities and vulnerabilities that black women and girls faced in their daily lives in the capital, but their actions show how they made Washington a site of liberty. Decades before these firms dominated the regional trade and abolitionist ferment erupted, enslaved women carved out pathways of escape.

In the early decades of the nineteenth century, enslaved women escaped from slaveholders in Washington, assembling the tools of navigation that brought together their knowledge of the region, its people, and potential networks of kin. Tied to the surrounding Chesapeake counties, members of the Virginia and Maryland slaveholding class frequented the new capital to search for fugitive women and found residents willing to identify runaways. Indeed, Alexandria still remained part of the District of Columbia until retrocession in 1846. In keeping with the Fugitive Slave Law of 1793, runaway enslaved women from the neighboring states were promptly jailed, returned to their owners upon capture, or sold farther south.[9] Two venues anchored the search for runaway enslaved people after the establishment of the capital on the Potomac: the jail, located less than a mile from the unfinished Capitol building, and the local newspapers with printing offices located in the District.

On New Jersey Avenue just between D and E Streets SE, news and advertisements were printed in the press at the building that housed the *National Intelligencer*—the news organ that featured the slave sales examined in the previous chapter. In 1810, Samuel Smith sold the paper to Joseph Gales Jr., who partnered with William Winston Seaton two years later. Smith, Gales, and Seaton would play leading roles in local politics and business throughout the first half of the nineteenth century, and newspapers more generally were important engines of surveillance and slave catching.[10] The beginning of the nineteenth century presented the editors with the unique opportunity to capture the most formative moments of the early republic and life in the capital. From early sessions of Congress to the War of 1812, the *Intelligencer* featured political debates, business ventures, local affairs, dispatches from war, and local advertisements. It boasted a significant readership and profited from paid advertisements for plots of land, as well as slave auctions and runaway notices.[11] Many of the advertisements mentioned in the previous chapter show that inquiries regarding the purchase of land and human property were made to the editor, demonstrating the ways that newspapers provided an essential medium for the speculative and commercial activity associated with the sale of enslaved women. These editors served not only as liaisons of the local trades but also as intermediaries in the hunt for fugitives. For enslaved women who decided to escape, the newspaper publications might feature a description of them and, interestingly, the ways that they fashioned new identities while in flight.

The local news reported "notices" that signaled when enslaved women escaped bondage and potentially sought either permanent or temporary refuge in the capital. This created a tense and persistent dynamic between the actions of enslaved women and the efforts of slaveholders to generate localized networks of surveillance.[12] The tensions sparked by announcements of flight also underscored the friction between the designs of racialized law and the ways enslaved women often engaged in extralegal processes of self-making. These processes manifested in altered physical appearances and dress, different names, possession of stolen goods, and new locations for living and work. While the lack of fugitive voices underscores critical silences in the newspapers, the announcements reveal an elusive glimpse into the kinds of choices and experiences that shaped their lives and informed their processes of self-definition. We also see routes of navigation that show how enslaved women might abscond temporarily or permanently escape within and outside the bounds of the District. If caught, they landed in the city jail—a facility that had required immediate construction if slavery were to remain a viable feature of the new capital.

In the spring of 1802, Thomas Jefferson authorized the erection of a new jail in the District.[13] Before this decision, a modest building composed of brick with small rooms characteristic of jails in Chesapeake towns served as the site of confinement. Jesse Torrey observed that the jail was "frequently occupied as a store house for the slave merchants," which reveals the interconnectedness between local municipal institutions and the growing local slave trade.[14] The first jail, located on a lot on C Street between Fourth and Sixth Streets NW, continued to be used by the levy court after the president proposed a new building, and that same year, Congress appropriated funds for the construction of an expanded jail comprising eight cells on each side that measured eight by ten feet.[15] The physical structures of policing and confinement functioned as the places where slave law and black codes were reinforced and protected. The jail, however, could also be leveraged in the strategies of navigation employed by African American women.

One summer evening in 1802, Millie, a black woman, along with a prisoner described as a "stout" and "lusty" Irishman, broke out of jail with a Dutchman named Charles; Thomas Naylor, a native of Virginia; and William Pickeron, an

Englishman.[16] Black women like Millie could find themselves in jail for a number of offenses stipulated in slave and black codes, while white inhabitants answered to a different set of laws. The notice did not indicate whether Millie was arrested with the men, and we have no way of understanding the nature of their acquaintance. Escape notices generally focused on descriptions of personality, race, ethnicity, place of birth, height, and age. A fifty-dollar reward incentivized the suspicion of people who met the descriptions, but it also certainly raises the question of whether a collective break across such racial, gender, and ethnic differences was a common occurrence. The provost marshal identified the Irishman, Daniel Heinesy, as particularly notorious and the most likely to lead an escape from the prison since he boasted an impressive record of breaking out of jail twice before in Alexandria. Records of jailbreaks appeared infrequently, and this incident was unusual. Jails typically confined black people, and black women in particular, separately from white male inmates. The white men involved would have had to intentionally collaborate with her since they were jailed apart from one another. Millie escaped prison, but no further information resurfaced that confirmed where she landed. Her escape shows the intersections of local lawbreaking and the racial complexity of early carceral spaces.[17] The jail served a number of functions tied to the enforcement of laws, as well as the interests of stakeholders in the slave trade. News editors employed the same tactics for capturing runaways in order to return inmates. These tactics involved publicly deploying intelligence about black women that put forth ideas about the notorious nature of their offenses and their conspiratorial personalities. But what if these descriptors were also insights into the processes of self-making or competing ideas about liberty? Editors, slave catchers, and slaveholders placed notices about these women in the news in an effort to uphold slave law and make a case for the criminal nature of their actions, but these notices also reveal black women's strategies for navigation and self-definition.

In early spring, Charlotte, a young enslaved woman, escaped Battle Town, Virginia, in Frederick County. After she had made her way past Prince William, Fairfax, and Alexandria Counties and across the Potomac River, she was committed to the Washington jail and a notice of her capture and the fees required to cover her confinement was soon published in the local news.[18] Similar to other notices in the early decades of the nineteenth century, the news about Charlotte reveals that enslaved women sought refuge within the District, perhaps to connect with people they were acquainted with. On February 20, 1802, officials arrested and jailed Sarah Ann Owens, an enslaved woman of approximately twenty-three years of age who belonged to William Foote of

Alexandria.[19] No explanation exists to clarify her potential motivations, although, for many, freedom itself would suffice as a significant reason. Perhaps the fact that she left tells us that she saw flight to the District as a conceivable enterprise. The scars on her breast bore a physical testament to what her treatment might have been like in Foote's custody. Just three days after Owens's arrest, Daniel Brent, marshal of the District, admitted another enslaved woman named Peggy after she fled a slaveholder in Port Tobacco, Maryland.[20] Described as "a dark Mulatto Woman" at five feet, four inches, Peggy also showed burn scars on her right arm, perhaps from domestic and cooking responsibilities or physical branding or abuse. Visible signs of pain, violence, and hard labor underscored that slavery proved far from lenient for enslaved women in Washington. The decline of staple crop plantation slavery and the subsequent rise in hiring out did not shield black women from abusive conditions. These women most likely shared cells with one another during their confinement. The jail served as a punitive space where they learned to navigate interactions with jailors, judges, slave traders, and one another. In the jails, they were reminded that their liberty was a crime. Some advertisements disclosed motivations for escape and clues about the living and working conditions they experienced.

In the late spring of 1802, Priscilla, a forty-five-year-old woman described as "very black" and short, escaped within the District. John Sasser, the slaveholder who placed an advertisement in the news, further noted that he couldn't verify her clothing and that "it is likely she may change her cloathing," demonstrating his own anticipation and understanding of enslaved women's sartorial strategies of self-making.[21] Women like Priscilla employed these rituals of liberty that allowed them to alter their appearance when they possessed the resources to do so. She also bore a "sore" on her right wrist, likely an outcome of repeated tasks from the labor demanded of her or evidence of having worn wrist shackles. He explained that she spent most of her life in Great Falls, Virginia, along the Potomac, and that he purchased her from a seller in the capital. Perhaps this was a relatively recent transaction and Priscilla found the conditions intolerable or the proximity to the District and the small free black community inspired her to flee. While we cannot verify the immediate stimulus for flight, Priscilla's actions indicate that she was a quick study for someone who spent most of her life across the Potomac.

During the summer of 1804, twenty-year-old Rachel escaped the custody of Francis Clark in Baltimore. Advanced in pregnancy and "stout made," Rachel didn't hesitate to take clothing belonging to her mistress.[22] This likely came as a surprise, since Clark described her as possessing "a bashful look when spoken to." A potentially shy young woman dressed in expensive cloth-ing and quite possibly exhausted from the late stages of pregnancy didn't fit typical descriptions of fugitive women. She embodied a new vision of herself in her navigation of both fugitivity and the possibilities of liberty for both herself and her unborn child. Baffled as they might have been, the Clarks con-tinued their search two years later, posting another notice. The second notice explained that Rachel had possibly fled to Georgetown, where "ALL her connec-tions" reside, and a place in which she "WILL pass herself for a free woman."[23] Rachel possessed connections in the District that reveal critical networks of kin and resistance that might have included relatives or friends who made her es-cape possible. Clark revised the reward for her capture from the ten dollars advertised in the first notice to fifty dollars two years later.

Another woman appeared recurrently in the local news because of her his-tory of repeated escape in the region. Massey Simms hired out Fame, an en-slaved woman in her thirties in Prince George's County. Simms described Fame as "very black, small featured," and noted that her face showed numer-ous scars and an eye defect from small pox and that she was last seen wearing "blue striped country cloth" and had reportedly been in Washington since she escaped.[24] He believed that she obtained a free pass from a black woman named Charity Shorty, who lived as a free woman in the city. Her relationship to Charity offers a glimpse into black women's local networks to show that they were willing to lend their support and quite possibly their literacy and writing abilities for another woman's escape. The following year, Simms posted another notice in search of Fame that revealed more details about her past and potential strategies of self-definition.[25] In the second notice, Simms described Fame as "very artful and cunning, having procured a free pass," and stated that before his purchase of Fame, she made several escape attempts over the course of eight years and was subsequently caught, apprehended, and sold to him. Simms decided to hire her out, and soon after he placed her with Thomas King of Prince George's County, she fled. He believed that after she secured a pass, she likely left for Calvert County, where her husband re-sided, revealing the role of family as a compelling motivation for flight. With the tremendous risks involved, passes, money, strategic relationships, and material goods were tools of navigation for intraregional and interregional es-capes. Hence, black women redefined their social designations, but they also gave new meaning to the emancipatory possibilities of the District well be-fore antebellum underground networks took shape.

At the beginning of the nineteenth century, enslaved women not only es-caped from owners within the District, but many of them possibly arrived from farther distances. In the spring of 1804, a woman named Phillis escaped a plantation owned by John Johnston in South Carolina. At the age of twenty-two, she left South Carolina with her husband, Strother. Johnston described Phillis as having a "medium build," "trim made," with a black complexion. Described as five feet, nine inches tall, "stout made," and "yellow complexioned," Strother was most easily identified by large scars on his back—scars inflicted from a severe beating. Johnston requested that the fugitives be admitted to any jail upon discovery.[26] What moved him to place an advertisement in Washington all the way from rural South Carolina? Before their escape, Johnston had purchased them from Edward Carter of Prince William County, Virginia. The couple met on Carter's plantation, but more importantly, Prince William County, located just thirty miles outside the District, was home. Their previous experiences furnished the knowledge required for navigating the region, but Prince William County also was the place in which their marital bond originated. As historians have noted, enslaved and free black people forged close-knit community ties that lasted through generations in northern Virginia, and Strother and Phillis's case was one of the rare instances in which enslaved people managed to sustain conjugal ties against the odds.[27] Not all fugitive women could claim ties to people in the region, however, and many enacted bold plans for escape with a limited sense of how to navigate local life.

Not long after her arrival from France, an enslaved girl described as a "dark mulatoe French girl" escaped at the age of fifteen.[28] Her owner did not list her name but simply referred to her as "girl." Why might an enslaved girl from France think to escape in a city completely foreign to her? What did she hear or learn about Washington and its people that made her chart her course toward liberty there? Her story is a testament to her ability to dramatically reorient herself in a strange place with strange customs, laws, and people. To take such bold action with limited resources and networks was characteristic of the ways black girls navigated Washington as a site of both bondage and possible refuge. Likewise, twelve-year-old Celia left the Virginia home of James S. Scott in the fall of 1805. Described as a "mulatto girl," she went by Nancy Adams—the alias she created for herself.[29] Black girls made the nation's capital a site of liberty where they employed their own strategies of self-definition, a place in which they were vulnerable, but a city where they could also redefine themselves, escape the terror of coming of age in a slaveholding household, or go by the name Nancy.

Escape notices underscore the ways that the perceptions of slaveholders and enslaved women collided, creating both a narrative of surveillance and a record of enslaved women's strategies for self-making. Just when slave owners thought they understood their human property, the women acted on ideas about themselves that conflicted with their behavior in bondage. One notice illuminates this point. On the morning of Christmas Day in 1804, Hannah, an enslaved woman wearing a green jacket and petticoat made of a thick kersey cloth for the winter months, toted a large sack filled with two pairs of shoes and stockings, a coarse hat, a "yellow ground calico habit," a white petticoat, a spotted jacket, and a raw bonnet.[30] In addition to a modest sum of money, she took much of what might be needed for a longer and more permanent journey than she led others to believe. Simon Sommers placed an urgent advertisement and warned the reader that "she is capable of great deception, sometimes she appears to be passive, and has but little to say when it is to answer her purpose, but at other times extremely impudent."[31] In a display of reticence and discretion not too dissimilar from those observed in the women mentioned earlier, Hannah changed her mode of conduct to avoid suspicion. Not until her escape did Sommers realize who Hannah really was. Hannah convinced the owner that her unobtrusiveness affirmed the unlikelihood of escape. Once the opportunity arrived, however, she absconded with the kind of boldness that incited an enslaved person to trek through the harsh winter of the Chesapeake with stolen goods. Hannah and the women who appeared in runaway advertisements show the manner in which they imagined and defined themselves and their lives beyond the purview of slaveholders. Hannah plotted her unflinching designs of liberty at a time when slavery functioned as the centerpiece of the labor economy in the struggling new capital. Lawmakers and leading locals continued to nurture the contradictions of liberty and bondage that defined life in Washington. One incident became the cause célèbre that reminded locals why slavery and the expanding slave trade posed a conundrum in the capital.

Just before dawn on December 19, 1815, slave traders from Georgia assembled a coffle of slaves on F Street near a local tavern owned by George Miller. Taverns located in the federal village often functioned as the sites of slave auctions and depots that marked the beginning of a grueling trek along key trade routes headed toward the Deep South. The Chesapeake slave trade geographically spanned south and west, and it demanded an intense journey that funneled scores of African Americans from Washington into the domestic slave market. Before the sun appeared on that wintry morning, an enslaved woman named Ann jumped out of a three-story window just above the designated starting point of the slave coffle. The men leading the coffle, however, would have to leave without her, as Ann was in no condition to walk with both arms broken and a shattered spine. "I didn't want to go, and I jumped out of the window; —but I am sorry now that I did it," she reportedly confessed.[32] Ann not only lamented the fact that she suffered life-altering injuries, but she remained separated from her husband and children, who were sold to the Carolinas. At the risk of her life, and in a moment just before the traders prepared to chain her to the other enslaved people in the coffle, she saw only one way out.

Ann used what limited power black women possessed at a time when their fate was often determined by a powerful law and the white men and women who wielded it. Such physical interventions changed the course of their lives in a split second and, in other instances, followed years of contemplating an existence beyond chains. Their actions show that the relationships torn apart by the domestic slave trade constituted a vital source of identity and belonging amid the day-to-day drudgery of bondage. Indeed, Michael Burton, Kwakiutl Dreher, and William Thomas III depict Ann's marriage in the film *Anna*, which visually dramatizes her husband walking countless miles to visit her and their children.[33] The length of this vignette is drawn out just enough to leave the viewer contemplating the duration of the walk. These bonds gave life in a place where death and separation loomed as an ever-present possibility. The perspectives of enslaved women shed light on the critical role that relationships played in their strategies for self-making and survival. At a time when the nation was embarking on a revolutionary political project, enslaved women in Washington envisaged lives that were not defined by bondage. Moreover, most black women during the early years of the capital remained enslaved, even as white Americans expressed discomfort and embarrassment when they witnessed coffles of enslaved people walking past or learned of the violence inflicted on enslaved women.[34] Ann's daughters were forced into the very coffle that awaited her, into the hands of the "Georgia man," the slave trader known among the enslaved as the notorious agent of their sale, separation, and subjection to violence.[35] Miller, the owner of the tavern near where Ann jumped, purchased her, and she later gave birth to more children with her husband. Although testimonies indicate that Miller permitted Ann to go about the city freely, legally she remained enslaved. She petitioned the court for her freedom with legal assistance from Francis Scott Key, attorney and author of "The Star-Spangled Banner."[36] The litigation of Ann's freedom suit also reminds us that more flexible terms of servitude did not change her desires to be free. As we will see in the following chapter, Key played an important role in enslaved women's local freedom suits. Although he freed seven enslaved people he owned upon his death, eight remained in bondage.[37] He

Ann Williams leaping out of the tavern. Jesse Torrey, *A Portraiture of Domestic Slavery, in the United States* [. . .] (Philadelphia: published by the author; John Bioren, printer, 1817).

embodied the contradictions that locals wrestled with as he continued to benefit from slavery while also arguing that free people possessed the right to legal protection of their freedom. His efforts to help Ann marked one of many cases in the legal fight for liberty. Immediately following the revolution, the number of manumissions and appeals for liberty increased with some measure of success.[38]

Despite the fact that Ann's initial attempt to escape failed, she never stopped trying and won her petition for freedom in 1832. Her actions formed the beginnings of local abolitionist legend. Before Miller's tavern burned in a fire in 1819, locals associated the place with "old Anna" as an expression of their objections to the slave trade.[39] Philadelphia doctor Jesse Torrey published Ann's story along with a woodcut illustration of her leaping out of the window in a pamphlet condemning slavery in the District. Torrey's publication was so widely read that John Randolph, congressman and slaveholder, found in Ann inspiration for the American Colonization Society, an organization that proposed deportation to initiate the decline of slavery.[40] Historians have emphasized the ways that Ann's story generated antislavery sympathy among District locals, including the mayor and his wife, who reportedly came to her rescue upon hearing her fall.[41] This approach portrays District residents as reluctant supporters of slavery burdened by the salacious demands of traders from Georgia and the cotton enterprises of the Deep South. The previous chapter, however, tempers this claim with evidence of the direct involvement of District residents in the steady exchange of the slave trade as they sold, hired, and bequeathed enslaved people both within and beyond the District. This is evident in advertisements such as one that inquired about a "servant woman," with a stipulation that "a slave would be preferred."[42] Local antislavery sentiment comingled with a vested interest in slaveholding. Ann's story stopped traffic for the moment, but locals mastered the art of complicity, the delicate balance between sympathy for the enslaved and the rejection of an emancipatory project based on racial equality. The story of "old Anna" stirred the founders of the American Colonization Society, but the society was not established with the freedom dreams of black women in mind. The reach of Ann's story was much broader than white Americans making sense of the contradictions of slavery and liberty. It is quite possible that Ann's very public attempts to become free, to the point of death, were discussed among enslaved women in the District. Her physical intervention reveals that the burgeoning slave trade constrained and shifted the currents of navigation that made escape possible. Enslaved women would need to be flexible and inventive in a city with a vigorous slave trade.

The decades following Ann's escape signaled the emergence of the capital as the heart of human trafficking where enslaved people were collected from the Chesapeake, incarcerated in the capital, and sent farther south. More cries could be heard from the growing number of desolate dens of bondage that appeared throughout the national mall and along prominent blocks of the city. Indeed, slave-trading firms appeared more organized and efficient than ever before, and the District of Columbia offered a number of opportunities for participants involved in the business of buying and selling enslaved and free black people.[43] Firms became increasingly integral to life in Washington, with establishments located along the national mall and near the Capitol. Enslaved people were marched to Center Market on Pennsylvania Avenue and sold alongside goods and wares. Slave trader Joseph W. Neale placed an advertisement in which he promised to pay "the highest prices in cash, for one hundred and fifty likely young Negroes, of both sexes, families included." He noted that he "can at all times be found at W. Robey's, on 7th street, south of the Centre Market House."[44] When they were not on the auction block, they were confined in slave pens such as the one at Robey's Tavern. Adjacent to Robey's, a pedestrian might spot an unassuming yellow building owned by William H. Williams, who funneled enslaved people to the infamous "Yellow House" just before they were forced to go to slave markets along the Mississippi River. Williams recommended that traders bring their enslaved cargo to the building at least a couple of days before boarding the *Tribune* or the *Unca*.[45] John Armfield placed a notice that stated, "Servants are intended to be shipped, will at any time be received for safe keeping at 25 cents per day."[46] Armfield's firm posted another advertisement that informed slave owners that the *Tribune* and *Unca* left the port every thirty days.[47] In addition to providing information about scheduled departures, they hoped to fill those vessels with more enslaved people. In an advertisement titled "CASH for 400 Negroes," the firm placed the following call: "Persons having likely servants to dispose of, will find it to be in their interest to give us a call, as we will give higher prices in cash than any other purchaser who is now, or may hereafter, come into this market."[48] Hotels and taverns doubled as accommodations for guests and reliable sites of confinement for slave traders in need of temporary quarters for enslaved people. The Southern Hotel was located at the end of King Street when the District of Columbia territory included Alexandria. One advertisement placed by the hotel offered "comfortable accommodation of travelers," with "particular provision for gentlemen from the Southern Country and for the security and support of their servants."[49] Lloyd's Tavern, the St. Charles Hotel, the United States Hotel, and the courtyards of the

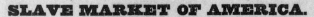

Slave market of America, 1836. Published by the American Anti-slavery Society. Rare Books and Special Collections Department, Library of Congress.

Decatur House, the Van Ness House, and Joel Barlow's Kalorama home ac-commodated slave traders with business ties to Georgia, New Orleans, and auction sites along the Mississippi River.[50] The emergence of more profes-sionalized trading firms and the ongoing activity of slave catchers who hunted fugitives and abducted black residents made the District a precarious site of liberty.

The geographical direction of escapes shifted after the first three decades of the nineteenth century, from flight within the District to long crossings farther north. Notices increasingly indicated that enslaved women set their sights on life as far as Canada rather than melting into the black population in the capital. Enslaved women undoubtedly understood the mounting surveil-lance efforts in the Upper South and in Washington in particular. The legal apparatus in place also coincided with the geographic significance of the capi-tal as a targeted corridor for fugitives and slave traders who capitalized on failed attempts at escape. As early as 1819, Washington implemented laws that allowed the immediate imprisonment of any black people unable to furnish proof of their freedom. By the 1840s, the U.S. marshal for the capital regularly sold off African Americans imprisoned for the inability to prove their legal status.[51] Appointed by the president, the local official sold black people, free and enslaved, repeatedly in the local trade and under full authorization of the law if they committed a criminal offense.[52] As Washington became a signifi-cant target of both abolitionist and proslavery interests, the city appeared in-creasingly hostile to black inhabitants. Enslaved women took note of this changing legal and political climate and employed strategies to evade the mounting surveillance of District marshals. For enslaved women, the nation's capital became a corridor for flight.

In Washington, D.C., and the neighboring slave states, enslaved women escaped with the hope of shaping a different life beyond bondage for them-selves and others. A variety of reasons informed an enslaved woman's deci-sion to run, including what Stephanie Camp refers to as "such 'push' factors as labor disputes, violence, and terror, on one hand, and the 'pull' of incen-tives such as reconnection with family and community, on the other."[53] En-slaved women, who remained subject to harsh punishment upon discovery, risked their lives and quite possibly the lives of loved ones should a slave owner decide to seek vengeance on their kin in their stead. In the moment of flight, women acted on their own understandings of what aspects of their lives, labor, and loyalty whites were entitled to. The kinship and antislavery networks forged across state lines, and the proximity to free soil, informed whether escape appeared within the realm of possibility for those willing to endure the perilous journey.[54] The study of enslaved women's escapes must be put in a regional context, using sources that reflect the experiences of those who traversed borderlands during their escape. Enslaved women fled from Maryland and Virginia to the District, and from the District into Maryland and on toward free states such as Pennsylvania. Ramped up efforts to return fugitives expanded the geographic scope of surveillance, and the District functioned as a corridor that fugitive women passed through to journey farther north.

"Negro thieves" or antislavery mediators within the District and outside the territory were associated with the runaway networks that assisted with enslaved women's escapes. These mediators, who included fellow slaves, abolitionists, and family members and acquaintances, were all criminalized as instigators of theft. An article titled "Negro Stealing" noted, "Horse thieves and negro thieves abound; and all efforts to catch them appear to be unsuccessful. We are of opinion that the only way to catch a negro thief is to watch the Northern routes."[55] Just as fugitives and abolitionists charted interregional and intraregional routes of escape, slave catchers theorized about the best avenues for capture. Indeed, the article confirms that enslaved women received critical support informed by their knowledge and networks. Some abolitionists estimated that they assisted with at least 150 escapes. These networks existed in pockets of the District that included places of worship. Churches in Washington, such as Mt. Zion United Methodist Church and Ebenezer Church (later renamed Israel Bethel Colored Methodist Episcopal Church), assisted with slave escapes. Locals lamented the fact that the capital had become the center of antislavery activity and, accordingly, supported efforts to retrieve fugitives.[56]

Notices of fugitive women reveal that their escapes were typically not solitary experiences. Enslaved women in Washington escaped by themselves, but some also fled with kin. Just a day after Christmas, Henny escaped from the household of Lewis Edwards with her twenty-one-month-old daughter.[57] After living some time in Georgetown, an enslaved woman, Anne, was purchased by members of the Diggs family.[58] The transaction likely inspired her escape, and she fled with her son Henry, who was not yet two years old. In another case, Betsey Adams, described as a "tall yellow woman," escaped from Alex Ewell with her two sons, Oliver and John, and her three-year-old daughter, Laura.[59] She managed to abscond while also pregnant with a fourth child. Violetta Graves also fled with her two sons, Chas and John, and daughters, Mary and Emma. The executor of the estate of Mary Bundy, the owner of the group, submitted the advertisement. His involvement in placing the notice offers an indicator that they likely escaped as a result of Bundy's death.[60] As discussed in the previous chapter, decisions regarding the division of assets and the resolution of outstanding debts often led to the separation of families, a leading cause for escape. An entire family comprising Geo; his wife, Sigismunda; and their eight-year-old daughter, Maria, not only fled their owner in Alexandria but also helped themselves to twenty dollars cash, a stopwatch, and clothing.[61] The roster of fugitives also included young people. Advertised as a "mulatto girl," twelve-year-old Parker worked as a hire for the Cathart household in the city for several months before she ran away "without the least provocation."[62] Enslaved women and girls, who experienced a range of living and labor conditions, discovered pathways to escape.

The close proximity to densely populated slave states made the District a key passageway of escape, particularly in the antebellum era, when the demographic transformations of the city reflected an increase in the free black population.[63] Enslaved women who fled to the nation's capital often attempted to temporarily pass as free people who resembled members of this expanding group of inhabitants. They found assistance from a growing network of free black residents in the District as early as 1830. As noted earlier in this chapter, enslaved and free African Americans, particularly family members, assisted in escapes as early as 1800 with the establishment of the capital on the Potomac. Escape networks formed between 1830 and 1850 reveal broader access to institutions and resources that transformed the scope of the District as a corridor to freedom. Women fugitives might encounter the growing network of safe houses and agents within and outside the region that appear in William Still's famous accounts. The underground activity of fugitive women and their allies gave the city another purpose and meaning.[64] Precise plans and networks of escape prove quite difficult to detect in the archive since such efforts entailed confidentiality. Abolitionist accounts, however, reveal that a network of free African Americans in the city made escapes possible. Countless unnamed black residents who worked for the government, owned businesses and property, and built churches and schools subsequently deployed their resources and reputations in ways that supported their covert efforts to offer aid for slave escapes.[65]

District resident Thomas Smallwood left accounts of an escape involving a family of four. A former bondman himself, Smallwood understood the precarious conditions enslaved women faced. He often partnered with well-known abolitionist Charles Torrey, who was imprisoned for infamously bombarding a convention of slaveholders in Annapolis, Maryland.[66] Smallwood met Torrey after an introduction from Smallwood's wife, who worked at the boardinghouse where Torrey temporarily resided. The pair shared plots of escapes and one such plan in particular. In late August 1842, Torrey planned to head north with the hope of taking a little over a dozen fugitives with him.[67] They managed to secure the necessary teamster from a huckster hoping to sell their wagon. The fifteen were instructed to meet at a specified location at a particular time. Sources from black abolitionists reveal coded language that refers to fugitives as "packages." These "packages" arrived at various depots that directed them to the next location. That evening, everyone arrived at the designated spot. Smallwood and Torrey ran into logistical issues, however, which led to delay. With plans driven to a halt, they proceeded to hide each member of the party throughout the District. In Smallwood's accounts of his activity, we learn that hiding fugitives at designated locations within the District was a common strategy used by those engaged in vigilance work.

The following morning, it did not take long for slave owners to realize that the women and men were missing. A search party spread out onto northern routes with the hope of tracking down the missing fifteen. Meanwhile, in the District, where the fugitives had taken cover, a woman and her two children hoped to join the group after her husband's futile attempts to purchase them failed. This presented a challenge for Smallwood, but an opportune moment for the woman. Ordinarily, assisting a mother and her children, according to him, was not ideal, but he managed to do so on many occasions. In this particular instance, Smallwood grappled with the danger of retrieving the woman's daughter, a little girl between five and six years of age. The little girl was forced to tend to the owner's infant, meaning that even at the age of five or six, she worked well into the night. "That child was required to set all night by the side of a cradle in its master's and mistress's bed chamber in order that if their child should awake, she should rock it, to prevent it from disturbing their slumbers," he recalled.[68] The mission of retrieving her was even outside the purview of Smallwood's extensive experience assisting fugitives. Aware of his own limitations, he admitted, "To get that child was the work of its mother, and to do it required some skill and caution. However, she did it admirably; it seemed, as if by special providence of the Lord, a heavy sleep had come upon her master and mistress so that she went into their bed chamber as she informed me since and took her child from the side of the cradle, without a stir on their part."[69] The slaveholder woke up the next morning only to find that the woman and child were gone. He immediately boarded a train headed to Baltimore. With a search party dispatched along the northern roads, the slave patrols returned empty-handed. The slaveholder returned that same evening, confounded by the pace at which the woman and her children escaped. To this, Smallwood remarked, "And no wonder for they had not left the City." Intraurban escape offered a temporary option for avoiding detection. Fugitives led patrollers on a manhunt while they remained in the city, a tactic that left slaveholders scratching their heads in aimless paranoia. Once the sun set, Torrey and the group commenced the long journey. The mother and her children arrived safely in Canada, "never to be placed there [in Washington] again, to spend a weary night for their [slave owners'] comfort."[70] Those "weary" nights that shaped the little girl's childhood in Washington came to an abrupt end. The mother and father of the little girl later testified that the man who owned them frequently boasted that no one could pull a fast one on him, but the family managed to beat the odds even with their daughter under his watchful eye.

Smallwood's narrative reveals important aspects of the local operations of covert networks. He explained that fugitives were guided to places of "deposit" throughout the region. Offering details about these "deposits," Smallwood explained, "The distance between Washington and the first was thirty-seven miles, the second was forty miles from the first, over these our passengers generally travelled in two nights, and the third night they cross the line, and accomplish a distance of nine miles into Pennsylvania, to another place of deposit."[71] Smallwood took immense pride in his role in vigilance work, but he shared William Still's sentiments that conveying women with children posed challenges. He noted that cases that involved women and children often required transportation and said, "We had to pay teamsters a very high price in order to induce them to risk themselves and teams in so dangerous an enterprise."[72] Such attitudes underscore an additional layer of uncertainty that enslaved women faced in their attempts at escape. Occasionally dismissed as precarious cargo, women did not always possess access to networks willing to assist with their journey. Well-known men such as Smallwood led groups of fugitives, but women with children likely had to improvise when they inquired of those reluctant to help.

Despite the challenges that enslaved women faced in the increasingly dangerous political and legal climate, they continued to pursue freedom and fled with loved ones. Just miles outside the District, on May 15, 1841, thirty-year-old Louisa escaped from Notley Maddox in Prince George's County, Maryland, with her two brothers, John and Dumpty. At least two of the siblings were considered to be literate, and all of them carried imitation free papers with close renditions of the required official seals. The rural areas of the Chesapeake did not always lend themselves to access to materials and resources associated with literacy and fabricated freedom papers. Liberty and the process of self-making, in this instance, began long before the date of flight; empowered by their literacy and knowledge of the trades, they understood what was required to successfully escape, most likely through networks of enslaved and free inhabitants within the region. Louisa, considered "handsome, with strong intellect," and reportedly in possession of good clothes, also helped herself to cash she took from Maddox. Her brother John was a carpenter and joiner hired out in the area—skills that commanded a handsome profit for the owner. John also took a large sum of cash from Maddox, but more importantly, he took one of the few high-yielding sources of income that his owner relied on—himself. Louisa was married to a free man named Jim Butler. Thus, Maddox lost not only the clothes and cash Louisa took but also the possibility of acquiring more property through reproductive increase should they decide to have children. Slaves attempting to escape typically took specific sums of money and clothing that provided startup resources for survival if they managed to make it to the place they planned to begin their new life. The notice in the local news instructed anyone who captured the three siblings to turn them in to the jail in Washington, D.C. The reward posted for their capture was the healthy sum of $1,000. Beyond the financial enticement the advertisement offered, the notice provided a physical and intellectual portrait of the fugitives—attributes that worked more to their advantage and less in favor of the attempts to assign criminality to them.[73] Some slave catchers suspected that slaves from the surrounding Chesapeake counties searched for refuge in the District during the initial phase of escape; however, antebellum legal transformations might bring the siblings as far north of Maryland as possible instead.

The encroachment of slave catchers shifted the direction of fugitive women in the region, and escape routes stretched beyond the North and across the Canadian border. The trajectory on which these networks operated and the paths these women traveled were not centered on one particular city or state and consequently muddled legal matters, as each case sparked disagreement about the rule of slave law. The Compromise of 1850 included legal provisions for tightened enforcement of the fugitive slave law that required the return of fugitives discovered in northern territories.[74] Several decades before the reinvigorated Fugitive Slave Act of 1850, the *Prigg v. Pennsylvania* case brought women's escapes to the national spotlight. Margaret Morgan, an enslaved woman living as a free person, ignited a legal firestorm against personal liberty laws in Pennsylvania. Born into slavery in Harford County, Maryland, Margaret married Jerry Morgan, a free black man. Her former owner, John Ashmore, did not formally free Margaret, but after his death she lived independently of his remaining descendants. Margaret resided with Jerry and their children before the family decided in 1832 to relocate to Pennsylvania. Five years after Morgan's move, Margaret Ashmore, descendant of John Ashmore, hired professional slave catcher Edward Prigg to capture and return Margaret and her children. In Pennsylvania, the personal liberty law of 1826 required that slave catchers obtain a certificate of removal from a local justice. Prigg returned Morgan and her children to Maryland without the necessary certificate of removal. For violating the Pennsylvania personal liberty laws, he was charged with kidnapping. He appealed the conviction, and by an eight-to-one vote, the Supreme Court decided to uphold the constitutionality of the federal Fugitive Slave Act of 1793, which overruled the personal liberty laws of the state of Pennsylvania.[75]

Prigg undoubtedly forced free states like Pennsylvania to reckon with the imposition of federal jurisdiction over local and state definitions of freedom.[76] The Fugitive Slave Act of 1850 further solidified this precedent in *Prigg*. These transformations, however, did not just transform the meaning of freedom in Pennsylvania. Enslaved women in the Chesapeake understood their heightened fugitivity and that federal support for the property interests of slaveholders now obstructed the geographic perimeter of liberty that they had navigated for the first few decades of the nineteenth century. Federal oversight in the free territories broadened enslaved women's resistance networks from regional to transnational in scope. The Supreme Court not only sent a clear message to Pennsylvania, but enslaved women in the Chesapeake too intercepted the dispatch that freedom remained contested even on free soil. An examination of enslaved women's navigation and self-definition in the context of fugitivity must be situated on this legal and geographic terrain.

By the 1850s, slaveholders in the region bristled as enslaved women continued to slip from under their noses. Harriet Shepherd offers an interesting case. In the fall months of 1855, Shepherd grew increasingly weary of the brutality she experienced from the man who owned her. Her will to survive through his unrelenting demands gave way to fantasies of a life of freedom for her and her children. One account explained, "She was chiefly induced to make the bold effort to save her children from having to drag the chains of Slavery as she herself had done."[77] She knew her owner's desires to keep her enslaved remained legally protected within the geographic bounds of Kent County, Maryland, so when she noticed four unattended horses and two carriages, she took her chances on a future elsewhere. Boldly, she packed her children, Anna Maria, Edwin, Eliza Jane, Mary Ann, and John Henry, in the carriages along with five others willing to risk their lives for a chance at liberty. Shepherd took off and headed to Wilmington, Delaware, where Thomas Garret, an abolitionist who assisted fugitives, led the large party to Pennsylvania. By the time she reached Pennsylvania, her former owner had wasted no time in offering detailed descriptions of each fugitive in the group. They strategically decided to divide up the group and assume disguises for the journey farther north.[78] She remarked that she never received "kind treatment" from her former owner, which inspired much of her resolve to take herself and her children, along with five other fugitives, to Canada.

Shepherd indicated that the slaveholder treated her harshly, and the brutality that would be heaped on her and her children, if caught and returned, certainly did not escape her. If she left her children behind, they too might be vulnerable to punishment as a result of her escape. Shepherd's decision to take her children put her at great risk. Still described her children as "young, and unable to walk, and she was penniless, and unable to hire a conveyance, even if she had known any one who would have been willing to risk the law in taking them a night's journey."[79] The decision to use the horses and carriages to make greater headway with a large group of runaways complicates perceptions of enslaved mothers as least likely to escape. In that moment, she forged a network for escape. Escape attempts could lead to separation, abandonment, or capture, and this highly visible method was no exception. Although the chances of successful entry into free territory with loved ones were slim, some mothers decided in favor of flight. For some, liberty might have to come at the cost of leaving loved ones behind. The profitable value of enslaved women's labor constantly threatened the lives of black women in Washington.[80]

Described as a "dark, slender built" woman with a stammer, Emeline Chapman ran away from the Washington home of Emily Thompson at the age of twenty-five. Upon learning that Thompson had made plans to sell her, Emeline escaped, leaving her husband, John Henry, and her two children, Margaret Ann and John, behind in her quest for freedom. Emeline had earned a steady income for Thompson as a local hire. While the hiring-out system afforded some distance away from owners and opportunities for earning additional income, Emeline made it known that her mistress withheld wages that she needed to purchase adequate clothing and necessities for her children—which Thompson dismissed as "non-essentials." In the local hire system, owners could obstruct access to extra income-earning opportunities associated with the practice. The advantages that historians associate with urban slavery did not always translate in the lives of enslaved women. Emeline lamented the fact that her labor conditions did not position her to provide the basic necessities for her children while her hard work supported the comfort of the woman who exploited her. Moreover, her experience navigating the District as a hire undoubtedly positioned her to cross paths with many women like her, as well as free people who possessed knowledge about how to orchestrate her flight beyond the District. Thompson exploited her labor to finance her own lifestyle, but Emeline refused to submit to her scheme to profit from her sale in the domestic trade. Emeline fled the District and headed farther north.[81]

Once Emeline arrived in New York, she went by the name Susan Bell, engaging in a meaningful practice that came with freedom—naming. Renaming provided critical protections to fugitive identity while enabling the fugitive to evade recapture, and it functioned as a ritual of self-making that empowered bondwomen to define aspects of their identity that had long been decided by slave owners. As William Still recounts his mother's escape, he notes that "life had to be begun anew," with new names, new identities, and a different sense of place.[82] Still's mother changed her name from Sidney to Charity. To consider and envision a life as a free woman marked a critical stage in an uncertain process that led enslaved women to defy the law and the boundaries that shaped nineteenth-century life in the region. Susan now charted the course of her life on her terms, but not without reflecting on those she longed for in Washington.

Perhaps prompted by questions concerning her decision to flee without her family, Still referred to her actions as a "serious sacrifice." Escapes that involved small groups occurred in the region, but such attempts depended on the circumstances of those traveling the distance. Perhaps bringing her children proved too much of a risk, or maybe her husband, John Henry, disagreed with the decision to escape with the children. Enslaved families typically made plans to reunite with kin at more opportune moments or when resources permitted. Still remarked, "The love of freedom, in the breast of this spirited young Slave-wife and mother, did not extinguish the love she bore to her husband and children."[83] The courage and desperation that led women to make the perilous journey out of the South often shaped the fate of their most treasured relationships.

As a young enslaved woman in Kent County, Maryland, not a day passed when Harriet Fuller did not think about the man she loved on a plantation nearby. Soon after their romance blossomed, Harriet married Cornelius and they had a daughter, but they remained separated on different plantations, as was the case for many enslaved couples. Unable to enjoy each other's everyday companionship and affection, they both lamented the fact that separation and the threat of the lash dashed their hopes for their union. The menacing realities of slavery stifled the prospects of being permanently united, especially since Harriet would not find a sympathetic ear in the household of her owner. She labored in the home of a major proslavery advocate, Judge Ezekiel F. Chambers of Kent County. Chambers, renowned for ousting suspected abolitionists from the state, served as a prominent local and state ally for wealthy planters on the Eastern Shore, where the slaveholdings were the largest per estate. Escape from the grips of slavery would be no small feat.[84]

Harriet and Cornelius acted on their bold plans for escape and stealthily navigated the Maryland terrain to reach Pennsylvania, but they also made the difficult decision to leave their daughter. Upon their arrival, they tapped into the networks of William Still and the Pennsylvania Abolition Society, and the couple proceeded farther north. After surviving a trek that took them hundreds of miles north of the Eastern Shore, Harriet and Cornelius lived as free residents in Saint Catharine's, a community of fugitives in Canada.[85] Knowledge transmitted among free and enslaved African Americans helped facilitate escapes in a region that sheltered a bustling slave trade. These local ties were one of many nodes in a transnational web of antislavery networks for fugitive women to tap into. One print source noted that in the summer of 1854, "some of the farmers in the neighboring counties of Maryland and Virginia have been losing many of their slaves lately."[86] Enslaved women escaped from notorious slaveholders in the region, and many of them also escaped in groups or with the assistance of covert networks strewn throughout the Chesapeake. These networks in the Upper South spanned beyond the boundaries of the District and well into the northernmost regions of North America.

Well-known abolitionists William Still and Harriet Tubman, among countless others, assisted fugitive women in the region. Still served as the chairman of the Vigilance Committee of the Pennsylvania Abolition Society, making financial arrangements and managing correspondence between agents such as Tubman. Tubman repeatedly returned to Maryland, from which she had escaped as a fugitive in 1849, building a legacy that scholars have yet to fully grapple with. Indeed, she is the epitome of self-making and navigation, having mastered the geographical terrain to evade capture and emerge as one of the most infamous fugitive women in the antebellum era. Advertisements described her as "Minty, aged about 27 years," "of chestnut color, fine looking,

and about 5 feet high."[87] By the time she returned to assist others in their escapes, she called herself Harriet, a tribute to her mother and a ritual of genealogical remembrance. Images of Tubman proliferated over the course of the
nineteenth century that gave shape to an iconography relevant to contemporary
discussions about the face of the American twenty-dollar bill. Tubman defined
her terms of liberty, an ethos grounded in a call to use what resources and insight she possessed to help others navigate their way out of bondage. Popular
histories of Tubman have rendered her as a romantic maternal heroine without
accounting for the fact that the society she lived in branded her as a criminal.[88]
Her notorious reputation likely reached the rumor mill of enslaved people in
the region. Her actions and the work of vigilance activists reveal a revolutionary political struggle that spanned regional and international borders across
North America. It is likely that enslaved women in Washington, D.C.,
Virginia, and Maryland heard of Tubman and Still's Pennsylvania Vigilance
Committee and employed similar networks that they used in assisting fugitives. Still's meticulous records and the legacy of Tubman enriched histories
of the Underground Railroad, but here, I examine lesser-known case studies
of escapes within the region to show a broader genealogy of black women's
navigation and self-making.[89]

Forebears of enslaved women's resistance appear not only in the cases Still
recounts but also in his own family history. Still's parents, Levin and Sidney,
were born enslaved in Maryland. Levin worked additional hours over a period of time and purchased his freedom. He managed to relocate to New
Jersey, where he secured a forty-acre farm, but Sidney and their children remained enslaved. Sidney escaped with four of her children, but slave traders
met her before she made it across the Mason-Dixon line. On her second attempt, she escaped with two of her children and successfully reconnected
with Levin. As mentioned earlier, once she arrived, "life had to be begun
anew. The old familiar slave names had to be changed, and others, for pru-
dential reasons, had to be found."[90] The Steels became the Stills. William Still
was born free because of Charity's decision to flee, and he subsequently devoted his life to the work of helping countless fugitives like her, invoking the
meaning of her name. When did Sidney become Charity? Perhaps she spent
years contemplating another name, or a "life . . . begun anew," before she arrived in New Jersey. Many more women pondered different names, homes,
lives, and futures in the region.

Local vigilance networks linked to northern abolitionist circles assisted
fifteen-year-old Anna Maria Weems in her escape from slave trader Charles M.
Price of Rockville, Maryland. The daughter of John and Arrah Weems, Anna

Maria Weems escaping in male attire. Schomburg Center for Research in Black Culture, Manuscripts, Archives and Rare Books Division, New York Public Library.

Maria managed to escape with the help of white abolitionist Jacob Bigelow, a widower who lived near his office on E Street. Bigelow appeared in Maryland in an effort to help Harriet Beecher Stowe purchase the freedom of an en-slaved woman and her two children. He shared that he met "the wife and children of John Weems, on their way to our National Man-market (Wash-ington)."[91] Bigelow and others like Lewis Tappan and Henry Highland Gar-net managed to raise funds to purchase the Weems family, but the market rate at the time meant that they could only afford to purchase Arrah and her daughter Caroline. Price set the value for Anna Maria higher than the going rate, and her three brothers also faced the threat of sale. Price refused to sell her, and to ensure that she did not escape, he forced her to sleep in his bed-room so that he could keep a watchful eye on her. When Price fell asleep, she escaped wearing men's clothing and assumed the name Joe Wright, a carriage driver.[92] She left Rockville and headed to Washington to wait for instructions to proceed north. In the District, she hid with a black family and, after an in-tense period of waiting, met a Dr. H near the White House to travel to Phila-delphia.[93] Price placed a notice in the *Baltimore Sun* announcing a reward of $500 for her capture and speculating that she "probably" left on a carriage driven by a white man.[94]

Anna Maria's mother, Arrah Weems, returned to Washington to rescue a fourteen-month-old baby and his older sister from the District. Still received a letter written in coded language stating, "To-morrow morning Mrs. Weems, with her baby, will start for Philadelphia and see you probably over night."[95] While the child bore no relation to Weems, she participated in this effort to reunite the infant and child with their mother, Emeline, who had escaped nine months before Weems's trip. Similarly, Bigelow wrote from Washington, D.C., requesting assistance with the "conveyance of only one small package."[96] Bigelow soon discovered that the removal "cannot be so safely effected without taking two larger packages with it," possibly meaning that he required assistance with the escape of a fugitive child and that two potential guardians planned to join the child. He noted, "I understand that the three are to be brought to this city and stored in safety, as soon as the forwarding merchant in Philadelphia shall say he is ready to send on." The three fugitives most likely came from Virginia or even as far south as the Carolinas, and the District functioned as a corridor for the route to Philadelphia and later New York.

Still received more letters from Washington, including one that informed him about the anticipated arrival of "ten packages" in Philadelphia.[97] A different letter from Washington also confirmed the departure of a large group from the city, stating, "I think it is now some four or five weeks since, that some packages left this vicinity, said to be from fifteen to twenty in number." Noting the mounting underground assault on the District, he observed, "It was at a time of uncommon vigilance here, and to me it was a matter of extreme wonder."[98] The coded language and the limited detail pose challenges for the historian attempting to map the movement of fugitives. The sources show the regional bearing of organized vigilance along borders in the Upper South, as well as the changing character of Washington, D.C., as an active site of fugitive geography. What the letters conceal about runaway women, slaveholders and catchers elaborated on in advertisements.

Details about the personalities and physical features of fugitive women appeared in runaway advertisements. Moreover, deformities of those who escaped disclosed details about working conditions, abuse, and the everyday physical challenges that enslaved women suffered. On July 16, 1845, a notice appeared in the weekly *Maryland Journal* featuring Rachel Davis, a twenty-three-year-old enslaved woman of "copper complexion" with a "bone felon" who ran away from the farm of Alexander Boswell in Montgomery County, Maryland. A bone felon, which is an inflamed growth, appeared identifiable on the young woman's finger. It was not uncommon for these tumors to form after repeated manual tasks required of the same part of the body. Deformities and marks created from violent abuse were also used to describe fugitive women in runaway advertisements.[99] Historians have also examined the importance of bodily inspection and the visible signs of scars in the process of marketing and selling slaves.[100] Rachel's bone felon exposed a source of physical pain caused by the ongoing demands of slave labor. Rather than view the deformity as a sign of the brutal conditions of enslavement, the slaveholder and those assisting with the search used it to underscore her criminality as a fugitive. Such deformities and other scars and marks of bondage and branding further guided the suspicion and surveillance of black women in ways that authorized public scrutiny of their bodies. Many believed that Rachel Davis ran to Alexandria or Georgetown, where some of her relatives resided.[101]

Several factors made Washington a target site of escape, one of which was the significance of networks of free kin. For instance, on February 16, 1851, three young women left the plantation owned by George W. Graham in Upper Marlboro, Maryland. Two of the girls, Susan and Jenny, were sisters, and the third was their friend Mary Anne. All of the young women could identify relatives who resided in the District, particularly the sisters, who were in contact with an aunt who lived there. That same year, Milly Tyler, at the age of eighteen, ran away from the plantation of R. H. Stuart of Prince George's County, Maryland.[102] Along with other family members, her father lived as a free person of color in Washington, D.C. Networks within the nation's capital provided critical support for executing intraregional escapes; however, the officials in the slaveholding territory recognized laws and policing practices that made fugitives vulnerable to discovery. While the District provided refuge in the context of family support, they were still legally susceptible to reenslavement and could easily be imprisoned and returned to previous owners. Some went to great lengths to ensure that they lived as far as possible from slave territories. As discussed previously, it was often assumed that women were less inclined to attempt escape mainly because of the risks associated with running with small children, especially if flight involved greater distances. This, of course, was not always the case.

Attempts at flight still remained a dangerous strategy of liberty in the capital. One summer evening, twenty-two-year-old Sophia learned that her owner had made arrangements for her sale. The mother of a nine-year-old boy and a seven-year-old girl, she was struck to the depths of her core at the thought of being separated from her children. Sophia took flight in the direction of the capital. Her hopes for freedom in the nation's capital, however, were betrayed by the surveillance of constables and local citizens in Washington willing to support efforts to capture her and subject her to the transactions of the slave market. After being placed in the Washington jail, Sophia and her children were sold for $1,700 to an unknown buyer. Her story would be one of many that told of the devastating capture and punishment of runaway women.[103]

These stories illuminate the ways enslaved women thought more expansively about their gender identities. Gendered expectations of African American women did not always preclude their responses to slavery and racial caste. Indeed, a mother might flee with her children upon learning of plans to have them sold, or she might find that death was the only option left. Some women left on their own, leaving lovers, parents, and children behind. The gender identities of African American women did not determinedly shape their decisions to flee. They interacted with complex, covert, and innovative networks that shaped the region during the antebellum era. In an article on black women's role in slave communities, Angela Davis states that black women were "essential to the survival of the community" and that "not all people have survived enslavement; hence [black women's] survival-oriented activities were themselves a form of resistance."[104] The women who did not escape or were recaptured represent a vital aspect of black women's genealogies of survival. The experiences uncovered here reveal that men were not the only arbiters of resistance, but that just as women were at the heart of surviving communities of African Americans in Washington, they also defied gender conventions that discouraged flight.[105]

The accounts of black women's escapes that appear in this chapter show that, in Washington, enslaved women mounted physical interventions, rituals of self-making, and claims to liberty. An expanded domestic slave market and the stringent application of fugitive slave laws made these efforts increasingly difficult. Moreover, these strategies appeared at the beginning of Washington's history and proliferated with the efforts of antislavery vigilance networks in the region in the antebellum decades. The hunt for fugitive women reveals a portrait of self-making that involved the rituals of naming, the preservation of family ties, the improvisation of escape, the locations of their new homes, and their continued activism after slavery. Brief descriptions such as the one that described the woman "who calls herself" Ann E. Hodges tell us more than the fact that her owner attempted to find her. At twenty-two years old, wearing a slate-colored merino dress and brown calico sun bonnet, "she says she is free, and served her time out with a Mr. Benjamin Daltry, of Southampton, VA."[106] The advertisement described several scars, one on the knee from the gnashing of a dog, one on the left wrist, and a burn on the breastbone. If housed in the Washington jail, the owner agreed to retrieve the woman and cover her prison expenses. The case of Ann Hodges elucidates the opaque demarcations between slave and free. Perhaps she was indeed free? Hodges arrived from Southampton, Virginia, where most of her connections remained. The city required a white resident of Washington to verify her legal status. Without assurance of good behavior and a certificate of residence, she could be imprisoned and sold back into slavery. While her legal status remains unclear, Hodges offers a glimpse into the self-making process that made locals suspicious of what black women "called themselves," the clothing they wore, the scars they bore, and the ways that all of these features coalesced to outwit, transcend, or make right the system that ensnared them. Someone in her position might even approach the courts to contest the terms of her enslavement.

CHAPTER THREE

Courts

A woman listed in an advertisement as Susan escaped from Washington after forty years of enslavement and likely landed in Baltimore, where her mother-in-law resided.[1] Those who crossed paths with her took note of the fact that "she called herself Sukey Boardley." Bordley navigated the District by employing the assistance and resources necessary to relocate to Baltimore. Like Bordley, other enslaved women were driven by desires for a life they defined, but also by ties to kin and community. Before she escaped, she petitioned the court for her freedom. Her children were included in her freedom suit, and her relatives gave testimony concerning her free status. Intriguingly, court documents indicate that she "called herself Susan."[2] A runaway notice reveals that either she did not win her suit or the verdict did not yield the desired results in time. Bordley also set in motion her own process of self-fashioning by instructing others to call her by different, preferred names that appeared in court documents and the runaway notice. Susan or Sukey Bordley shows us legal and extralegal pathways to self-making that materialized in the courts.

African American women appeared before the civil and criminal courts of the District of Columbia throughout the first half of the nineteenth century for a number of reasons. Judges decided on cases ranging from freedom and manumission suits to criminal charges of disorderly conduct and theft. These appearances before the court tell a story about black women's strategies of improvisation. Like Bordley, women made both legal and extralegal claims to survive and become free. They navigated a legal apparatus of slave codes and black codes designed to circumscribe their lives and uphold the rule of law.[3] The law often determined the potential opportunities and consequences associated with black women's navigation of the courts. They could petition the courts for freedom or take slaveholders to court for their unlawful enslavement. Laws were amended and strengthened over time with the growth of the free black population and agitation of antislavery activists. At the same time, abolitionists were making legal arguments for the demise of southern slave laws. In *The Power of Congress over the District of Columbia*, Theodore Dwight Weld argued, "Slaves are not '*property*' and wherever held as property under law, it is only by *positive legislative acts*, forcibly setting aside the law of nature, the common law, and the principles of universal justice."[4] In other words, laws created to maintain slavery and organize people by race and gender were derived from positive law and established through deliberate ideas about how society should be organized. This chapter examines African American women's encounters with the local courts and how the legal culture of the District created both opportunities and constraints in women's efforts at self-making. An array of causes, claims, and offenses reveal that black women across a legal spectrum of identities and experiences appeared before the courts. Thus, this chapter consists of cases involving manumission suits and violations of the fugitive slave law, as well as theft, disorderly conduct, and prostitution—themes typically treated separately by historians. Rather than reading these cases in the contexts of civil and criminal law, this chapter explores the impetus for black women's appearances in the courts to understand their worlds. In each of these cases, self-making and navigation involved improvisation on the part of the women, who experienced the courts both as a place of emancipatory possibilities and a site of discipline and punishment.

The first black codes in Washington, D.C., enacted in 1808 based on the laws of the surrounding slave states of Maryland and Virginia, limited the movement and activities of black inhabitants, banning "idle" and "disorderly" behavior. These codes made the District a particularly complex location for black women to reside in, whether enslaved or free. While the District afforded black people freedoms similar to those in northern free states, such as limited access to education, the city was suffused with the heavy traffic of the slave trade, and the black codes merely reinforced and supported the existence of this institution.[5] Black codes became more restrictive by 1827, when city officials expanded the legal strictures imposed on black inhabitants. Indeed, these regulations tied certain activities to criminality only when applied to "black and/or mulatto" people. On May 31, 1827, the mayor of the city of Washington, Joseph Gales Jr., issued an ordinance of the Corporation of Washington referred to as "An Act: Concerning the Negroes, Mulattoes, and Slaves" outlining the code of conduct for black people in the District of Columbia. This act—publicly announced and distributed throughout the District—demanded that every black inhabitant carry identification permits at all times or else pay fines triple the amount required in 1808.[6] In fact, free African Americans who boarded trains from the North with the District as their final destination were required to show verification of their freedom in order to purchase their tickets. Further, it restricted the "idle assemblages of negroes" and prohibited free and enslaved black residents from playing games such as cards or dice, hosting dances and privately held gatherings in homes, remaining outside after ten o'clock at night, harboring or concealing a fugitive slave, or engaging in profane or obscene language.[7] In this regime, free and enslaved women frequented the pages of the police precinct records and newspapers for violation of these codes. The laws reflected an attempt to control the physical, economic, and social mobility of the black population, which aroused ongoing suspicion of black inhabitants, enslaved and free.[8]

The black code required "all free black, or mulatto persons, males of the age of sixteen, and females of the age of fourteen years, and upwards, who may then reside in the city of Washington, to exhibit satisfactory evidence of their title to freedom to the Register of this Corporation."[9] This stipulation included a bond required of every African American who resided in the city and fostered close record keeping and surveillance of individuals and family members. As Francis Powell's statistical research demonstrates, black female-headed households reached an all-time high in antebellum Washington.[10] Interestingly, the law established different age requirements for male and female residents, tracking black female residential status earlier than that of males. This may be attributed to the fact that slave status was inheritable through black women. If they were found without free papers, women, along with potential offspring, could be returned to slavery—further serving the interests of area slave-trading firms. More plausibly, tracking young black women earlier aligned with efforts to prevent black children from claiming legally free status in an already expanding free black population.

The practice of requiring a permit of every free black person in the city made the suspicion of black inhabitants a common feature of day-to-day life in the capital. A fourteen-year-old black girl in the District, therefore, found her very existence under legal scrutiny before any potential crime could be committed. The codes, moreover, mapped out numerous avenues through which enslaved and free black people were made subject to police arrests, fines, and workhouse sentences. This same legal scaffolding was also designed to protect the property interests of slaveholders and at times protected individuals who illegally trafficked black inhabitants. Black women, however, resisted and countered these measures in the courts. Scholars have shown that throughout the early years of the nineteenth century, black women managed to appeal for their freedom with relatively high rates of success in instances in which they were wrongfully enslaved.[11] Black women's experiences more broadly, however, varied depending on the reasons for their appearance. Judges in the District of Columbia heard cases relevant to Washington City, Georgetown, and Alexandria.

The president appointed the justices of the peace for the courts of each county (Alexandria and Washington) to enforce slave and black codes and address civil and criminal matters and any additional issues concerning the "conservation of the peace."[12] The courts consisted of one chief judge and two assistant judges who resided in the District. The county justices administered judgments in social disputes and appeals made to the local courts, and enslaved and free black women in the District also interacted with these justices in instances involving manumission, criminal charges, civil disputes, inheritances, and sale of their labors.[13] The court held four sessions annually in each of the District counties; in Washington County, they met the fourth Mondays of March, June, September, and December; and in Alexandria County, judges held sessions on the second Mondays of January, April, and July and the first Monday of October.[14] In disputes and issues concerning children, a judge of the orphans' court managed the placement of enslaved and free black children subject to various labor arrangements and further commoditized in the resolution of estates. Additionally, an appointed marshal managed the county jails, which housed a number of black inhabitants. The appearances of African Americans in the courts reveal the ways that local governance preserved and sustained sites of slavery. If given the opportunity or resources to do so, enslaved women appealed to the courts for their freedom.[15]

In the early years of Washington, D.C., enslaved women, with the assistance of free African Americans and white lawyers, challenged slavery through legal measures.[16] In particular, enslaved women and men who claimed white maternal parentage challenged a slaveholder's legal claim to their labor since the law recognized slavery as inheritable through women of African descent. *Quia partus sequitur ventrem*, "That which is brought forth follows the womb," was the legal phrase that reverberated throughout the lives of all enslaved people, but particularly enslaved women.[17] The freedom petitions or manumissions of enslaved women could potentially discontinue generations of captivity. In Washington, enslaved women and their descendants reflected deeply on this concept with the hope that they might successfully make legal claims to freedom.[18] Historians refer to this time as a moment of "liberalization" or "egalitarianism."[19] As a result, more African Americans became free from manumission by will or deed, or legal claims to free mothers.[20] In Washington, black women employed every measure at their disposal to legally claim liberty.

Two women, Priscilla and Mina Queen, worked with Francis Scott Key to petition the Circuit Court of the District of Columbia for their freedom.[21] As the June 1810 term of the court convened, Key argued that Priscilla Queen was the descendant of Mary Queen, a woman believed to be legally free, and therefore the mother of free children. The Queen women, like members of the Queen family who appear in previous cases, leveraged *partus sequitur ven-trem* to affirm their freedom. The defendant, Rev. Frances Neale, was a Jesuit priest preparing for his new appointment as president of Georgetown College.[22] Key faced the challenge of providing evidence of Mary Queen's legal status at the time of Priscilla's birth. In earlier cases involving the Queen family, the courts admitted the testimony of witnesses who verified Mary Queen's free status, but some of these cases were tried in Maryland. As early as the mid-1780s, Maryland courts allowed hearsay evidence from witnesses who attested to the free status of deceased women in African American families.[23] In Mina's case, the defendant, John Hepburn, argued that Queen's great-grandmother Mary was enslaved. The court sided with Hepburn on the basis that hearsay evidence was inadmissible. Mina, who also included her daughter, Louisa, in the suit, then appealed the decision and the case appeared before the U.S. Supreme Court in 1813.[24] Key understood the parameters of the Queen sisters' claim clearly since he and his uncle Philip Barton Key helped many members of the Queen family and a number of other African Americans file freedom suits.[25] Mina Queen appealed to the U.S. Supreme Court on a writ of error, arguing that hearsay evidence was wrongly omitted from the case. From Mina's point of view, this worked for other relatives in the 1790s, so why wouldn't the court take hearsay testimony under consideration in her case?[26] In 1813, the Supreme Court heard the case and upheld the lower court decision. Chief Justice John Marshall penned the majority opinion and argued, "Hearsay evidence is incompetent to establish any specific fact which is in its nature susceptible of being proved by witnesses who speak from their own knowledge."[27] He warned, "The danger of admitting hearsay evidence is sufficient to admonish courts of justice against lightly yielding to the introduction of fresh exceptions to an old and well established rule the value of which is felt and acknowledged by all."[28] Earlier precedents in the Queen family and in Maryland, however, complicate the assumptions about the "old and well established rule."[29] Indeed, the real fear surfaced when he offered, "If the circumstance that the eye witnesses of any fact be dead should justify the introduction of testimony to establish that fact from hearsay, no man could feel safe in any property a claim to which might be supported by proof so easily obtained."[30] The issue was not a deviation from established rules but rather the consequences that could come with setting yet another legal precedent concerning the admissibility of hearsay evidence.

In instances involving claims to freedom, the use of hearsay evidence could lead to a proliferation of freedom suits based on deceased women of

African descent.[31] Justice Marshall understood the implications clearly, and so did Gabriel Duvall, associate justice who wrote a dissenting opinion.[32] Duvall argued that hearsay had long been acceptable evidence in petitions for freedom where the ancestor had been deceased for a length of time. He stated further, "If the ancestor neglected to claim her right, the issue could not be bound by length of time, it being a natural inherent right."[33] At this particular moment when the rhetoric of inalienable rights coursed through courts of the new republic, such rights seemed to appear that much more beyond the reach of African Americans. Indeed, Duvall concluded that "people of color, from their helpless condition under the uncontrolled authority of a master, are entitled to all reasonable protection."[34] Priscilla, Mina, and Mina's daughter, Louisa, remained legally enslaved. And so the late eighteenth-century moment that permitted hearsay evidence in freedom suits came to an abrupt end for these members of the Queen family, just a decade before the country saw an upswing in freedom suits known as the "golden age."[35] With limited recourse, hearsay evidence had long been a critical strategy for enslaved women initiating freedom suits. By the first decade of the nineteenth century, this avenue toward freedom appeared less effective. Some enslaved women, however, received deeds of manumission in instances that involved a slaveholder willing to agree to their freedom, and others benefited from financial and legal assistance from existing free residents of the District.[36]

The freedom suits of Priscilla and Mina Queen offer indicators of the ways that enslaved women looked to the courts as a path toward liberty and opportunities for self-making. Indeed, the suit was filed under the name Mima, but she petitioned the courts under the name Mina.[37] Self-making occurred in formal actions, with names and information that black women created for the courts to consider, even if the verdict went for the defendant. These shards of information provide insight into the ways that black women maintained information about themselves and their families. The work of historian Loren Schweninger shows that enslaved women were critical interlocutors of oral genealogical traditions that courts took under consideration in freedom suits.[38] Women passed down the names, relationships, and information about their lives from one generation to the next.[39] When presented with the opportunity, enslaved women referred back to their stores of local and familial knowledge to prove their freedom. Moreover, the Queen family experienced relative success with the submission of freedom petitions that claimed that Mary Queen was free. At least twenty-four members of the Queen family sued Georgetown College founder Rev. John Ashton.[40] While some members of the family won their suits, others like Priscilla, Mina, and Louisa were not so fortunate. Still, enslaved women shaped the "cultural, social, genealogical, and economic relationships" of their respective communities.[41] Priscilla and Mina Queen were no exception to this pattern. Women were integral to understandings of familial ties in the District, and that network became apparent when the Queen family approached the court with claims to kinship.[42]

Freedom suits in early Washington also underscore the fact that outcomes of legal recourse appeared increasingly inconsistent throughout the early republic.[43] Historians point to the significance of the timing of the verdict of Mina Queen's case.[44] The postrevolutionary moment marked a departure from more flexible interpretations of the law and, in particular, the admissibility of hearsay evidence in freedom suits. The era of egalitarianism lasted for a critical moment, but new legal interpretations appeared to reinforce the racial and gendered hierarchies that shaped life for black women in Washington.[45] When legal avenues to freedom led to a dead end, enslaved women improvised ways to realize their liberty in a city undergoing a critical moment of transformation.

By 1820, the capital appeared slightly more established, with newly completed buildings erected along a few more finished avenues. Washington looked like an up-and-coming southern city. The growth of the domestic slave trade and the propagation of slave hiring markedly shaped the economic development of the nation's capital and the experiences of African American women. Black women worked in homes, workhouses, and local commerce in the District as they did at the beginning of the nineteenth century, but the black population was changing. The free African American population could be found on any given Sunday as black inhabitants of the city made their way to church or Sabbath schools. Black women could be found congregating in the alleys, laughing, washing, working, or calling after young children, "with cotton handkerchiefs twisted round their heads."[46] The presence of enslaved, fugitive, and free African Americans meant that kinship ties and local networks were forged in a moment when black codes were tightening restrictions on their daily lives and the slave trade remained a menacing threat. Nevertheless, black Washington was taking shape.

Before black women appeared in the courts, there were communities, homes, and churches that informed their epistemologies of what life could look like outside slavery. African American churches were the heart of black social life and activism in early Washington. They provided spaces for spiritual edification, but they also constituted the very networks that made resources and opportunities available to black women for self-making. In 1820, black residents pooled their resources to erect a log building on Fourth Street East near Virginia Avenue.[47] At the church, known as Ebenezer Church, the members held services and organized both social and educational gatherings. Some of the members helped found another church, Israel Bethel Colored Methodist Episcopal Church, the first church led by black clergy.[48] When Israel Bethel faced financial obstacles, Alethia Browning Tanner, along with her brother-in-law, purchased the church. Tanner also paid for the freedom of her family members and likely shared her knowledge of the system that made purchase and legal freedom possible for enslaved or free black residents searching for answers about the possibilities of liberty. Tanner's nephew, Rev. John F. Cook, a minister and leader in the church, helped found Union Bethel African Methodist Episcopal Church. The decision to establish the church was largely a result of the long distances members were required to travel in order to attend services. In addition to walking conditions during inclement weather, the resolution mentioned the "limited time allotted to us as a colored people to pass with safety at night, without being subject to molestation," as a primary reason for meeting at a different location.[49] Indeed, this might explain the proliferation of fourteen different black churches founded in Washington before the Civil War.[50]

As congregations grew, black women found opportunities for leadership. According to records at Union Bethel, the member register listed Alethia or "Lethee" Tanner as the first woman to join the church and noted that she served as "a Class Leader."[51] When the committee for purchasing the new plot for Union met, they recorded a list of contributors that included Tanner as the only woman and the donor who made the second-highest contribution.[52] Harriet Felson Taylor, the second woman listed on the membership roster, "distinguished herself as the First Female Exhorter and Local Preacher."[53] Her role as "exhorter" and "preacher" serves as a testament to the ways Union embraced the leadership of women at a time when men dominated most clergy positions in black churches. At one point, however, Taylor appeared at odds with some of the male leadership when she raised funds for the new location of the church without board approval. The same document that listed the generous gift Tanner pledged toward the new site also included a rebuke of Taylor's efforts to lead a fund-raising campaign. Clergy embraced black women's philanthropy, but their leadership and initiative might be checked without adequate support from male leaders. Patriarchy pervaded religious life even as women parishioners outnumbered men. Indeed, of the list of 104 members, over half were women.[54]

Both enslaved and free black women joined the rosters of early black churches in Washington and participated in joint worship services, experienced shifts in leadership, and helped establish new congregations. One church in particular became a haven for free, enslaved, and fugitive women. Located between Eleventh and K Streets NW, Asbury African Methodist Episcopal Church boasted more than six hundred members. Dissatisfied with their experiences at Montgomery Street Church (now Dumbarton United Methodist Church), nearly 125 enslaved and free black parishioners founded one of the oldest black churches in the city.[55] Once they purchased the lot of Mill Street, the place became known as "the Meeting House" and "the Little Ark" until the name was changed to Mount Zion Methodist Episcopal Church. According to church oral histories, the vault of the burial ground of the Little Ark served as an important hiding place for fugitives.[56] African American churches were sites of self-making and meeting places of emancipatory possibilities that often catalyzed the liberty claims, activism, and self-fashioning of black women. One faithful member of the Little Ark landed in court against the legal forces of the slave trade in the District.

In 1837, Dorcas Allen lived with her husband, Nathan, and their four children in Georgetown. Much to her surprise, slave trader James H. Birch acquired possession of her and her four children late that summer. Dorcas lived free with her husband, who worked as a waiter at Gadsby's (National) Hotel, located on the corner of Pennsylvania Avenue and Sixth Street NW.[57] A man named Gideon Davis owned Dorcas and her children. He agreed to formally manumit her upon his death, but failed to make the necessary legal arrangements. Consequently, when his wife, Maria, married Rezin Orme, she refused to manumit Dorcas and instead arranged for her sale. Dorcas occupied a liminal status between enslaved and free as her life served as one of many examples of the opaque demarcations of liberty that black women navigated in a city still tied to slavery. The uncertainty of verbal promises of freedom meant that Dorcas created a life and marriage amid the looming threat of slavery. Undoubtedly, when Nathan walked along Pennsylvania Avenue, he regularly witnessed scenes of enslaved people in coffles on their way south, but he hoped he'd never see the day when his own wife and children bore those same shackles. Everything changed when Orme sold Dorcas and her children, Mary, Margaret, Maria, and William. Birch immediately made arrangements for their incarceration at George Kephart's slave market on Duke Street in Alexandria.

Birch confined Dorcas and her children at the three-story Duke Street pen previously owned by the infamous firm Franklin and Armfield. A former agent of the firm, George Kephart, assumed ownership of the pen after Isaac Franklin and John Armfield retired.[58] Kephart began preparations for their sale as Dorcas and her children remained imprisoned in the buildings that housed women and children separate from men.[59] Later that evening, shriek-ing cries could be heard from Kephart's market. Dorcas had decided that the lives of her children would end that night. She killed her two youngest children, Maria and William, and before she could end the lives of the re-maining two, their cries caught the attention of people nearby and Dorcas's plan was aborted. This was neither the first nor last incident of infanticide recorded in the history of American slavery.[60] Dorcas confronted limited op-tions but perhaps considered a fate in a spiritual afterlife the best possible outcome for her children. Motivated by the transaction that led to her con-finement, she wielded the limited power she possessed over the futures of her children.[61] Indeed, Dorcas nourished her faith as a committed member of Little Ark Church in Georgetown, an institution where spiritual self-making happened without the oversight of slaveholders.[62] Her conviction that heaven awaited her children was rooted in Methodist beliefs in eternal life. With two of her children laid in their final resting place, she calmly testified before jus-tices of the court.

The court tried her case with a jury comprising twenty-three people, pri-marily slaveholding residents of Alexandria.[63] Birch hoped that Dorcas might receive acquittal on the basis of insanity. While a "defective" enslaved woman did not command a lucrative price, he might be able to recover some of the costs associated with her purchase rather than lose the entire sum he paid. Well-connected attorneys William Brent and Francis Asbury Dickins pre-pared a defense and argued that Dorcas acted in a moment of insanity. The jury found her not guilty, and historians have considered the exceptional cir-cumstances to play a role in the verdict.[64] Not guilty, however, did not mean free. Rather than Dorcas receiving the death penalty or imprisonment, the slaveholder regained possession of her and her two surviving daughters. Birch resumed his efforts to sell them, but news spread of her actions and posed significant challenges for him. Very few buyers were interested in a "de-fective" or "rebellious" enslaved woman. These purported defects reveal the very physical interventions of navigation that Dorcas employed in response to being torn from the people who shaped her ideas about identity, home, and community. The controversy, however, bought her husband, Nathan, more time to recover his wife and children. District Attorney Francis Scott Key, who assisted with at least a dozen freedom suits prior to his appointment to this post, proposed that Nathan collect subscription funds to purchase his family.[65] Nathan managed to raise the sum of $475 with assistance from contributors such as former president John Quincy Adams. The Allens moved to Rhode Island, where they found comparatively more protection. Birch went on to become the trader famously complicit in the sale of Solomon Northup, a free black man kidnapped from the north and incarcerated in a local pen.[66]

The legal climate of Washington appeared increasingly hostile to African Americans by the 1830s. Drawing on laws established earlier in the Chesapeake, slave codes and court cases were adjudicated in ways to ensure that black inhabitants were in no position to undermine slavery and the racial hierarchies that shaped social relations in the city. Nonetheless, many like the Allens managed to strategically maneuver and improvise through this legal apparatus to obtain their liberty. Under the most devastating circumstances, women like Dorcas found a way to respond to a sense of powerlessness. Many others also landed in court for criminal offenses. Enslaved women demonstrated an awareness of opportunities for flight, as well as the legal risks associated with fugitivity in the region. This web of legal knowledge appears evident not only in the transportation of fugitive women but also in the rumor mill that alerted them of forthcoming opportunities for flight. The escape of seventy-seven enslaved people on the schooner *Pearl* appears regularly in histories of Washington. The incident offers insights into not only the most notable escape attempt in history but also the ways black women navigated the opportunities for self-making through collective resistance.

The daughters of an enslaved mother and a free father, Mary and Emily Edmonson were two of Paul and Amelia Edmonson's fourteen children. Paul was manumitted by his former owner, and by "economy, industry, and thrift" obtained and maintained forty acres of land.[67] One of the Edmonson sons, Hamilton, had already been sold south, and five of their daughters were manumitted through purchase and resided in the District.[68] When she was fifteen years old, Mary and her sister Emily were hired out by their owner, Rebecca Culver, to work for wealthy families in the District. They likely found moments to interact with their free siblings and soon discovered plans for an escape on the merchant schooner *Pearl*. The six of them decided that they would make the journey together, along with seventy-one other enslaved women, men, and children who boarded the *Pearl* on April 15, 1848. On the docks of the nation's capital, they joined the largest documented slave escape in American history.[69]

Mary's and Emily's stories of self-making were tied up in the efforts of others who tried to become free. It all began with Daniel and Mary Bell. Daniel earned enough to purchase his freedom at $1,630. Mary and her children were freed according to the terms of their former owner's will, but when they attempted to claim their freedom, the wife of their former owner contested the manumission terms of the will. When the courts failed to produce the desired results, African Americans did not shy away from extralegal strategies to become free. With no other option than to arrange an escape, Daniel Bell covered the necessary expenses for Daniel Drayton to secure a vessel that would take them north. The Edmonson sisters also joined the escape because they had recently learned that they might be sold off as prostitutes in the fancy-girl trade in New Orleans.[70] Their experiences with being marketed as both sexualized and fetishized human property reflected many of the ways enslaved girls and women were commodified as potential prostitutes or high-end servants in the domestic slave market. Word of mouth reached the girls just in time for them to evade such a future. As one news account noted, someone "communicated the opportunity to them and to several others; they communicated it to their friends; and when captain Drayton came to sail, instead of having seven passengers, as he had expected, he had ten times that number." These were the networks of navigation—free African Americans, local white allies, and northern friends willing to spread the word, risk discovery, and finance the excursion along the Atlantic Seaboard.[71]

Interracial cooperation and communication networks throughout the District made Emily and Mary's escape possible. As Stanley Harrold points out, interracial antislavery resistance characterized much of the abolitionist ferment in antebellum Washington.[72] Networks of communication among enslaved and free black inhabitants created an even longer tradition of antislavery activism in the capital. Black inhabitants such as Daniel Bell and Paul Jennings, a formerly enslaved servant owned by President James Madison, spread the word, informing black locals of the organized escape attempt to take place on the *Pearl*. White supporters such as Gerrit Smith, William L. Chaplin, and the ship's crew members Daniel Drayton, Edward Sayres, and Chester English secured the vessel for their transport. The planned route took the schooner 100 miles down the Potomac River, and then 125 miles north on the Chesapeake Bay toward the free state of New Jersey. The morning after their departure, reports of missing fugitives erupted in the city. According to John H. Paynter, an enslaved man named Judson Diggs furnished the mob of outraged slave owners with information about the plans for escape. A group of angry slaveholders sailed out on the *Salem* to find the vessel near Point Lookout in Maryland.[73]

Emily and Mary and the seventy-five other enslaved people on board the *Pearl* were imprisoned, and Drayton, Sayres, and English were tried in the

Portrait of Mary and Emily Edmonson. Prints and Photographs, Library of Congress.

Criminal Court of the District of Columbia for "stealing."[74] English was dismissed largely because he worked as the hired cook and help on the crew and claimed that he didn't completely understand the intent of the voyage. Sayres was acquitted on two counts of slave stealing but, having incurred fines and legal fees amounting to over $10,000, had to remain in jail. Drayton pleaded guilty to the transportation of slaves outside the District and was convicted on two counts of slave stealing. Drayton and Sayres were imprisoned because of the hefty fines and legal fees they incurred while on trial, but were later granted a pardon from President Millard Fillmore at the endorsement of Massachusetts senator Charles Sumner.[75] Slave traders confined the Edmonson siblings at a slave pen in Alexandria in preparation for the voyage to the slave markets in New Orleans. Traders sold Samuel Edmonson in New Orleans, but the remaining siblings were returned to Baltimore as a result of a yellow fever outbreak. Philanthropic efforts led to the purchase of Richard Edmonson, who reunited with his wife and children in Baltimore. The slave-trading firm undoubtedly regarded sisters Mary and Emily as too lucrative an opportunity to pass on. They held the potential to generate a handsome profit if they sold in the fancy-girl trade in New Orleans.[76] If they did not attract buyers in the fancy-girl trade, they certainly retained their value as potential servants in some of the wealthier homes of Louisiana. In the meantime, the two sisters were forced to labor as washerwomen and kept in the local prison during the hours in which they were not employed at work. Persistence from their father, Paul Edmonson, eventually led to an arrangement with the firm that allowed him to purchase his daughters at the impressive sum of $2,250.

On November 4, 1848, the Edmonson sisters traveled to New York, and with the assistance of the Beecher family, they attended the Young Ladies Preparatory School at Oberlin College in Ohio.[77] At Oberlin, they began the process of self-making as legally free young women. Education offered both social and economic mobility in preparation for possible careers in teaching. The Edmonson sisters traveled throughout the North to attend abolitionist rallies and protest the Fugitive Slave Act of 1850. Antislavery activism became an important aspect of their new worlds as free women. But for one of them, this new season quickly came to an end. In 1853, after having survived the dramatic developments of the *Pearl*, Mary died of tuberculosis at the age of twenty.[78] Her death led Emily to return to Washington, where she worked with a school for African American girls and married her husband, Larkin Johnson. They lived in Anacostia, where they became founders of the Hillsdale community and retained closed ties to Frederick Douglass.[79]

Unlike the Edmonson sisters, most of the fugitives on the *Pearl* remained enslaved, but some managed to become free. Ellen Stewart, daughter of a woman named Sukey, who labored as Dolley Madison's attendant, was included among the list of fugitives.[80] At times, records show her as Hellen, Mary, and Ellen Ann with a last name of Steward or Stewart. The variations of her name might be of her own doing or the result of errors made by those drafting the records that include her name. An earlier chapter discussed Madison's dependence on Sukey to maintain the persona associated with her life as America's favorite first lady. Although she expressed remorse at the thought of participating in the slave trade, Madison infamously sold enslaved people in times of financial crisis. By the time of the escape on the *Pearl*, Madison had managed to sell all of Sukey's children except for Ellen. When Madison invited a potential buyer to her home to arrange for her sale, Ellen absconded and joined the enslaved people on the *Pearl*.[81] Once the *Pearl* fugitives were caught, slave traders prepared Ellen for Baltimore, but a number of sympathizers attempted to purchase her freedom.[82] A local physician paid for Ellen to be free and helped her move to Boston. Madison unleashed her financial frustrations on Sukey and sold her to another woman in the city. Sukey had served the Madisons since birth, but at fifty years old, she would have to reconstitute her life and work in a new household.[83] When her services were not required, Washington offered opportunities to forge new bonds. Enslaved women who traveled on errands and passed through different homes discovered chances to interact with free black locals.[84] Access to the people, churches, and neighborhoods that shaped black life in the capital were vital to black women's survival and self-making. As the *Pearl* incident shows, through their own networks of kin, girls like Mary, Emily, and Ellen learned of both opportunities for escape and avenues to evade sale farther south. Family and abolitionist networks rallied behind the girls to support the purchase of their freedom.[85] The escape on the *Pearl* marked the District as an important site of antislavery activity that stretched throughout the different parts of the region and into national debates about slavery. To the local slave owner, vigilance lurked everywhere.

Enslaved women traversed the Mason-Dixon line, evaded slaveholders and slave catchers, and challenged the power of federal law in the courts. One such case involved an enslaved woman named Jane Johnson. John Wheeler purchased Johnson and two of her children from a slaveholder in Richmond, Virginia. Wheeler owned a house on Eleventh Street on the corner of I and Tenth Streets. He was a proslavery and states' rights advocate from North Carolina. A confidant of President Franklin Pierce, Wheeler traveled to Philadelphia as a stop along the journey toward Nicaragua, where Pierce had appointed him to serve as the U.S. minister.[86] Johnson served as the personal attendant to his wife, Ellen Sully. One observer described Johnson as "a fine specimen of the best class of Virginia housemaids, with a certain ladylike air, propriety of language, and timidity of manner that prepossesses the audience in her favour."[87] The writer spoke of her "very polite manners," a demeanor some mistresses found very appealing in elite political circles. Perhaps these

descriptors capture Johnson's own ethos of self-making and survival. Her "ladylike air" demonstrated her own self-fashioning amid the conditions and
indignities associated with bondage. Wheeler took Johnson and her children
to Philadelphia with the plan to arrive in Nicaragua to meet with his wife. He
instructed Johnson to "have nothing to say to colored persons," and if they
asked, to say that she was a free woman traveling with a minister.[88] Wheeler
remained focused on Johnson's every move, but at the precise moment when
he became distracted, she whispered to a free black man, "I and my children
are slaves, and we want liberty!"[89]

This one lucid declaration led to the confrontation Wheeler had taken
careful steps to avoid. When he retired to his quarters, William Still and Passmore Williamson, of the Philadelphia Vigilance Committee, along with six
dockworkers, approached him, stating that they wished to communicate to
Johnson her rights. The men informed her, "You can come with us, you are as
free as your master, if you want your freedom come now; if you go back to
Washington you may never get it."[90] She followed them, and Wheeler tried to
plead with her and convince her that he would grant her freedom. "But he had
never promised it before, and I knew he would never give it to me," she recalled.[91] She took her children by the hands and walked off with the group.
She declared to the judge that, far from being naively enticed by Williamson,
she "went away of [her] own free will."[92] While the event reportedly took
place over less than an hour, the legal battle over Jane Johnson and her children
was far from over.

Like the *Pearl* escape, Johnson's case brought the underground battle
against slavery to the courts. The legal implications of the event ensured that
Johnson's story and Wheeler's property rights loomed in the spotlight. William Still and six dockworkers appeared on trial for charges of assault and
battery after Wheeler claimed that the group physically restrained him during
the confrontation. Judge John Kane of the federal district court, with whom
Wheeler maintained cordial ties, summoned Williamson to court with specific instructions, under habeas corpus, to bring Johnson and her children
before him.[93] Williamson refused to disclose information regarding her
whereabouts and subsequently spent time in jail for contempt of court. News
of the incident galvanized abolitionist sympathies, but it also reveals how black
women's decisions to escape generated questions about the reach of federal
law.[94] In Johnson's case, the court had to decide whether Wheeler could right-
fully claim his human property on free soil. Passmore and abolitionists, on the
other hand, continued to defend the personal liberty laws of Pennsylvania that
recognized Johnson's claims to liberty. At the risk of confrontations with local

Portrait of Jane Johnson. Schomburg Center for Research in Black Culture, Manuscripts, Archives and Rare Books Division, New York Public Library.

mobs, Johnson appeared before the court to testify that Passmore did not kidnap her, as Wheeler's accusation led the court to believe. Saturated with tension, the crowded courthouse intently listened to Johnson as she testified that she had always desired to be free.

The court served as the place where Johnson debuted her voice and her claims in the face of her detractors and the looming threat of the fugitive slave law. Indeed, at a time when the testimony of enslaved women mattered very little to the slaveholding class, the indictment of her defense drove Wheeler out of the courtroom. He secured two warrants for her arrest as a fugitive and a thief of the clothing she wore. District Attorney Robert Mann called on city police to ensure that she did not fall into the hands of the federal marshals who awaited her. As she left the trial, law enforcement descended on the courthouse, with one mob intent on protecting her and another targeting her for arrest. She managed to escape the grip of slavery a second time. Johnson absconded and remained undetected in various locations, including the home of antislavery activist Lucretia Mott. For his steadfast refusal to incriminate himself or Johnson, Williamson served time in jail for over three months, during which abolitionists paid countless visits and even took a photograph to distribute and garner support.[95] Kane ruled that Pennsylvania's free laws only applied "to persons resident and persons sojourning" and not those in transit or "passing through" the state.[96] But the verdict came too late. Johnson made her way to Boston, where she assisted with the escapes of women like herself. For her, self-making meant a life devoted to helping others do the very thing she dared do after serving the Wheelers in Washington. An etching of Johnson shows her modestly dressed in a dark blouse with an elegant tie that rests on a crisp white collar. Her hair, parted directly down the middle, is tied in a loose and wavy bun that rests at the neck to show the gold hoop earrings in her ears. Her gaze is one that is both warm and definitive at the same time, conveying to the observer that her liberty is hard fought, and her self-fashioning deeply rooted in her imaginings of her life well before she defended her actions in court. Johnson navigated outside the District with an understanding of the legal and geographical implications of travel to Philadelphia before her encounter with Williamson. Her repeated attempts to defiantly communicate with free African Americans and her assertion that she "always wished to be free and meant to be free" underscore this point.[97] Johnson's experience as an enslaved woman in Washington enlightened her about the possibilities well before Still and Passmore approached her. Johnson served the household of a political figure and diplomat and likely overheard conversations about the fugitive slave law as well as local escapes of women with children. Such discussions undoubtedly resonated with her as she considered the possibilities of her own liberty. Wheeler perhaps did not realize the ways Johnson's decisions would embroil his own vested interest in the enforcement of the fugitive slave law. Although these antebellum confrontations among fugitive, slave catcher, and abolitionist tell a heroic narrative of the antislavery movement, Johnson's case reveals the countless ways that fugitivity operated in the world of criminal courts. Indeed, criminal court records provide much more evidence of activism, survival, and self-making in a nineteenth-century world that relegated African American women to the margins of society. Abolitionists lauded African Americans for their participation in local vigilance work, but they likewise faced hardships and risks associated with antislavery activism. Their actions were treated as legal offenses, which certainly placed pressure on their lives as free black people in the District. A reputation for lawbreaking at a time when the onus of impeccable behavior fell on the free black inhabitants of Washington meant that such risks could affect their prospects for employment, housing, and safety. Nevertheless, black women in Washington looked to legal and extralegal avenues to navigate and define life in the capital.

In their strategies of navigation, black women did not always land in the places contextualized by uplift. Their living conditions were precarious since they confronted not only stringent financial circumstances but also the possibility of abduction.[98] The precarity of life and subsistence meant that they often navigated a very narrow set of options and appeared before the courts for an array of reasons. Nothing captures this point better than the records of criminal courts where African American women were brought not only for escape but also for theft, disorderly conduct, drinking, gambling, and soliciting sex. This spectrum of offenses reminds us to think broadly and carefully about the application of nineteenth-century ideas about criminality and the ways they affected black women. If enslaved women became free or lived as fugitives within the District, the black codes made it quite possible for them to end up in jail and brought before the justices of the criminal court.

The escape of one woman reveals the complexity of the criminal courts and the ways that the paths of women from various walks of life might intersect. Harriet, a girl described as a "very handsome yellow + worth 600$," escaped from her owner, Voltaire Willett. The court held a session where they charged Mary Juniper and Eliza Butler for aiding and abetting in the escape. Butler had appeared before the criminal court on several occasions for owning a bawdy house and committing actions associated with disorderly conduct.[99] The emphasis on Harriet's appearance and value might suggest that Willett feared that Harriet might enter the local sex and leisure economy, but evidence doesn't seem to confirm that Juniper's and Butler's intentions were to lure her into prostitution. Besides, the records confirm that Harriet escaped and no longer resided in the city. The court found for the plaintiff on charges of aiding and abetting an escape.

Throughout the nineteenth century, black women in Washington increasingly appeared in the criminal court for "keeping a house of ill fame," more commonly referred to as a bawdy house. For instance, on April 15, 1836, judges examined Butler, along with her husband, Henry, for managing "a certain common bawdy house, situated in the City of Washington." Police charged them with maintaining the said house "for filthy lucre and gain." Legal documents described those who maintained a house of ill fame as "divers evil disposed persons, as well as men and women, and whores." Eliza was listed first in the official documents, and Henry was listed second, which may indicate that he was an accomplice. A free black man named Henry Butler also appears in the property tax record as a waiter who owed taxes on a small lot. The city directory of black residents lists Henry's occupation as a waiter, while Eliza appears in the tax record without a "profession." It is quite possible that the same Eliza and Henry Butler listed in the tax record are the ones who appear in the criminal court docket, but other free men and women with the same last name were accounted for in the property tax record, and some were listed with better-paying jobs that enabled them to avoid financial ties to a bawdy house.[100]

The wording applied by the courts offers evidence of the link between law and nineteenth-century discourses of morality. The jurors further stated that the Butlers committed "whoredom and fornication, whereby divers unlawful assemblies, riots, routs, affrays, disturbances, and violations, of the peace of the United States, and dreadful filthy and lewd offences, [occurred] in the same house." The contrast between the description of "dreadful filthy and lewd offences" and the expectation of good "manners, conversation, morals, and estate" underscores the moral overtones that shaped expected social norms in the District. According to the jurors, their crimes ultimately caused "destruction and corruption of youth, and other people, in their manners, conversation, morals, and estate, and against the peace and government of the United States." The meanings tied to the legal phrases of the courts were also read on the bodies of those charged for said offenses. The juror statement became the formulaic way to document cases of women accused of keeping a bawdy house. Despite the constant risk of arrest, fines, and terms served in the workhouse, free black women continued to maintain prostitution enterprises in key locations throughout the District.[101]

Antebellum Washington was a city in a constant state of transformation and a person considered of ill-repute might reside in the same neighborhood of those viewed as the elite classes. Consequently, it was nearly impossible to experience the new city without walking past women and men from various walks of life. In 1833 Ann Simms, Mrs. Wurtz, and Mary Wurtz went to jail for keeping a bawdy house on Pennsylvania Avenue near Fourteenth Street. The three women ran an operation located near Lafayette Square, a neighborhood where prominent white families resided. One historian noted that in this neighborhood "lived most of the local establishment—old-line families, ranking politicians," and that "in this fashionable circle, etiquette followed the traditions of the slave-owning chivalry of nearby counties." Court records with details of these cases accused participants in prostitution of causing "great damage and common nuisance of all the good citizens," and thus reflects the desire of lawmaking officials to cordon off disruptive behavior. Black women's sex commerce near sites of elite white residences and businesses burdened the efforts of those who hoped to embody the class sensibilities of cosmopolitan urbanity.[102]

The presence of both black prostitutes and the notorious slave pens situated nearby further complicated the polite designs of elite neighborhoods and federal offices. Slave pens, which dotted the landscape but clustered near the location where Simms, Wurtz, and Mrs. Wurtz were arrested for keeping a bawdy house, disrupted these designs less disturbingly for the whites already accustomed to the power dynamics of slaveholding. The slave pens between Fourteenth and Constitution Avenue encouraged the constant presence of slave traders and slave owners. These same men who participated in the slave trade were target clients for prostitutes. Likewise, slave traders might also target black prostitutes for the fancy-girl trade. The synchronicity of the local slave trade, sex commerce, and the establishment of elite families that characterized this prominent enclave meant the constant flow of criminal and civil disputes in the local courts. Lafayette Square, named in honor of Marquis de Lafayette, boasted St. John's Church and federal-style homes such as the Decatur House and Dolley Madison's residence. The "questionable character" of black women disrupted the cosmopolitan landscape that reputable white families and politicians struggled to imagine. The looming presence of the slave trade also presented frustrations in their attempts to fashion the square as a refined space. The local market demand, whether for slaves or for sex, illuminates the degree to which certain areas of commerce were far from marginal but rather fully integrated into the urban landscape and social life of the capital.

Black women not only operated dens of sex and leisure that allowed gambling, cards, and drinking, they also enlisted the efforts of family members and spouses to meet market demands. Interestingly, like Mrs. Eliza Butler, some women were listed with a social title indicating that they were legally married. Marriage did not necessarily presuppose the likelihood of black women's involvement in commercial sex, nor did singleness predetermine a path to prostitution. Cases pertaining to black women confirm a theme found in the criminal court record, that of collaborative prostitution, which at times engaged kinship networks. The specific nature of the relationship between Mrs. Wurtz and Mary Wurtz is unknown, but given the scope of the free African American population in the city, we could assume that they were related in some form. Married couples like the Butlers also collaborated in sex commerce, often combining resources to finance their respective establishments. Such resources proved critical for the operation of the bawdy house in addition to paying the fees incurred from arrest.[103] If local authorities caught black women, combined earnings provided a possible avenue for payment of fines demanded in the court proceedings.

Survival and self-making fostered a sense of economic collaboration among African Americans in Washington regardless of reputation and class standing. The fact that those accused of keeping a bawdy house incurred the highest fines did not dissuade black women from maintaining independent prostitution operations, but it further positioned them to cover the fines that most prostitutes working alone did not possess the means to pay. For example, Eliza Warner and "Eliza Warner the Younger" (her daughter) were both convicted for "keeping a house of ill fame."[104] In any line of work, it was common for nineteenth-century families to employ the labor of younger members in the family to contribute to the household income. In this case, the sources remain unclear as to whether the "Younger" solicited sex or assisted with the duties associated with the upkeep of the house, but both appeared before the criminal court and both fines were fully paid. Furthermore, black women might work with other black women or family members who solicited in the same ward or from the same bawdy house to build on client networks and resources. Ann Johnson and Hannah Contee went to jail for "keeping a house of ill fame" near the third ward of the city. Sally McDaniel, Patty Pallison, and Kell Simpson were all arrested as a group as well.[105] Collaborative enterprises expanded the potential reach of each establishment while also providing a degree of protection. The person who managed the bawdy house might organize women in the same location, maximizing the opportunities for women to make money based on the reputation of the house as a reliable site for sex services. The presence of other sex workers provided some semblance of security in the face of the potential threats to safety involved with prostitution or in the event that a client withheld payment.

As a punishment to prostitutes, courts might impose a fine of anywhere from one to a little over five dollars for such offenses, whereas those identified as madams paid as much as twenty dollars. Nearly every workhouse sentence ranged from thirty to ninety days. Susan Ross, arrested and charged for keeping a bawdy house, paid a fine of fifteen dollars. During the summer of 1850, Elizabeth Ware went to jail for "keeping a house of ill fame and a house of assignation." The distinction made here between a "house of ill fame" and a "house of assignation" suggests that Ware provided not only a place for solicitation but also a place for prostitutes working independently of a madam and an organized bawdy house. Ware avoided the workhouse and paid a fine. Women arrested for keeping bawdy houses or houses of assignation paid a higher amount in legal fees than those convicted of crimes associated with prostitution, such as gambling, drinking alcohol, disorderly conduct, being out after hours, profanity, or unlawful assembly. The risks and financial costs associated with sex commerce help us understand not only the premium they placed on economic incentives of the work but also the lack of access to alternative avenues for income. Survival demanded income, and employment prospects for black women were limited. For some women, managing a prostitution ring was less about defying sexual mores and more about refusing to work as servants or in the range of low-wage jobs black women were narrowly confined to. The unusually high fines paid by those who "operated" a bawdy house and the fees paid by prostitutes who violated laws associated with sex work indicate that such women had financial incentives for working independently of white households. In some cases, prostitution supported strategies of self-making at variance with respectability.[106]

The extralegal nature of sex and leisure commerce in the District complicates ideas about liberty and self-making as they relate to moral respectability. Marriage and kinship shape our understandings of the aspirations and motivations for freedom, but they also worked in tandem with extralegal avenues for income that provided some measure of economic mobility. For instance, George W. Gray and Celia Gray, his wife, faced charges for "keeping a house of ill fame, commonly called a whore house," on F Street near the Methodist meeting house. Sources remain unclear about whether Celia herself worked as a prostitute, but the record does demonstrate that they both operated the bawdy house. Marriage and family cohesion among free blacks proved particularly important in shaping their home life in a way previously denied them as former slaves. As historian Erica Ball argues in her work on antislavery life and the black middle class, marriage and emphasis on the family were also strategies of respectability to convey moral virtue, particularly among free black women.[107] In this case, however, George and Celia Gray both embraced legal marriage and disregarded the precepts of moral virtue championed by many free African Americans at the time. The couple even solicited clients near a Methodist church. Rather than subscribing to the tenets of moral virtue demanded by the courts and by racial uplift initiatives, some black women elaborated their own ideas about family identity and enterprise.[108]

By the 1850s, many black women in charge of bawdy houses increasingly appeared before the courts to face charges of disorderly conduct, selling liquor, playing cards, gambling, and unlawful assembly. After many of them paid fines or worked a term in the workhouse, they returned to sex and leisure commerce. The experiences of black women prostitutes and bawdy house owners show the obstacles to self-making that they confronted in the courts and the local labor economy. As Cynthia Blair demonstrates, racial inferiority was still inscribed in the exchanges and expectations of black prostitutes, including through lower compensation for sexual encounters.[109] This points to the degree to which black women's survival depended heavily on the market demand for their labor, and the sexual commodification of their labor in particular. Black women confronted challenges in the sex and leisure economy and yet found ways to improvise as they formed strategies for earning money and acquiring material goods.

The records of the criminal court reveal that self-making and the improvisation that came with this process at times involved theft. Advertisements and descriptions of fugitive women show the ways they employed practices of theft in order to claim material resources for self-making and to earn money to go toward their travel. These women took both women's and men's clothing as disguises or to build a new wardrobe, as well as money, housewares, ribbons and fabric, blankets, and shoes. When black women became free, they might help themselves to more goods in the event they did not earn enough income. Jane White was accused and found guilty of stealing three chemises and three shifts from Maria Dives.[110] Ann Joyce allegedly took two sheets, two blankets, one bolster, and two quilts from James C. White.[111] But Joyce apparently didn't end her excursion at White's; she moved on to the home of R. G. Purdy, where she took a vest, a pair of pants, and a cotton apron. Two years later, Joyce appeared before the court again and the jury found her guilty of stealing two pieces of cotton.[112] The court found another woman guilty of stealing a toilet cover, two knives, a sheet of paper, one dress, and eighteen napkins.[113] Jane Holly, who also went by the name Jane Hanson, received a guilty conviction for allegedly taking two silver dollars, six half dollars, and one purse.[114] A number of women sentenced to the workhouse were funneled right back to serve terms for recurring offenses. While serving a term for a previous conviction, Ellen Lindsley appeared before the court again, but this time she stood before the judges and jury on charges of arson.[115] According to court documents, she set fire to the barn attached to the local almshouse, where she worked for the term of her sentence. One news report stated that she committed the act out of "revenge for being given the shower bath, by the Intendant."[116] Lindsley confessed to the fire, and the court found her guilty of arson. A few months after she served her sentence, the court found her guilty of stealing one quilt, two dollars, one blanket, and a bonnet.[117]

African American women appeared before the courts for both legal and extralegal actions that illuminate the hurdles of navigation and self-definition that they encountered in early Washington. Some enslaved women appealed to the courts for legal freedom, and others were also brought before the court for unlawfully attempting escape from slavery. Even as black women became free, they struggled to live in a city with limited opportunities for economic mobility, which often led women to sex and leisure trades that involved activities traditionally criminalized in the antebellum era. Life after slavery did not always translate into uplift and respectability, and the criminal court records reveal African American women's complicated racial and gendered status within the law. In other words, their criminality was implied whether they were enslaved or free, as the slave codes and black codes circumscribed life and economic opportunities available to them in the capital. The courts became the place where those laws were enforced. The proceedings of the courts also provide insights into black women's opportunities and obstacles to self-making and navigation of the capital. When they encountered such obstacles, they improvised in ways that led them to the courts.

During these antebellum decades, the black population experienced a dramatic shift marked by a decline in the population of enslaved people. In the 1850s, free African Americans increasingly shaped the contours of black life in Washington. Although the Fugitive Slave Act of 1850 banned the slave trade in the District, agents evaded these restrictions by trading on the borders of Maryland and Virginia, and many enslaved women were sold off to cotton and sugar plantations farther south. Enslaved women also found ways to secure their legal manumission through the courts or discovered an avenue for escape. Consequently, free African Americans formed just over 73 percent of the black population at 10,059 and the number of enslaved people declined from 33 percent of Washington residents in 1840 to 26 percent in 1850.[118] Sectional strife left enslaved and free black women waiting in the wings of compromise, contemplating whether to chart their course elsewhere. For those who remained, the racial tensions of the District escalated, and white mobs confronted a changing city where institutions of black achievement dotted the urban landscape. From the underground to the eye of the public storm, black women and girls emerged in the mounting racial debate in antebellum Washington, D.C.

CHAPTER FOUR

Schools

Living in Washington required an awareness of social customs that involved strict observance of the local black code and attitudes of moral virtue that featured prominently in black institutions. Amid these parameters, African Americans carved out an educational tradition in the nation's capital that fostered a sense of social mobility. Black girls emerged as the descendants of free and formerly enslaved people into a burgeoning middle class. This social designation did not necessarily constitute social distance marked by economic means alone but was also defined by the mores, education, and aspirations associated with antebellum black middle-class communities. Nor were they afforded the protections from labor and sexual exploitation available to middle-class white girls.[1] Thus, black women and girls faced limited access to economic and social mobility, but an education opened up possibilities for a vocation in teaching and participation in social reform. For African American women and girls in Washington, schools became the institutionalized venues for self-making.

During the first half of the nineteenth century, free black women and girls emerged as benefactors, teachers, and pupils who set in motion the rich tradition of black education in Washington. African Americans and white allies in the District built a thriving set of private schools for black children, some specifically designed for African American girls. Black leaders across the country did not always agree on the curriculum of educational institutions for women and girls.[2] Debates looked similar to those sparked around white women's education.[3] Black leaders in Washington deliberated the degree to which women and girls should pursue what contemporaries referred to as an ornamental education focused on the domestic arts. An ornamental curriculum comprising needlework, penmanship, art, music, and decorative arts emphasized women's obligations to family and implied membership in the middle class. Unlike their white peers, black girls received an education that did not necessarily presume a life focused on domestic responsibilities, as many antebellum black women juggled familial obligations and work outside the home. Thus, the schools for girls in Washington focused on literacy and religious instruction, and at times subjects such as geography, philosophy, and the sciences in preparation for employment as teachers. At a time when access to an education was limited for girls of any race in the South, most African Americans viewed schools that catered to black girls as a worthy enterprise.

This chapter looks at the participation of African American women and girls in Washington's antebellum black schools and the ways their educational experiences shaped their processes of self-definition. The early history of black education in the District shows the ways that black women emerged as leaders in the work of uplift, setting in motion the traditions of educationally centered strategies of self-making that shaped black Washington. Furthermore, the sources that shed light on schools for black girls provide a rare glimpse of their voices and the manner in which they were groomed for such work. The foundation laid in establishing black educational institutions in Washington prepared black girls for the privileges and realities associated with freedom. African Americans found ways to create community and pursued the cultivation of their intellects by establishing, financing, and attending their own institutions. The education of black girls had broader implications beyond vocational endeavors that emphasized the role of women outside the home.[4] Placing a premium on moral virtue and education, free black girls' rejections of larger narratives about racial inferiority shaped their commitments to learning. Faced with budgetary constraints, local harassment, and a popular discourse that regarded black women as inferior, few found education an easy endeavor in a locale legally and geographically confined to the customs of the slaveholding South. The education and socialization of black girls in local churches and schools reveal the kind of intellectual and social development that subverted the hostilities designed to intimidate them. The determination of black girls to elevate their position in society clashed with the commitment of District residents to preserve distinctions between the races. Mounting racial tensions in antebellum Washington signaled a new era in which black girls were factored into the fold of the race debate.

Historians of antebellum education largely link schools for African American children and adults to the abolitionist movement and the broader work of social reform. Schools for black girls in Washington certainly fit this mold. Reform constituted the framework of not only black education but also the social activist tradition of black Washington more broadly. Schools catered to both enslaved and free attendees even at the risk of harassment and mob violence. The political significance of obtaining an education was therefore not lost on black children. Although historians have pointed to the ways that African American women and men were infantilized in public debates about equality, we also see that enslaved and free children learned firsthand the realities of inequality and racism, particularly in their efforts to attend school.[5] If infantilization shaped their treatment as adults, racism, sexism, and mob violence demanded the kind of maturity required to survive such daily assaults as children. An education in nineteenth-century Washington involved a curriculum in literacy and scholarly subjects, as well as an informal education focused on the social development of the pupil. Liberty for black schoolgirls involved a set of socializing norms that underscored their abilities, their protection, and their futures. The emphasis on conduct and character shows the ways that teachers were attentive to issues of race, gender, and sexuality in the self-making process. Indeed, the schools were designed to prepare them for a society threatened by their very existence. During the 1850s, black girls witnessed firsthand the public outcry and violence targeted at them for pursuing an education. The growing tradition of black education in antebellum Washington threatened the social order of the day, and black girls found themselves defending their endeavors both verbally and physically. Before the schools for girls appeared, black women and men, many of whom were former slaves, began laying the foundation for literacy and learning in the nation's capital.

Schools in Washington were established with ties to local religious organizations, as in nearly every antebellum city. Religious movements throughout the mid-eighteenth and early nineteenth centuries encouraged literacy and the ability to read the Bible as an important path to salvation.[6] Some southern planters permitted enslaved people to learn to read to comprehend the biblical scriptures or to conduct skilled labor that required rudimentary reading abilities.[7] Indeed, leading antebellum African American activists such as Thomas Smallwood and Elizabeth Keckly learned to read while enslaved.[8] Planters did not find religious instruction in tension with slavery, but developed a theology that applied scripture to planter paternalism and demands for obedience from enslaved people. Various denominations launched initiatives to teach basic literacy skills to poor and enslaved people at the dawn of the century, but toward the antebellum decades race riots and hostilities inhibited black access to literacy and education. Slave rebellions, antislavery ferment, and the dissemination of abolitionist literature led southerners to pass or strengthen laws prohibiting literacy among slaves in states such as Virginia, North Carolina, South Carolina, Alabama, and Louisiana.[9] Former slaves penned autobiographies that underscored the lack of education as one of the most frustrating aspects of bondage.[10] This led scholars to develop the widespread belief that every state and city that permitted slavery also outlawed reading and writing among the enslaved.

In the District of Columbia, the black codes did not prohibit enslaved people from learning to read and write.[11] Moreover, as Myrtilla Miner, a northern white woman, later considered where to establish her new school, she explained that Washington made the most sense since it "contained the greatest proportion of untaught colored people of any city in which prohibitory laws did not exist."[12] Washington more closely resembled southern cities with social hierarchies that discouraged literacy among enslaved and free black inhabitants. One historian aptly noted, "Where laws were not a discouragement, custom was," and any slaveholder could punish attempts to read or write under his or her own authority.[13] The local slave code prohibited any gatherings of enslaved people and outlawed the circulation of "insurrectionary publications."[14] While prohibitions on learning to read and write did not appear in the code, the possibility of attending a school or reading literature attracted the wrong kind of attention, as white locals expressed hostilities toward black schools. Some enslaved women and girls managed to find creative ways to learn to read, whether from other black residents, from a willing white accomplice, or by painstakingly teaching themselves. At the risk of arrest and punishment, some teachers even allowed enslaved people to attend the local schools. The demands of labor and the tendency to hire both enslaved and free children posed challenges to children's attempts to learn to read and write in antebellum cities.[15] The avenues toward literacy that existed, however, reveal insights into the possibility that some enslaved women and girls learned to read and write before the Civil War. Learning became a hallmark of black life in antebellum Washington. During the 1850s, Washington boasted more private schools for African Americans than any other southern city.[16]

The origins of black education in Washington can be traced to the beginning of the nineteenth century. In 1807, George Bell, Nicholas Franklin, and Moses Liverpool built the first school for African Americans in the District. They were born enslaved, and once they became free, they collectively pulled their resources together one year following the establishment of the first all-white public school in the District.[17] The Bell School opened its doors at Second and D Streets SE with a matriculation of both enslaved and free pupils who resided in the city.[18] Bell and his wife, Sophia Browning, were enslaved when they had three sons and a daughter. Browning managed a "market garden" and regularly sold her produce at the Alexandria market during the hours she didn't labor for her owner, Rachel Pratt. Eventually, she saved $400, which she entrusted to a Methodist minister to purchase her husband. Once freed, Bell purchased Browning from Pratt and they secured the freedom of their four children, with their daughter being freed upon the mistress's death.

At the time they built the school, Bell and his comrades couldn't read or write, but with the help of Browning, they started a tradition of learning that shaped black Washington throughout the nineteenth century.[19]

Pratt also owned Browning's sister, an enslaved woman named Alethia Browning Tanner. Tanner also sold goods in the local market at President's Square and generated enough revenue to purchase her freedom to the tune of $1,400.[20] Her ability to earn a substantial amount of income shows the potential for enslaved women's informal economies. Such entrepreneurial activity required the consent of the slaveholder and the shrewdness of enslaved women like Tanner and Browning. After Tanner became free, she generously purchased her oldest sister Laurena Cook, along with her five children. The stories of Browning and Tanner illuminate not only the possibilities that came with enslaved women's entrepreneurial economies but also the ways their generosity helped usher in institutions that encouraged the intellectual endeavors of African Americans in Washington. Tanner purchased the freedom of John F. Cook, renowned educator and minister in Washington, who was one of her sister Laurena's five children.[21] She became a legendary arbiter of liberty and even paid for the freedom of the remaining enslaved members of the Cook family. Tanner and Browning made contributions that initiated the formation of key religious and educational institutions of black life in Washington.

Leading black men including George Bell and William Costin organized local societies like the Resolute Beneficial Society, and members of the group established another school for African Americans in the District. Students received lessons in reading, writing, arithmetic, and grammar, and the school boasted a regular attendance of "fifty or sixty scholars, and often more." One John Adams, a local shoemaker, became the first African American man to teach in the District. On the corner of F and Seventh Streets, Henry Potter opened the third school available to free black students.[22] These schools accommodated the pupils who built schools and trained teachers at future institutions. Potter taught teachers such as Anne Marie Becraft, who later opened the first school for black girls in Washington. Schools for black students eventually appeared in a number of neighborhoods. Between Old Capitol and Carroll Row on First Street, Anne Maria Hall started a coeducational school just steps from the halls of Congress and Senate. Hall was born in Prince George's County, Maryland, and attended a school in Alexandria. She taught large numbers of students for several decades while supporting her family following her husband's death. As a single mother, Hall became one of the first African American women to lead a school in the nation's capital.

Portrait of Alethia
Browning Tanner.
Cook Family Papers,
Moorland-Spingarn
Research Center,
Howard University.

In 1810, an Englishwoman named Mary Billings started a school for locals
on Dumbarton Street in Georgetown. Initially, Billings taught white students,
with the intention of forming an interracial school, but ultimately admitted
black students exclusively after locals protested. She opened an additional location on H Street in Washington at the home of a black man named Daniel
Jones. Henry Potter took over her Georgetown school and an Englishman
named Shay assisted with the Washington location. Shay eventually maintained a school of his own on the corner of I and Seventeenth Streets. He
likely taught enslaved residents to read and write, since he was arrested in
1830 for assisting a fugitive and served time in the workhouse.[23] Although his
arrest forced him to temporarily suspend his teaching responsibilities, a former pupil of Mary Billings named Henry Smothers opened a school near the
location of Shay's school. The school reportedly maintained an enrollment of

"more than a hundred and often as high as one hundred and fifty scholars."[24] Smothers served as the head of the school until a man named John W. Prout assumed leadership and transitioned the institution to a "free school" for a couple of years, allowing students to attend at an affordable cost or no cost at all. During the 1830s, the political and social climate shaped the constraints black educators worked under. The career of John F. Cook offers a case in point.

In 1834, Cook assumed leadership of the Smother's School. After Alethia Tanner purchased Cook's freedom, he worked as a shoemaker and later secured a job as assistant messenger in the Land Office. Cook increasingly became interested in pursuing education at the Columbia Institute, and he matriculated with the financial backing of his aunt Alethia.[25] When he didn't work at the Land Office, Cook committed to learning as much as possible and eventually left his position to become a teacher and minister. African American schools fell under intense scrutiny following the Southampton Rebellion in 1831, when Nat Turner and enslaved women and men of Southampton launched a campaign of violent resistance in Virginia that reverberated throughout the country.[26] The rebellion occurred three years before the start of Cook's teaching career, but tensions remained high in the nation's capital, where the implications of the revolt were rehashed in countless debates over the future of slavery and the Union. Locals opposed any efforts to elevate the social position of black Washingtonians. Georgetown enacted a black code particularly directed at antislavery efforts "calculated to excite insurrection or insubordination among the slaves or colored people." The heightened sense of insecurity led directly to stricter enforcement of the slave and black codes in antebellum Washington. In this context, Cook taught for a year before a race riot broke out. Following allegations that an enslaved man named Arthur Bowen had entered the bedroom of his owner, Anna Maria Thornton, the political climate placed even greater pressure on racial uplift in the capital.[27]

Anna Thornton, the wife of William Thornton, the renowned designer of the Capitol building, owned Bowen and at least three generations of his family. Although enslaved, Bowen built relationships among the city's free black leaders, including Cook. Bowen found moments to steal away to lectures hosted by the Philomathean Talking Society, a group composed primarily of free black men interested in discussing abolitionism, temperance, and economic independence. Bowen understood the mounting debates about slavery and expressed his own resentment about his legal status. Allegedly, following a night of drinking, Bowen grabbed an ax and reportedly stumbled into the room where Anna, her mother, and Bowen's mother slept. When Anna became aware of his presence in her room, he immediately fled, and Madison Jeffers, a police constable and local slave trader, launched a search to arrest him. Bowen confronted Anna Thornton to protest his enslavement, and the idea that he was entitled to freedom likely had something to do with the philosophical debates and lectures he attended at the Philomathean Talking Society. Bowen's story illuminates the possibilities that existed for enslaved people to participate in intellectual communities. Exposure to such societies in the era of the Southampton Rebellion triggered the anxieties of white locals.[28]

On August 12, 1835, an estimated three thousand white residents congregated in the capital demanding that Bowen be hanged. A free black man observed in his diary that "their object was to get Mrs. Thornton's mulatto man out and hang him without Judge or Juror."[29] The Washington correspondent for the *Richmond Enquirer* reported, "One of the men who seemed most anxious and resolute in raising the mob said they only intended to cut off both his ears and give him a good coat of tar."[30] Andrew Laub, the son of John Laub, a slave owner and clerk in the Treasury Department, led the angry mob. Anna Thornton apparently did not believe that Bowen intended to kill her, and she repeatedly sent letters to President Andrew Jackson to petition for a pardon on his behalf. After a highly publicized trial and a campaign to damage black homes, institutions, and businesses, the judge sentenced Bowen to be hanged for attempted murder. Thornton's efforts to petition the president led to his pardon and sale to an owner in another state. *Niles Weekly Register* reported that in the year 1835, a total of fifty-three riots related to slavery erupted in the country, compared with just four in 1833.[31] The racial climate remained tense and shaped the challenges that free African Americans experienced in antebellum Washington—a place of growing hostility toward black people.

Panic gripped the Chesapeake as white locals and political elites in the District expressed rage at the thought of an attempted murder of a white woman by an enslaved man. Bowen's entry into Thornton's bedchamber fed into nineteenth-century fears of black masculinity and imperatives to protect white womanhood. Despite the fact that Thornton made several pleas for pardon, images emerged of Bowen as a drunken murderer and a sexual predator who had targeted a prominent white woman's bedchamber. Condemnation of the incident translated into violent repercussions for the black community more broadly and, in particular, efforts to undermine economically successful black residents such as Beverly Snow, a popular restauranteur in the city. Mob violence broke out, damaging black schools, churches, businesses, and homes as a means to intimidate black residents and white allies in the city. Mary Wormley's school, located near the corner of Vermont Avenue and I Street, was destroyed by the mob after they set it on fire.[32] Georgetown enacted its first black code that punished the possession and circulation of abolitionist literature, and the city council of Washington passed a corporate ordinance that prohibited black locals from obtaining shop licenses, confining them to businesses contained in drive carts and hackneys.[33] Mobs targeted John Cook, who managed to flee before they reached his home. They showed no mercy on his school, however, and "destroyed all the books and furniture and partially destroyed the building."[34] Cook remained in Pennsylvania for a brief period before returning to reorganize his school into Union Seminary. The race riot left an indelible imprint of antiblack sentiment that was particularly aimed at burgeoning black middle-class institutions in the city.

In the wake of the 1835 riots, white mobs identified as "Plug Uglies" or "rowdies" consistently targeted black schools in the District in their determination to undermine the uplift efforts of African Americans. The *Evening Star* noted that they assembled between I and K Streets every afternoon "to play bandy and impose on helpless colored persons" and that "no age is spared." Black children frequented I and K Streets to attend Cook's school located at the Fifteenth Street Presbyterian Church. The report noted, "Not long since a poor old colored man was beat, by these boys, and it usually for these young Plug Uglies to amuse themselves—after their games—on their way home, by running down helpless colored children and beating them." Notices of their terror frequented the pages of the press. Following a Sabbath School Convention held at Dumbarton Street Church, a reporter noted the "reckless and lawless spirit" of these young men and commented, "It is far from being an uncommon thing to see many of this class, during the early hours of the night, prowling about the streets—either wholly or partly intoxicated."[35] Despite the violence and harassment he faced, Cook proceeded with leading Union Seminary, which enrolled an average of one hundred women and men a year.[36] Cook maintained the school until his death in 1855, and his sons John and George continued the family tradition of leading African American educational institutions in Washington. This lineage of black education serves as the backdrop from which schools for African American girls emerged.

Antebellum ideas about race and gender shaped conversations about respectability and the ideological purpose of schools for black girls. In 1827, Anne Marie Becraft opened the first school for African American girls on Dumbarton Street in Georgetown.[37] Born in 1805, Becraft attended Henry Potter's school for a year in 1812 and the school organized by Mary Billings until 1820. At the age of fifteen, Becraft received support to establish a school from a Catholic priest named Father Vanlomen of the Holy Trinity Church. Her school drew the attention of Vanlomen, and he offered to find a larger building for the school on Fayette Street, where Becraft offered both a day and boarding school for the girls in attendance. Between thirty and thirty-five girls enrolled at the school, and oral histories from the nineteenth century describe catching a glimpse of "the troop of girls, dressed uniformly," following "their pious and refined teacher to devotions on the sabbath at Holy Trinity Church."[38] Becraft demonstrated a consummate commitment to her own spiritual development. In 1831, Pope Gregory XVI approved the establishment of the Oblate Sisters of Providence, a convent of African American women in Baltimore.[39] Feeling pulled to the formation of this new black female Catholic community, Becraft trained one of the pupils who attended the school to assume leadership and responsibility of the institution so she could join the convent in Baltimore. As a member of the Oblate Sisters of Providence, she served as the lead teacher and made such an impression that the convent made plans to appoint her as mother superior. She died of illness not long after she moved to Baltimore, but her vision for a school for African American girls led to more efforts to create similar institutions.

Becraft remains, like Alethia Tanner and Sophia Browning, one of the foremothers of social activism in black Washington. She was described as "a woman of the rarest sweetness and exaltation of Christian life, graceful and attractive in person and manners, gifted, well educated, and wholly devoted to doing good."[40] She embodied the ideals that many leading antebellum black families hoped to instill in their daughters. The work of uplift was inextricably tied to identity, character, and conduct, and African Americans with aspirations for social mobility looked to these tenets as a guide for young women.[41] The formation of Becraft's school and the stable enrollment indicate an emerging black middle class invested in the ideals of moral improvement. Sources note, "The school comprised girls from the best colored families of Georgetown, Washington, Alexandria, and surrounding country."[42] The educational offerings of Washington evolved enough to create the demand for a school designed specifically for African American girls. Such schools in particular reveal the ways that uplift work shaped the gender conventions of an emerging black middle class and its corresponding institutions of self-making.[43]

Black middle-class inhabitants in Washington invested time and energy in building educational, social, and religious institutions throughout the nineteenth century. These institutions served the purposes of self-making and made broader contributions to the race. One source noted, "The colored people who first settled in Washington constituted a very superior class of their race."[44] Demarcations of class appeared early in the establishment of the capital. The source stated, "Many of them were favorite family servants, who came here with congressmen from the south, and with the families of other public officers." These families, which were distinguished in histories of black Washington, contributed their resources to organize schools, churches, and local societies. The framework for such institutions reinforced uplift ideologies with origins in Protestant black liberation theology. Individuals from prominent free black families supported the development of Christian character through moral reform, abolition, temperance, and economic independence. This prescribed path to uplift formed the foundation for demands for liberty on the basis of equality. The social project of uplift, however, made moral demands of black women that bore implications for themselves and the race.[45]

The public conduct of African Americans fell under scrutiny in the black press as writers called not only to improve the perception of black people but also to ensure their safety and survival. Implicit in antebellum black codes was the pervasive idea that black residents and their mobility warranted suspicion and even surveillance. Black leaders instructed members of their race on public conduct not because they held any suspicions of them but because they understood the ideological underpinnings of racism.[46] A recurring theme in black print culture was the need for "moral improvement" and "politeness." In 1849, the *North Star*, published by Frederick Douglass, included a feature titled "Free Negroes in Virginia," which stated, "The condition of the Free Negroes of the South is scarcely preferable to that of the slaves." Life in the South made black institutions like churches, schools, and civic organizations incredibly precarious to manage. He noted further, "They are objects of contempt and suspicion. They have but few privileges, no incentives to either mental or moral improvement, and no hope beyond the most contracted circle of domestic servitude."[47] In antebellum Washington and the bordering slave states, "contempt and suspicion" pervaded the locale with the enforcement of black codes, the fugitive slave law, and notices in the local press. As Stanley Harrold points out, "Most whites regarded free blacks as an immoral, criminal class that endangered property and chastity." The imperatives of survival and acceptance shaped ideas about respectability, which at times translated into intense demands for strict moral conduct. Respectability was based, in part, on designating the mantle of virtue as the responsibility of black women.[48]

Black women articulated the tenets of virtue as part of the work of racial uplift but recognized that not all women embraced these ideals. The Israel Church Sabbath School Association of Washington, D.C., made the argument for an ethics of charity, manners, and modesty. Rebecca Moore, a member of the local association, penned an essay titled "Goodness and Sobriety," writing, "Again, there are females in this world who seem to think that politeness is an ostentatious parade. Their rudeness, which they are pleased to term plainness, never stops to think obnoxious life is made happy by our good, sober, modest action."[49] Moore's ideas met with skepticism from those who regarded her approach to black womanhood as "an ostentatious parade," but her statement reveals that black womanhood did not constitute a monolith but rather was characterized by myriad ideas about what it meant to live as a free black woman.[50] Many of the free black women typically disassociated from the black middle class did not always express a preoccupation with moral reform efforts and largely represented the target audience for uplift proselytizing. Moore's plea struck at the core of the tensions that might appear among black women's choices and ideas about how they defined themselves. Women like Moore deployed the idea of respectability as an important measure of racial progress, but the concept also functioned as a label for other black women. Economically, however, the aims of both the free black middle class and black women working in extralegal economies appeared not all that opposed—their activities collectively encouraged survival, self-making, and economic independence.[51] Moore stated further, "Females should dwell together as one common band of sisterhood, whose sole object should be to do good, having wisdom, friendship, which begets peace among all mankind, as their chart: the same is life to those who possess it, death and misery to those who do not."[52] Her charge to embrace this prescribed idea of "goodness and sobriety" gestured toward the intraracial and class-centered fissures that black women grappled with.[53] According to Moore, the ramifications were grim, but a broader view of black women shows that they lived lives of greater complexity than her distillation of proper conduct accounts for.

Many black women who attended local schools regarded moral virtue as an expression of racial progress, and thus a weapon against popular perceptions of African Americans as depraved and unfit for citizenship. White Americans typically did not associate enslaved and free black women with the white middle-class ideals articulated in the cult of "true womanhood."[54] Antebellum black women assumed a standard of womanhood with broader implications and convictions in mind. Scholars such as Erica Ball have reinterpreted respectability as one of many strategies in the arsenal against slavery. Ball argues that respectability politics transcended the white gaze and "is better understood as something valued for itself, irrespective of the presence or absence of whites, and as continuing to shape the conduct of elite and aspiring African Americans in spite of a hostile white republic."[55] Education for black girls required a pedagogical approach that fostered a sense of empowerment through learning. The strain of empowerment evident in schools for black girls underscored the imperatives of moral improvement and the framework from which they were encouraged to see their identities taking shape. Attending school shaped not only the scope of what they knew but also how they began to understand themselves.[56]

Contemporaries of African American women teachers like Becraft included more widely known antebellum women such as Sarah Mapps Douglass.[57] Like Becraft, in Philadelphia, Douglass also specifically taught African American girls. Douglass notably removed her school from the Philadelphia Female Anti-slavery Society, an interracial yet predominantly white abolitionist organization. Douglass felt that the academy no longer required white support and assumed management of the school.[58] Her pupils learned in an environment she controlled and that catered to their experiences as African American girls. Aware of the pejorative stereotypes of black women's sexuality, Douglass taught science with watercolors of flowers to allude to female genitalia as aspects of the body to be cherished and valued.[59] Such ideas were a radical departure from prevailing attitudes that associated black women's and girls' bodies as distorted physiological anomalies.[60] One of the first black women to develop a curriculum of sex education, Douglass was a woman before her time, charting a course of epistemic revision. Historian April Haynes remarks, "She used physiology, art, and poetry to portray black women's bodies as themselves delicate—neither hardened against pain nor immune to desire."[61] Douglass used brightly colored paintings of flowers as both emblems of modesty and indicators of their natural beauty. Black girls' bodies were neither an aspect of themselves of which to be ashamed nor available and disposable for anyone else. In this particular context of modesty and self-control, they were empowered by a pedagogy of self-making to exercise autonomy over their bodies, even in the face of racial caste.

Black women and girls in the District sought education, moral improvement, and mobility within the confines of the law and at tremendous personal risk. Thus, careful observance of the law did not offer a shield to their divergences from social customs and attitudes. Faced with white resentment and retaliation, black women and girls could not accept the perceptions of white Americans as the only stakes of respectability. A life of virtue and moral improvement rested on an ethic of self-making that emphasized how they perceived themselves. Such convictions manifested in their pursuit of education. The project of encouraging the intellectual development of women and girls prepared future generations of black women activists.[62] The work of educating girls exclusively reveals a tradition of learning and enrichment among black girls in Washington leading up to the Civil War. The ideas and perspectives offered by these girls appeared in Miner's Normal School for Colored Girls.

In the decade leading up to the Civil War, white New York native Myrtilla Miner opened a school for African American girls in Washington. What might compel a white woman from the northeast to move south and open a school for black girls? By the 1850s, the abolitionist movement was in full swing, with various factions of antislavery activism launching visible and covert campaigns to end slavery. Moreover, white women, particularly from free states, played a significant role in the fight against slavery and for women's rights. The antebellum decades marked an era of reform that took the nation by storm. White and African American women pursued single-gender education, since many schools exclusively admitted boys and men.[63] Schools and seminaries became increasingly available to middle-class women and girls in both the North and the South.[64] Most schools for white girls in the South focused less on preparations for careers in teaching and more on enhancing prospects for marriage.[65] The intellectual development of women in the South corresponded with a woman's ability to maintain the interest of her husband and those she entertained. Between 1840 and 1860, school attendance declined in the New England states compared with mid-Atlantic and southern states.[66] Still, the North maintained a tradition of women's education that trained women teachers later appointed to the South. Miner's own intellectual journey shaped her desires to teach African American girls.

Miner's education and training were influenced by exposure to interracial education. In 1840, she enrolled at Clinton Seminary, a school for girls that abolitionist Hiram H. Kellogg established in 1821 in Clinton, New York, not long after educator Prudence Crandall opened the doors of her school in Connecticut. Crandall established a school for girls in Canterbury in 1831. The school gained a reputation for excellence and claimed pupils from prominent New England families. When an African American student named Sarah Harris enrolled in the school, families protested and removed their daughters from Crandall's institution.[67] Crandall decided to exclusively admit black girls, and the local government responded with a new law that prohibited schools for African Americans. Crandall was arrested and convicted after several trials. When she tried to resume the operation of her school, local protests grew so violent that she closed the school for safety reasons. Miner undoubtedly knew of this controversy when she began her studies at Clinton. During her time at the seminary, at least three of her classmates were African American women.[68] Following her graduation, Miner taught at Clover Street Seminary, a girls' school in Rochester, New York. Celestia Bloss, the founder and headmistress of the school, was acquainted with abolitionist and reform circles in upstate New York. Most white women teachers did not possess abolitionist or reform sympathies, but regarded education as complementary to gender conventions.[69] Nonetheless, Miner lived in a region that the Reverend Charles Grandison Finney called the "burnt district," which became a hotbed of abolitionism.[70] By the time she was employed to teach the daughters of planters in Whitesville, Mississippi, her exposure to the realities of slavery had inspired her to open a school for black girls. She remarked, "Wherever I go, horror and despair offend me, and I do not wish to become any more acquainted with a people who shock me by their injustice and place such sights and sounds before me."[71] Moreover, women like Miner expressed concerns that white southern children "must be contaminated and their consciences and sensibilities perverted by such things."[72] Some white women teachers from the North arrived in the South only to be repelled by the realities of slavery.

Miner's antislavery ideas were also influenced by her experiences in upstate New York. Learning at Clinton alongside three African American peers revealed to Miner the ways they contradicted racist myths about the intellectual capacities of black girls. Furthermore, Miner maintained correspondence with leading African Americans in North, so why not establish a school there? Besides, the slave South often sparked culture shock among women from New England seminaries. Nevertheless, Miner chose Washington instead—a contested city that drew the political passions of people from all over the country. Thus, she joined the ranks of a small coterie of white women teachers willing to risk social and political ostracism to teach African Americans in the South. Miner chose the nation's capital as the location for her project of educating African American girls at the heart of the nation. Her plans, however, did not take off without resistance.

Unable to see the viability of a teaching career in the white schools of the South, Miner set out to "sap the slave power by educating its victims."[73] The school afforded black girls in the District a quality education, and Miner hoped to position the graduates of the school to work as teachers.[74] She believed that black girls might benefit the most since they possessed "fewer resources for an independent subsistence."[75] In the winter of 1851, with just one hundred dollars to start, Miner opened her Normal School for Colored Girls in a home owned by an African American man named Edward C. Young, located at Eleventh Street and New York Avenue NW, that comfortably accommodated six students.[76] By the end of the second month, as many as forty girls packed into the limited space. Although black private schools already existed in the District, debates about the role of black education in the city erupted when Miner's school opened.

Miner's efforts to offer an exceptional education exclusively for black girls exacerbated the frustrations of Walter Lenox, the mayor of Washington, with black schools. In response to Miner's school, Lenox remarked, "In my judgement, these two objections—the increase of our free population and the indiscriminate education of them far beyond their fixed condition—are sufficient reasons for us to oppose this scheme."[77] The idea of "their fixed condition" was the very idea that black schools refuted. Claims to liberty on the basis of equality meant that education served a vital function in dispelling myths about the intellectual capacities of black people. Education was a means through which black girls contradicted prevailing ideas about their "fixed condition." Miner made visible her intentions in the District, but black schools often materialized in covert locations in the city. Churches typically took part in this clandestine effort to propel black children "far beyond their fixed condition." John F. Cook Jr. opened a school in the basement of the Fifteenth Street Presbyterian Church located between I and K Streets, an area frequented by both free African Americans and white mobs. George Cook's school held classes in the basement of the Israel Bethel Church on South Capitol Street. Sabbath schools also appeared at Enoch Ambush's Wesleyan Seminary on C Street South between Ninth and Tenth Streets. Black businesses and any buildings where African Americans paid leases provided critical venues for black schools as well. C. Leonard's school was located on H Street near Fourteenth Street. Black-controlled spaces, veiled from public view, served as key sites of education and socialization, and perhaps these unassuming locations appeared less threatening. But the fact remains that African Americans also launched a more public initiative that added to Lenox's frustrations. Black residents protested the disparities between tax funds allotted to black schools and the public funding of schools for white residents in the capital.

Congress exercised federal oversight of the commissioners who regulated public schools in the District. Two years before Miner's school opened, black residents petitioned city commissioners for the establishment of public schools that admitted black children. They argued that black residents paid nearly $200,000 in local taxes and lacked the same access available to white residents.[78] As early as the 1820s, the District included at least 23 black owners of property, but by the 1850s there were as many as 168 black property holders who paid taxes that funded white public schools.[79] Racial discrimination, black codes, and local white reactions did not deter black activism and claims to racial equality. The board of common council rejected the petition even as the private schools exhibited degrees of success and enrollment comparable to those of white peer institutions. The contest among residents confirmed that the local and federal government had no intention to assist with expenses associated with African American schools. This made the efforts of black and white educators that much more exceptional as they offered a quality education with limited resources.

While the petitioners stood firm on the validity of their claims, many black locals did not find the response surprising. As Miner reflected not on the black local but on the political leanings of white District residents, she identified an "extremely Southern and proslavery" "tone of society." Upon learning about her plans, Frederick Douglass warned Miner that Washington was "the very citadel of slavery, the place most zealously watched and guarded by the slave power."[80] Miner expected the resistance that Douglass described, and she recalled that even upon her arrival, white women refused to offer her board because of her efforts to teach black girls. The petitioners demonstrated that the free black population had managed to build socioeconomic influence in the District, and while they represented a growing community with modest means, they deployed what leverage they possessed to make demands of the local government. Amid racial hostilities, black Washingtonians and white allies continued the work of building African American schools and consistently maintained a hard line against inequality and any opposition they faced in the capital.[81]

In the absence of public schools, financial contributions needed to be collected in order to offer an education of higher quality. In 1853, Miner traveled throughout the northern states to raise funds to purchase a lot between Nineteenth and Twentieth Streets and N Street and New Hampshire Avenue.[82] The lot comprised a small frame house and barn, along with fruit and shade trees. She received monetary gifts privately among her network of philanthropists who shared abolitionist sympathies, including Harriet Beecher Stowe, who donated at least $1,000 of her proceeds from *Uncle Tom's Cabin*. Although Miner's local ally Gamaliel Bailey owned the *National Era* newspaper, they decided against any editorial appeals for contributions because of local resistance.[83] Bailey knew better than anyone the risks that came with such efforts, as his printing office had barely survived the wrath of white mobs during the *Pearl* affair. Frederick Douglass characterized Miner's effort as "reckless, almost to the point of madness."[84] In the meantime, students with the means to pay tuition contributed $1.50 each month; according to Miner, out of forty students, twenty-five paid fees to attend the school.[85] Miner covered the remainder of the expenses incurred for materials and upkeep of the school through private donations. With that support, she managed to build a notable school for African American girls in the nation's capital.[86]

African American girls enrolled in Miner's Normal School for Colored Girls with the understanding that the education they received afforded them training to become teachers themselves. They were being instructed to model moral and intellectual excellence, and Miner hoped to prepare them for leadership in education. The coexistence of slavery, racism, and sexism in the capital created an environment that threatened such endeavors. Some of the girls who came from "the more well-to-do families of the city" were described as "mulattoes and quadroons for the most part, though some were obviously of pure African blood, and others could with difficulty be distinguished from whites."[87] "Some have red hair and blue eyes and slightly tinged complexions—They learn very fast and some of them are so smart, it seems quite wonderful indeed," wrote Miner.[88] The blurring of racial and economic lines that these girls embodied agitated many of the white residents of the District who were slaveholders or simply rejected any idea of racial equality and advancement. Social reformers too, with principled motives, could easily slip into postures of condescension. A white woman leading the process of adolescent socialization for black girls raises issues concerning how we think about race and power in the antebellum classroom. Given that the content of moral and religious instruction tapped into the most intimate part of the girls' lives, a level of trust had to be established. Even with the realities of these power dynamics present, Miner fostered a bond with the girls, and they discovered ways to learn as much as they could under her charge. Letters between the pupils and their teacher reveal insights into their experiences.

Students at the school wrote letters, always addressed to "My Teacher," to Miner when she toured the northeast to visit with donors and share updates on the progress of the school. Indeed, epistolary composition appeared in the required curriculum of most schools for girls, and Miner's school demanded the same. The letters give us a sense of their ideas, opinions, and interests. Many students who attended antebellum black schools started with limited or no exposure to reading and writing. As Mary Thomas reminded Miner,

"You will remember that I could not write anything fit to be read one year ago for I could neither write intelligently nor think anything sensible enough to pay for the trouble of writing."[89] Thomas marveled at the progress she had made in her writing, skills she hoped to pass on to others. She noted, "I think if I had an education I would not be as contented, but I should try to do all I could to help those that have none."[90] For Thomas, an education for herself was not enough, since she aspired to use her training to help others. In her pedagogy, Miner embedded an ethos of uplift that entailed applying their learning for the benefit of everyone.

The letters reveal that the girls not only recognized the exceptional opportunities that a school for black girls afforded in the 1850s but also had a sense of responsibility associated with sharing that knowledge with others. An education designed to train them to pursue a career in education meant their futures pointed in the direction of the middle class. Moreover, membership in the black middle class in Washington, D.C., also came with the imperatives of uplift and social reform. Thus, Mary Brent declared, "When we have obtained our complete education I hope we may use well the means God has given us and not desire the favor of men rather than God, but that we may teach the ignorant how to read as well as we, no matter how rich, we may be." Brent not only communicated the essence of uplift work but also shunned the trappings of materialistic success for virtue. Thrift, frugality, and hard work defined her idea of the duties of black girls afforded an education and opportunities for leadership. She offered, "I hope none of us will be ashamed to work for our living, though we have not many privileges yet we can be useful and do some good if we try for I think nothing defects earnest effort."[91] The girls understood that to be a privileged African American girl did not carry the same meaning it did for upper- and middle-class white girls. Their work would not solely be confined to the domestic sphere, and did not translate into economic security.[92] Like many middle-class African American women at the time, they juggled the demands for moral virtue and domesticity with the necessity of earning an income.

Conversations about reform and uplift were often tied to the girls' engagement with antebellum politics and race relations, which prepared the girls to be conversant in issues pertaining to public life.[93] This awareness was particularly acute when students learned about the ramifications of slave revolts and the waves of racial repression that shaped public discourse. As we have seen, after the Southampton Rebellion, many southern states passed laws further restricting literacy among slaves (since Nat Turner wielded his knowledge of the Bible in ways that emphasized a liberation theology for the enslaved).

One student offered a critique of such laws, noting, "I think that no government or State of men has a right to make a law to hinder any human being from seeing and reading the Bible."[94] She argued, "Giving the Bible to any slave is the best means of preparing the way for their elevation," and it served as the road map to virtue. Nonetheless, she believed that every person should possess access to biblical scripture "as a necessary means of salvation" and a spiritual right. She proposed a theology that made salvation and literacy accessible to everyone, but also understood the possibilities of resistance associated with biblical texts. Biblical study invited numerous interpretations among nineteenth-century African Americans that tied the moral and spiritual state of the race to their political destinies.

One student, Marietta Hill, was particularly engrossed in the political affairs of the Union. In 1854, Congress passed the Kansas-Nebraska Act, which allowed those who settled in the territory to decide whether to permit slavery there. The girls remained attuned to the latest political debates about slavery, understanding that the fate of the institution shaped the contours of their own experience in the District. Hill shared, "Sometimes a dark cloud seems to overshadow me and since the Nebraska bill has passed the cloud appears thicker and darker and I say will slavery forever exist?"[95] Slavery seemed to meet no end as Congress went back and forth with one compromise after the next. As long as slavery existed, and African Americans lacked equal rights to citizenship, their lives remained circumscribed by rigid legal and social parameters. But Hill's resolve remained steadfast, and she declared, "It shall cease! It shall and must be abolished! I think there will be blood shed before all can be free, and the question is are we willing to give up our lives for freedom? Will we die for our people! We may say yes." Hill's assessment of the political climate was eerily prophetic. Bloodshed not just in Kansas but in Harpers Ferry and eventually at Fort Sumter would usher the Union into war. In the meantime, Miner provided an intellectual environment that made space for the girls to share their thoughts and frustrations, as well as their candid opinions, about the national state of affairs. They offered critiques on topics that ranged from national events to everyday insults they experienced in Washington. One student noted in response to a white woman's exclusion of black women from a local event, "She gains the heart of some white people, but does not gain the heart of God. I would rather gain the heart of God than of people."[96] These spiritual dimensions to their appraisal of the state of society offered an avenue through which they confronted the demeaning treatment they remained subjected to.

The girls' political, spiritual, and social convictions appeared poignantly in their creative works as well. A few students enjoyed creative writing and sent their short stories during Miner's trips north. The girls imbued moral and spiritual lessons in their narratives, ideas most likely shaped by their instruction at the school. Matilda Jones particularly exhibited an interest in crafting these moral tales. She wrote a story titled "The Widow and Her Children" about a woman who lives in the western part of New York with her three children, Eva, Rodolpho, and Ella. The story shows her aptitude for character development, beginning with fifteen-year-old Eva, a girl similar in age to herself. Eva "was beloved by all because she was so gentle and good, and when she wished to make the children mind her, or when they had done wrong, and she wished to make them know that they had she did not storm and scold at them, but spoke to them in gentle and mild tones fulfilling the scripture in the Bible that declared, 'Soft words turneth away wrath.'" She is the eldest daughter and embodies all of the virtues celebrated by antebellum reformers. Invoking the text found in the book of Proverbs, Jones incorporates religious teaching into her description of characters. The second sibling, Rodolpho, however, serves as a contrast to Eva. Jones describes him as "a dark-eyed high-spirited boy, instead of minding his gentle sister when she reproved him, he often went away to think of some mode of revenge for he was a revengeful boy just like his father." Jones condemns the behavior of the men of the family when she describes their father as "a reckless young man" who "died early from dissipation." Contrastingly, she characterizes his widow as "a gentle woman" and notes that "the daughters were like her. She was hard-working and industrious. She was obliged to be so to keep herself and children clothed, fed, and educated."[97] In Jones's story, men are tragic figures in need of salvation, while the women serve as the arbiters of virtue. The women are not responsible for the shortcomings found in the male members of the family, yet they are highlighted as the guides through which we understand the imperatives of moral self-making.

Jones strategically deploys gendered ideas of racial uplift in her narrative with a juxtaposition between the siblings as contrasting figures that serve an instructive purpose. The attributes that Eva embodies underscore the wisdom of the biblical book of Proverbs and the industriousness of the woman famously cited in the thirty-first chapter. Contrastingly, Rodolpho reads like the nineteenth-century "confidence man," as he fails to embody the virtues expected of Christian men with his inherited "recklessness."[98] Jones thus demonstrates her familiarity with a nineteenth-century sentimentalist literary tradition and its emphasis on hardship, feeling, and character. Eva dies of consumption, and soon after the widow dies from grief, overwhelmed by the loss of her youngest daughter. Jones captures the realities of nineteenth-century life, highlighting the vulnerability to disease and the countless tales of trials and survival, particularly among black families and women who struggled to support their kin. These cautionary tales underscore the tenets of virtue that the girls themselves strove to model. The moral lessons infused in the short stories mirrored the religious scaffolding of the education offered at Miner's school.

The girls sent letters filled with lessons that might aptly reflect the theological underpinnings of Miner's pedagogical approach. One student, Sarah Shorter, offered, "I think there is a spirit which teaches us to do right, and there is an evil spirit which teaches us to do wrong. I think we ought to hearken to the good spirit."[99] Shorter deferred to the "good spirit" in order to appear more pleasing to God. Another student, Mary, opined, "I think obeying parents is a great commandment but I think we should obey God above all and keep his commandments."[100] She then added that she believed that she should obey parents and teachers next, after she'd given priority to God. The dynamic between flesh, spirit, and submission appeared in a story one student wrote about two little girls who live in a city. The main character receives specific instructions from her guardian to go directly home from school, but she goes to a pond first, where she falls and nearly drowns. The author concludes, "Her distress shows that little girls should not disobey their parents."[101] The story serves as a metaphor for the religious convictions of sin and righteousness, or obedience and rebellion that could lead to life or death. Still, salvation allowed for the grace that came with the trials of spiritual life that made a mishap like drowning only a near-death experience rather than impending doom. Moral tales and imaginings of an afterlife filled the spiritual context of the girls' education and established a road map from which to cultivate their identities and beliefs.

In some instances, Miner prompted the girls with a broad theological or political question. When asked whether they believed they would go to heaven following their death, the girls sent responses that exhibited aspects of their theological training at the school. Caroline Elizabeth Brent remarked, "I think heaven is a very pure place and nothing holy or unclean can enter there. I think it is a place prepared by God for those who love and serve him here on earth."[102] Brent remained steadfast in the idea that heaven required a lived experience of righteousness, but such a life remained available to all regardless of race or gender. Uncertain as to whether she qualified, she offered,

"I think if I ever get there I will be so happy for the Bible says the righteous will sing the songs that angels cannot sing." Another student, Catherine, confessed, "I have not done the will of God, but I hope that I shall in the future. I am trying to serve him with my whole heart."[103] In her reply, another student simply listed off her offenses, stating, "I have been angry with girls, just for little [offenses] and cherished my anger for weeks. I think that I was wrong." She confessed, "I have disobeyed my teacher sometimes, I talked in school, all of which I know is wrong. Sometimes I do things without thinking. I do not know whether that is wrong, but I have an idea. That is because it involves carelessness." Each student, a bit unsure yet hopeful that any crooked path could be made straight with righteousness, made space for spiritual reflection. This contemplative activity, however, was a series of self-critical disclosures that reveal the intimate degree to which Miner gained access to their inner lives. The same student lamented, "I must repent and give up all my wicked ways, and try to do everything that is good and right, and then I think the Lord will forgive me and receive [me] into his blessed abode."[104] Even with their commitment to spiritual growth, the girls expressed uncertainty about their own worthiness of a glorious afterlife.

To what degree did Miner serve as a spiritual intermediary? Undoubtedly, antebellum teachers, as facilitators of these self-reflections, made such inquiries from a place of authority. The premise of white missionary-oriented education rested on the idea of their own moral and racial superiority. The girls' responses to questions of their worthiness of salvation mirrored the racialized power dynamic between teacher and pupil. The consistent posture of repentance and spiritual insecurity quite possibly reflects their personal sentiments or perhaps the manner in which they were taught to view their salvation. Miner undoubtedly fostered a culture of deference, as was the custom of headmistresses of antebellum schools.[105] The intimacy from which these responses to such personal reflections were drawn underscores the degree of power Miner exercised in facilitating their spiritual beliefs. Conversely, the girls' visualizations of an afterlife appeared in their literary descriptions of what heaven might look like—a process of imagining that took them momentarily out of their racialized and gendered environment.

Theological queries about a happy afterlife pulled at the religious ideas that such introspective concerns sparked in the literary imagination of the girls. Martha Jane wrote, "I think that heaven is a beautiful place above the sky where all good people and good children will go when they die." In contrast to the unrealized grandeur of the capital, Martha Jane explained that in heaven, the "streets are paved with gold, where [there] are beautiful gardens with children in them, changed into angels, robed in shining garments singing sweetly, with wreaths of flowers about their heads, and everything holy and happy about them." Rather than the busy sounds of the antebellum city or the shouts of white mobs waiting outside the school, she offered that "there is music, O such sweet music! Not like ours, but softer and sweeter, gushing forth, making beautiful melody."[106] Not only did Martha Jane demonstrate a knack for literary prose, but perhaps we gain through her writing a sense of why such spiritual concerns resonated with black girls in the District. Martha Jane and her peers lived in a region that reminded them daily of their vulnerability to a life quite the opposite of their visions of heaven. Moreover, even as they looked within to consider their own worthiness of such an afterlife, they understood that their pursuit of righteousness only tempered the realities of the daily injustices they confronted as black girls in the nation's capital. Still, such considerations inspired hope that someday, the world around them might change, and if it didn't, a better life awaited them. Despite the tempestuous climate that shaped the country, the students at Miner's school showed their determination to model intellectual and spiritual prowess in the face of a society resolute in the idea that black girls should remain on its margins.

African American girls attended Miner's school during a time when the debate over slavery was intensifying in the halls of Congress and filling the pages of national and local newspapers.[107] Everywhere, Americans grappled with the growing chasm that shaped politics during the 1850s. The antebellum political climate and anxieties about racial equality created an atmosphere of hostility for the girls at Miner's school. Miner noted, "It is hardly necessary to say that the vast majority of the white population were bitterly opposed to their having any education whatever."[108] She stated further, "The class of free blacks was looked upon by all supporters of the system of slavery with peculiar suspicion and dislike." Emily Edmonson, a survivor of the *Pearl* escape in 1848, attended Oberlin College and returned to the nation's capital to work with Miner on school grounds.[109] White northern abolitionist Emily Howland, along with former pupil Emma V. Brown, also assisted Miner with everyday operations of the school.[110] Employment at the school came with vulnerability to local harassment—an all too familiar reality for Edmonson. Miner recalled, "Emily and I lived here alone, unprotected, except by God, the rowdies occasionally stoning our house at evening."[111] Miner and her teaching assistants aided God in shielding the campus from mob violence. Miner noted, "Since then our high, hard-to-get-over fence has been built, Emily and I have been seen practicing shooting with a pistol."[112] Forced to defend themselves daily, the women also went to great lengths to ensure that the girls returned home safely. Gangs of white men congregated near the school and shouted insults at the students as they went home.[113] Black girls in the District learned early in their socialization the disdain that whites held for people of their race. With each day they attended Miner's school, the girls were offered a glimpse of what racial equality might look like.

In 1856, Miner set out to build an edifice worthy of the school and the girls' achievements.[114] The current school held classes in a basic, framed school-house with poor air quality and limited capacity. With the new property, she hoped to attract "applicants pressing upon it from the numerous free colored blacks in the District and adjacent states."[115] Miner launched a campaign to raise funds for a building that could accommodate an enrollment of 150 students.[116] This new campus would provide homes for teachers and aides who assisted with the operations of the school. Indeed, Miner envisioned a stately institution unlike any educational initiative launched for the matriculation of black girls. In addition to the new design and accommodations, she hoped to introduce a new curriculum that offered the equivalent of preparatory and college departments. This initiative offered an inspired vision for the expansion of educational opportunities for African American girls, but it also revealed the degree to which black girls were prepared for higher education. Black schools in Washington prepared students for careers in teaching as well as advanced learning. The next step became evident in the campaign to further develop Miner's school. The initiative conveyed the message that black girls were positioned to surpass the social thresholds of their white peers. Miner's plans set off an alarmed response from Washington's municipal leadership.

In response to the initiative to build a new school, Mayor Walter Lenox wrote a scathing exposition on the school's impact on the city. Lenox was a slaveholder who echoed much of the political sentiment found in southern cities.[117] He anchored his editorial with fears that "our District will be converted into the headquarters of 'slavery agitation,'" pointing specifically to the rapid rate at which agitation escalated during the *Pearl* escape and the Snow Riot. Lenox acknowledged the success of the school but expressed fear that the "scheme was started some years ago in humble guise, and in the foothold it has already gained it feels secure of its future progress." He argued, "Earnest, prompt action can now arrest it peacefully; tumult and blood may stain its future history."[118] Like most whites in the District, he regarded free blacks as a nuisance, and a disturbance of the peace. Their educational success, he warned, posed a grave threat to the stability of the nation's capital and the Union.

Making education accessible to black girls stirred social and political anxieties among white locals concerned with the future of the country. Lenox pleaded, "We cannot tolerate an influence in our midst which will not only constantly disturb the repose and prosperity of our own community and of the country but may even rend asunder the 'Union itself.'"[119] He appealed to the local government to wield its influence to undermine the work of Miner's school. Lenox implored, "Such a protest it is the duty of our corporate authorities to make. Its beneficent effect may be to persuade the supporters of this scheme to abandon its further prosecution." Lenox claimed that Miner and her students left white residents no choice, warning that "the responsibility will be with those who by their own wanton acts of aggression make resistance a necessity and submission an impossibility." Thus, the mayor of Washington validated the violent response of white mobs that the girls confronted on a daily basis.

Why did white locals find the establishment so threatening? Lenox began the tirade with a demographic assessment. He expressed fear that the growth of the free black population outpaced the desired number and status of African Americans in the District, stating that "their number, originally too large in proportion to our white population, is increasing rapidly both by their natural increase and from immigration."[120] Georgetown mayor Henry Addison echoed similar concerns about the African American population in the capital.[121] White District inhabitants protested the presence of slavery, but not because they wished to see African Americans realize their aspirations for liberty and citizenship. Lenox proposed that in order to enact "justice to ourselves and kindness to them," "we should prohibit immigration and encourage their removal from our limits."[122] Lenox's article was republished in several northern newspapers, and many of Miner's donors withdrew their support for the new school.

In a context where few girls exercised the privilege of attending private school and most black girls were expected to serve at the pleasure of white families, Miner's success challenged the racial and gender hierarchies of the District. African American girls found in the normal school a rigorous curriculum that prepared them for careers in education. Black families from the Chesapeake found in the school a thriving environment that appealed to their aspirations for their daughters. Lenox stated further, "Now, it is plainly manifest that the success of this school enterprise must largely increase our negro population by the inducements it offers." Not only did the school promote a problematic representation of what he regarded as an inferior race, but such a message could portray the capital as an inviting refuge for black people. He argued, "The schools will be increased with demand. It will bring not only scholars to remain temporarily, but ensure families, until our District is inundated with them."[123] Taking Lenox at his word, it seemed as though Miner achieved precisely what she set out to do. She set out to "sap the slave power by educating its victims." The slave power and its advocates identified such a threat in Miner and the girls at the normal school.

Miner's school inspired violent retaliatory responses that involved racist and sexist epithets aimed at the girls. One white pedestrian balked at a group of the students and referred to them as "impudent hussies," demanding that the landlady "turn out that nigger school or be mobbed."[124] The use of the term *hussies* invoked sexualized imagery of seductresses and nineteenth-century coquetry as though the girls' very presence invited such insults. The man projected a sexualized and wayward representation of them in the broader public to justify their removal. Students' responses to local harassment do not appear in the existing record, but perhaps their thoughts remained confined to their private lives. Indeed, historian Darlene Clark Hine explains the ways that nineteenth-century black women embraced a culture of dissemblance in which they protected their inner lives and reactions to sexualized insults.[125] These girls most likely deployed a number of strategies for survival, many exhibited by African American women within their respective communities. Sources allow us to see that students took seriously the work of learning and regarded such efforts as an indictment of the society that deprived them of the basic privileges afforded their white counterparts. When lectured by the white wife of a clergyman on the importance of being educated according to one's social status, Lizzy Snowden responded, "I would rather be learned than be contented and be ignorant. I will be learned. I must be learned! I would not ask this as colored people should not enjoy every right as white people."[126] Lizzy's commitment to education coalesced with her claims to citizenship. This inextricable connection between learning, enlightenment, and rights underlines the pedagogical project of the Miner school. Miner hoped to provide the kind of education that positioned the girls to articulate claims to equality in the capital. This was the pedagogy of political self-making. The intellectual outcomes of the institution are reflected not only in personal letters and essays but also in the observations of visitors who marveled at the caliber of education offered at the school.

Miner welcomed countless visitors to view the classes in session, perhaps in an effort to prove her detractors wrong. Eben Norton Horsford, a chemistry professor at Harvard University, observed morning exercises during the winter months of 1852, just a year after Miner founded the school. The students in attendance ranged from ages eight to sixteen. Regarded as "neat, orderly and plainly dressed," students received instruction in spelling, reading, geography, penmanship, composition, analysis of authors, moral philosophy, and translations from French.[127] Additionally, Miner took students to witness a demonstration of a science experiment that showed the power of air. In a letter to Miner, Mary Thomas opined, "I think you were very kind to take us to see these beautiful wonders of air. I think air is full of power I had no idea that air would make such great noise and do such wonderful things."[128] The curriculum, decorum, and interactions of the students were also imbued with "healthful, moral, and religious tones."[129] Horsford was impressed: "I do not hesitate to add, that I have never attended a School exercise that interested me more deeply than that of Miss Miner's at Washington, nor can I escape the conviction that if the School can be maintained, its usefulness in the great cause of humanity will be more marked than if the pupils were white instead of colored."[130] Lessons for white girls who could afford an education in the South included penmanship, reading, and composition, but most of the instruction focused on skills for domestic life, including sewing, cooking, and rigorous biblical instruction.[131] Here, Miner exposed her students to the study of aerodynamics. Exceptions to ornamental education existed particularly in advanced schools such as white seminaries and colleges devoted to higher education.[132] One such institution in Washington taught "Sherwin's Algebra, Davis's Legendre's Geometry and Trigonometry, Cartee's Physical Geography, Weber's History, Kames's Criticism, Cleveland's English Literature, Whateley's Morals and Christian Evidences, Thompsons's Outlines of the Laws of Thought, Butler's Analogy, and Haven's Mental Philosophy."[133] The institution certainly conveyed its intention to shape its pupils as intellectuals, but the advanced seminary did not offer admission to black girls. Miner's school offered an avenue for rigorous study, and Horsford took note of this when he pointed to the exceptional nature of the course of study that diverged from curricula solely associated with domesticity.

Guests at Miner's school offered a counternarrative to the mayor's polemic. She invited visitors who offered glowing reports of the achievements of the students and the impact of the school in the fight against slavery. One man, W. H. Channing, noted that "the plan of establishing in the capitol of the nation a Normal School for colored teachers, is admirable, alike for its originality and for its good sense and humanity."[134] He recognized that the demonstration of these educational exercises and its evidence of success undermined arguments of racial inferiority and broader justifications for the protraction of slavery. With regard to the quality of education offered at the school, he noted that it was "the place to demonstrate by culture, their intellectual and moral power, and thus justify their aspirations for refinement and usefulness." The girls were on stage during these visits as guests assessed the quality and effectiveness of Miner's institution. Channing viewed the girls as "powerful instruments in the peaceful solution of our great National Problem." The students appeared composed and proficient as local pressures propelled their experiences into the national spotlight.

As the girls confronted resistance, their strategies of self-making emerged at the forefront of antebellum political debates. In response to one white detractor, Matilda Jones argued, "We need it [education] more than your people do, & ought to strive harder, because the greater part of our people, are yet in bondage." Protest became a strategy of self-making as the girls were thinking about a future of African American liberation and the role of education as a counterpoint to bondage. "We must get the knowledge and use it well. I expect the day will come, when the voice of my people, shall be heard and felt, as strong as the voice of your people."[135] George Sampson, the pastor of E Street Baptist Church, marveled at not only the "proficiency of the pupils" in elementary and advanced education but the development of their moral character as well.[136] Having been acquainted with many of their fathers, he noted that they were "enterprising and intelligent men" and that "their honorable and Christian aspirations for the improvement of their daughters, and their deep interest in this School, are a sufficient guarantee of its character and worth." The school proved a testament to the efforts not only of Miner and the students but also of the families associated with the girls. They understood that the future rested on the preparation of the younger generation. Parents and communities of kin also did the work of educating and socializing their daughters in ways that defied white expectations of them. Miner, too, based her pedagogical approach on an ethos reflected in antebellum free black communities. The establishment of an educated class of black Washingtonians resulted from the notion that the privilege of an education translated into a broader responsibility of sharing knowledge and modeling achievement for others. This approach required the collective resources, participation, and convictions of people like John Cook and Anne Marie Becraft and, even more so, women like Alethia Tanner and Sophia Browning who made such institutions possible from the beginning. Miner's aim of training black girls to be teachers and leaders served as an extension of this philosophy.

About the same time that Miner founded her school for girls, other schools led by African American women teachers appeared. A pupil of St. Frances Academy in Baltimore and former student at the Billings School in Georgetown,

Arabella Jones founded a school for black girls in Washington. St. Agnes Academy was founded on model similar to those of St. Frances Academy and Becraft's school, with religious and moral instruction at the heart of the curriculum.[137] Jones's ties to Washington were long-standing, and as a child she worked as a servant for the family of John Quincy Adams when he served as secretary of state. Jones enjoyed Shakespeare, played the piano, occasionally published poems, and "wrote and spoke with ease and propriety the French tongue." Jones taught and modeled the kind of self-making that black women reformers found valuable in an education for black girls. She kept the school open until she began a sewing business. At the time of her death in 1868, she worked as a clerk for the government.

Emma V. Brown was a former pupil at Miner's school. Her education prepared her for further study at Oberlin College, and she returned to Miner's school to work as an assistant teacher.[138] She never received a degree from Oberlin, and this might be attributed to her inability to cover the costs of tuition, since she was required to take on additional work in order to subsidize some of the fees. When Miner's health began to decline, Brown and Emily Howland maintained the school for a year. During Howland's travels, Brown managed the operations of the school.[139] In a letter to Miner, Brown wrote, "When I see one of the scholars eyes suddenly brighten with some intelligent idea that I have conveyed to them—then it is that I feel true happiness."[140] Brown established her own school in the basement of a Methodist church located in Georgetown during the Civil War, and by 1865 she had become one of the first teachers for the new public schools available to African Americans in Washington.[141]

Another Miner student, Matilda Jones, maintained correspondence with Miner. She praised Miner's efforts, offering, "We can scarcely be grateful enough to you, & the strengthening Power that supported you through the obstacles & trials, that you have had to surmount & endure in teaching us the only true way to escape from this galling bondage."[142] Jones held the conviction that true liberty began in the mind, and the intellectual liberation that came with an education would sustain African Americans in generations to come. "I trust that all might soon come to a knowledge of the truth & then we will be in a fair way to break the chains that confine us," she declared.[143] In 1861, Jones established a school above her father's store on K Street between Twentieth and Twenty-First Streets. The early traditions of black education paid off with the emergence of black women teachers who established schools in later decades.

A descendant of Alethia Tanner and John Cook, Eliza Anne Cook attended Miner's school and soon after did the very thing she'd been groomed to do. After a brief stint teaching at the free Catholic school at Smothers's schoolhouse, she opened a school in her mother's home. On average, she taught between twenty-five and thirty pupils, and eventually built a modest schoolhouse on Sixteenth Street between K and L Streets. She taught for the rest of her life as long as her health permitted. In 1857, Anne E. Washington, one of Cook's peers at Miner's school, opened a school nearby. Sources described Washington as a woman of refinement, with an "excellent aptitude for teaching." She gained notoriety for the way she operated her school, "with a system and superior judgment, giving universal satisfaction, the number of her pupils being only limited by the size of her room." The room, located in her mother's home, speaks to the resourcefulness of black women teachers without the philanthropic connections that Miner employed. Washington's mother was a washerwoman who made limited income in a labor economy that relegated black women to the bottom of the wage-earning spectrum. Sources offer that her mother, "a widow woman, is a laundress, and by her own labor has given her children good advantages, though she had no such advantages herself."[144]

African American women culled their resources in ways that made the education of black girls possible. Partnered with leading black men and white allies, they established a robust tradition of education that came to mark the nation's capital as a special place for black liberty. Locals resisted and even mocked the efforts of teachers to educate African Americans, but the proliferation of schools marked an undeniable development in the racial and gender dynamics of the city. The idea that the education of black girls might threaten the very fabric of the Union meant that black girls like Marietta Hill were right. Slavery remained at the forefront of national political turbulence, and black Washington stood ready to fight for liberty as bondage remained a looming threat. "We may say yes!" indeed. In his fears of the implications of the school for African American girls, Mayor Lenox was thinking about the future of the Union, a future that the girls planned to be a part of.

Before the Civil War, African American Washingtonians had already boasted a lineage of scholarly activism. Formerly enslaved women and men had financed and led the creation of black schools in the city since the first decade of its founding. These schools, often subsidized by black women's informal economies in the District, give us the starting point from which we can begin to understand black Washington's rich intellectual institutions.

Women like Becraft began a tradition that Myrtilla Miner and countless others continued with the establishment of their schools toward the end of the century. In 1938, W. E. B. Du Bois remarked that all of these early schools established for African Americans provided "the foundation upon which the present magnificent Negro school system of Washington is built."[145] The reputation of African American schools that thrived in late nineteenth- and early twentieth-century Washington was rooted in traditions of uplift that made education a critical tenet of self-making.[146] Black women and girls assumed the mantle of leadership in many of these schools as they envisioned the possibilities for inclusion in a society that rejected them. Many of the girls who attended Miner's school worked as teachers in Washington's African American schools. They continued to advocate for equal access to public resources for black education as Washington underwent tremendous transformation.

Schools for African Americans in Washington served as critical sites of self-making for black women and girls who resided in the city and the neighboring counties. When Alexandria won the battle to retrocede from the District of Columbia, black schools were immediately forced to close its doors.[147] Those seeking an education in the northern corners of Virginia were required to travel into Washington for such opportunities. Participation in learning and advancing the notion that they possessed the same capacity for intellectual achievement as white Americans prepared the pupils of these antebellum schools for the postbellum fight for equality. The oral histories and genealogies of this rich educational tradition showcase the persistence and determination of African Americans in the city who withstood daily insults in their efforts to obtain an education. The race riots of the antebellum decades attest to the mounting assault on the black schools in the District. African Americans, with assistance from white allies, laid much of the institutional groundwork from which black residents of the District made claims to racial equality in later decades.[148]

African Americans continued to face unequal access to public funding for schools. During the Civil War, white public schools received $29,000 in government funding in 1862 and $36,000 in 1863. Black schools received a mere $265 and $410 during those fiscal periods, despite the fact that African Americans paid significant sums in property taxes.[149] Still, the work of black education continued in Washington, and so did the mission of Miner's school. Miner died in a carriage accident in 1864, but the legacy of the normal school for girls continued in the form of the Institution for the Education of Colored Youth, a school granted a charter by the Senate and later affiliated with Howard University.[150] In 1879, the school merged with the District of Columbia public school system as Miner Normal School, and it received accreditation as Miner Teachers College in the twentieth century. At Miner's antebellum school, African American girls formulated their own critiques of slavery and inequality before the prospect of emancipation and citizenship seemed a possibility. The imaginings of identities and aspirations beyond the antebellum configurations of society prepared them for the ways they navigated social transformations in subsequent decades. The schools offered spaces for thinking through complex issues that plagued the race and their own gendered position in society. Even at the risk of violence, and under tremendous pressure, the girls, along with countless other pupils who came through Washington's black schools, formulated ideas about liberty, equality, and themselves.

Black girls and women faced a number of social and economic hurdles in their efforts to live free in the capital. It took the shrewdness of washerwomen like Anne Washington's mother to cover fees for their girls to attend school. A career in education offered an opportunity for a select few, and the economic challenges that black women faced grew increasingly acute as the Union stood at the brink of war. Black women, however, navigated various and at times divergent avenues of survival. Whereas the girls at Miner's school followed a course of uplift that demanded strict moral conduct, some black women leveraged opportunities that emerged in the wartime sex economy. The growth of the free African American population meant that black women and girls increasingly contended with the limitations of liberty in the nation's capital, and they navigated these social and economic challenges in different ways. Miner's girls were afforded opportunities to attend school, while some girls and women earned a living in the local entrepreneurial, sex, and leisure economies.

CHAPTER FIVE

Streets

As the country stood at the precipice of war, black Washington appeared more established with institutions, businesses, and organizations, as well as opportunities for leisure. The prospects for leisure and recreation available to African Americans largely depended on the entrepreneurial activity of black women. Black men operated restaurants, grooming salons, and hackney services that typically catered to white clientele. Black women sold goods, took in washing, and started sewing businesses also patronized by white families. Black women, however, participated in the sex and leisure economy that catered to both African Americans and white men. They provided spaces for sex, gambling, drinking, and socializing throughout the District. Furthermore, the outbreak of war not only shaped the significance of the nation's capital politically and militarily but also transformed the ways African Americans navigated social and economic life in the city. African American women mingled with black and white Union soldiers and migrants throughout the conflict. As white men drifted in and out of these "dens of infamy," Union military officials and locals grew frustrated in their efforts to stave off the rampant opportunities for sex and recreation. Indeed, leading black Washingtonians and reformers also regarded these spaces as counterproductive to the work of uplift. The wartime sex and leisure economy shows the ways some black women responded to the economic opportunities that came with the war. Although they typically faced relatively narrow prospects for financial stability, they improvised, and the influx of men that came as a result of efforts to mobilize the army made sex commerce a lucrative enterprise. This chapter shifts the focus to the streets to show the complexity of nominal freedom and the ways that economic self-making unfolded in a city transformed by the developments of war.

The realities of survival and the motivations of black women's work underscore the economic and social inequality that shaped their lives. Thus, these public-facing women reveal less about how they defined themselves and more about the ways they navigated the economic limitations of freedom. Freedom involved different ideas about earning income to cover the basic necessities of life. The economic mobility that came with successful outcomes in local businesses afforded black women the financial resources for self-making in the capital. Overcrowding and the growing military significance of the capital sparked a hike in rents and the overall cost of living in the capital, making money and accommodations hard to obtain in a job market that limited black women's employment and earning prospects.[1] A discussion of the sex economy therefore necessitates an examination of black women's labor economy more broadly and the strategies they employed as they solicited in the streets of the nation's capital to make ends meet. In fact, black women who worked in sex and leisure at times juggled additional jobs as washerwomen and cooks. Sex and leisure did not provide the only avenue for income, since black women found entrepreneurial ways to meet the local demand for labor, goods, and even space. Still, the employment options that existed did not always offset the financial obligations of black women, and the war created conditions in which the demand for sex increased.[2] For these black women, sex and other ventures regarded as immoral became the commodified services and experiences that put food on the table, which, for some, took precedence over the moral implications of their participation. Sources offer limited information about the relationship between black women's sexual encounters and desire, but much needs to be understood to consider the possibilities of their erotic lives.[3] Since these accounts are entangled in the criminal record and local news, black women's sexual desires are less apparent, but we should not assume that they are absent. This chapter examines how activities involving leisure, sexuality, and extralegal economies underscored the ways that black women negotiated their lack of access to social and economic power and took to the streets to improvise. The economic incentives, however, came with vulnerability to sexual violence and exploitation, along with repeat encounters with local police. Although prostitution was not illegal, the activities associated with it were, and black codes made black women frequent violators.[4] Thus, police precinct records and newspaper notices offer a very public window onto the streets and the private worlds of dens.

African American women did not enjoy the same degree of privacy as white women, and both groups experienced significant impositions on their personal lives and social worlds. Middle-class white residents of Washington reserved their socializing for public venues or, for women, the intimate spaces of property they inhabited or owned. Indeed, the term *public women* was reserved for women associated with sex for economic survival in a variety of contexts outside marriage.[5] Middle-class white women likely engaged in transgressive behavior, but their socioeconomic position afforded a measure of privacy from the local police, as policing was done most effectively in the streets.[6] This layer of protection from police surveillance was unavailable to women who were not members of the elite, and black women in particular. While middle-class and married white women might be shielded from arrest, socializing, sex, and leisure still fell under the purview of paternalist men. Accordingly, historians have advanced an extensive body of scholarship about nineteenth-century American women through the framework of public and private spheres with an emphasis on domesticity. These themes appear even in what we know about fashionable white bawdy houses, particularly those designed to cater to an elite clientele. African American women's experiences are harder to place within this framework.

Black women's lives took them through various private and public intervals of work and leisure.[7] For instance, their conversation, laughter, or occasions of passionate debate were subject to scrutiny in public spaces, including the streets, as "disorderly conduct" or "unlawful assembly." When black women congregated just outside their cramped dwellings or their places of employment to engage in autonomous forms of leisure, policing officials exercised discretion to determine whether such actions constituted public disturbances. Indeed, a black woman walking along the grand avenues of the District for the purpose of taking a leisurely stroll, soliciting potential clients, begging for money, or assembling with others might easily be subject to arrest with a subsequent payment of fines or a term served at the workhouse. Thus, leisure and everyday attempts to carve out black spaces became highly criminalized and associated with vice in the city's streets.

Black women confronted surveillance not only in public spaces but within their homes as well. The local black code, which restricted any enslaved or free black person from "playing cards, dice, or any other game of an immoral tendency," criminalized private spaces that black people owned or leased. Jane Johnson, a cook residing in the District, was arrested for "allowing gambling in her home."[8] Johnson creatively sought ways to make ends meet, which might involve extralegal measures like transforming her home into a gambling den. A few months after her arrest, she reappeared before the court for receiving stolen goods, which she could sell for a decent profit.[9] Women like Johnson juggled the work of cooking during a specific time frame and organizing her home into a space of leisure after-hours. She could offer alcohol, sell and receive stolen goods, or prepare food for a modest fee, and if police apprehended her, those fees were put toward the payment of fines that went directly to the precinct. Black women did not occupy the private spheres that characterized white women's relationship to space and place; rather, their lives were always regarded as public. White middle-class understandings of socializing, which might differ from black cultural practices of mingling and leisure, largely shaped police interpretations of disorderliness and idleness. Throughout the course of the Civil War, police exercised a substantial degree of discretion, which often involved recurring visits to sites of black leisure.

Wartime transformations led to the reorientation and appropriation of streets, alleys, and enclaves among an increasingly expanding and transient population.[10] Police worked to recontain the mobility, as well as the social and sexual interactions, of an unwieldy population composed of soldiers, African Americans, women, and immigrants.[11] The influx of recently freed and refugee black people during the war and the boom in the sex economy heightened not only existing concerns about the population but also fears of the racial "amalgamation" implied by interracial sex.[12] The interracial character of the sex economy mirrored trends in other southern cities such as New Orleans, Charleston, and Savannah.[13] The nineteenth-century American city gained a reputation as a repository of vice, and the streets offered a space where race and gender appeared more fluid.[14] Interracial sex certainly existed throughout the Chesapeake before the Civil War, but the impending destruction of slavery exacerbated the apprehensions of white locals.[15] Since the founding of Washington, white men had easily and legally maintained sexual access to black women's bodies, but wartime conditions revealed an illicit dynamic between black women and white men. Moreover, how might the sexual relationships between black women and white men in the context of freedom and commerce shape discussions about race?[16] The records only provide a vague sense of possible answers, but they do show that black women took advantage of the opportunities presented by the war, and an interracial sex economy took shape as a result. Union soldiers arrived in Washington at the outbreak of war and, supported with better salaries than their Confederate counterparts, paid for the sex and leisure offerings available in the city.[17] What was once a sleepy and sparsely populated southern village soon transformed into a bustling, overcrowded, and lewd entrepôt. For black women, the streets were sites of improvisation that allowed for their economic survival.

Black women navigated a limited set of income-earning options in the mid-nineteenth century. Free black women in the District typically worked low-wage, service-oriented jobs that limited their income-earning potential and often undercut their abilities to meet their material needs. During the mid-nineteenth century, black women primarily appeared in local records as slaves, servants, washerwomen, seamstresses, cooks, and prostitutes. Enslaved women earned virtually nothing for their labor unless a slave owner allowed them to collect additional earnings from being hired out or selling produce and goods they collected on their own.[18] Such opportunities, however, were more common for those considered "skilled" laborers, such as seamstresses, while cooks and market women likely found opportunities to supplement their wages as well. According to tax and court records, free black women worked as seamstresses, teachers, and housewives before the Civil War, and those same women were often associated with an emerging black middle class.[19]

Employment prospects in Washington were designed to preserve the racial and gender hierarchies of society, but African American women found creative ways to maneuver through the challenges of the job market. Domestic service, and the intimacy and oversight that such work involved, meant that free black women often labored in conditions similar to those of enslaved women working for local families.[20] By independently employing the skills they already performed in these homes, free African American women found economic opportunities as entrepreneurs. Some women did the sewing for local families and over time advertised their services to attract consistent clients. Such women included Sara Anderson, who took in sewing projects that she completed in her home, located in an alley community near F Street.[21] Others such as Louisa Wanser on L Street, Martha Washington near Eleventh Street W, Elizabeth Rhodes on K Street, Margaret Ross on I Street, and Mary Pierre were just a few of the names that appeared in a local directory.[22] The labor required hours of sewing, mending, and meticulous stitch work, which allowed women a measure of independence from white homes.[23] Women like Maria Brown, Ellen Shaw, and, more notably during the war, Elizabeth Keckly were specifically known for their abilities as dressmakers.[24] The social seasons of Washington, along with the list of prominent political families that split their time in the capital, meant that the skills required to design, cut, and sew quality garments were in demand. Throughout the Civil War era, roughly 250 African American women worked as employees of the federal government.[25] They worked as attendants in hospitals, sweepers, manual laborers in the printing office, and clerks.[26] As the work of Jessica Ziparo reveals, the historical record poses challenges to fully understanding the breadth of their experiences, since employee data did not consistently specify race. Nonetheless, these coveted positions afforded some financial stability and social mobility. The labor of black women brought them into regular interactions with white residents of Washington.

Black women took to the streets and neighborhoods, knocking on doors to hire out their labor to local families. The daily management and various social engagements of middle-class households in the city created a demand for reliable cooks. Black women like Elizabeth Bowers, Mary E. Brown,

Alice A. Ferguson, Ann Green, Letitia Ingram, and Harriet Jackson were advertised as cooks.[27] They experienced various degrees of intimacy with their clients, but in many cases, they also exercised the right to live independently of these households. Elite white women throughout the District took note of black women's cooking abilities and expressed the difficulty of finding good cooks, which might have offered avenues for black women to negotiate more favorable wages. Given the level of discretion exercised in feeding white households, a measure of trust and dependence on black women often resulted from these arrangements, and white women expressed frustration when forced to replace them.[28] Black women like Sukey, who appeared at the beginning of this book, marketed their abilities with an entrepreneurial shrewdness that promoted their culinary talents.

Nursing was another profession that demanded discretion, skill, and attentiveness. The directory shows a modest number of black women employed as nurses, who likely gained reputations as healers and, in some instances, gained some exposure to basic medical knowledge from established institutions.[29] Women such as Treasin Burgess, Maria Dines, Charlotte Dunlop, Jane Garrett, Ellen Jenkins, Ellen Smith, Sarah Thomas, and Matilda Wormley appeared among the small group of black women nurses in the capital.[30] Many of these women likely belonged to the local black middle class. For instance, Dunlop married George Dunlop, a teacher in the city's African American schools. They both occupied professions highly regarded by African Americans in Washington at the time. Similarly, Wormley was a member of the prominent Wormley family, which included leading educators, ministers, and black women known for their philanthropy. These women worked as nurses and midwives who catered to African Americans in search of care at a time when many of them were distrustful of white doctors and nurses. Black women's entrepreneurial strategies afforded African Americans services and goods independent of white households, businesses, and institutions. Moreover, independent and semi-independent forms of employment allowed for greater flexibility to manage multiple tasks, including care for children and elderly kin.

Washerwomen performed much of the backbreaking labor of washing in streets and alleys near their own homes or in the small courtyards of white residences. According to one study, nearly half of the black women in Washington were washerwomen.[31] Of the women listed in the local directory, the number of black washerwomen exceeds the number that appears in the U.S. Census.[32] Indeed, one study reveals that nearly 46 percent of black women were listed in the census with no occupation. Even an examination of the local directory shows that some women decided not to disclose details about their employment. Both records reveal inconsistencies and gaps, but we can glean from the limited information available that informal and entrepreneurial economies contributed to black women's abilities to support themselves financially. Washerwomen remained in demand throughout the nineteenth century since most middle-class women avoided the labor-intensive and time-consuming work of laundry. One particular white woman disliked the idea of using the latest washing technology and remarked that she possessed "no faith in anything but hard knuckles and a cherry board; and in regard to time, it must be from sun to sun—steam and soap-suds, from morning till dusky twilight."[33] White women took pride in being able to efficiently manage households; this ethos rested on the exploitation of black women's labors. Washerwomen were paid anywhere from fifty cents to one dollar for a day's work.[34] Black women negotiated wages, particularly if the client increased the load or the woman felt she delivered consistent and high-quality service. If black women performed responsibilities associated with caring for family or loved ones, entrepreneurial economies afforded them various degrees of flexibility. Working independently of households also positioned them to seek out multiple customers in the broader local market to grow their incomes.

In addition to domestic service, black women promoted and sold goods in stands they leased from the commissioners of the District markets. Women such as Ann Herod, Betsey Thompson, and Elizabeth White sold goods in stands they leased at the Centre Market.[35] Elizabeth Diggs lived in Georgetown, but she sold products at 52 Centre Market.[36] Silby Hall lived in the city and operated a stand at 44 Centre Market, and Ann Hines sold goods at 11 Centre Market.[37] The local directory did not always specify the type of merchandise the women sold, but Francis Lee, who lived between I and K Streets, regularly sold "flour and feed" at the Centre Market.[38] Lucinda Meyer operated two stands, one at 87 and another at 88 Centre Market, which quite possibly functioned as one shop with much more space.[39] Rosa Tilman operated what appears to have been two separate shops in the market, one located at 69 and another at 10 Centre Market.[40] The market was organized into four branches, the Centre, Western, Northern, and Eastern Markets.[41] The stalls featured everything from meat and vegetables to wood, hay, and even goods made at the workhouse and asylum. Vendors were required to pay for leases of their stalls, and commissioners appointed by the mayor supervised the operations of each location.[42]

Black women primarily sold goods at the Centre Market, where the leases were more expensive, but the foot traffic heavier than the other locations.

The fact that black women were positioned to pay for the higher leases at the Centre Market indicates that they experienced some degree of success. Depending on the goods a vendor sold, rents could range from twenty dollars for a stand in the Eastern Market to one hundred dollars to secure a location in the Centre Market.[43] The lease fees were paid annually and could be submitted to the respective commissioners in installments. The official ordinances do not give any indication that black women were subjected to different treatment, but as history reminds us, after the Snow Riot, the local black codes placed restrictions on and introduced legal obstacles to obtaining a shop license.[44] No parameters or restrictions were put in place to prevent commissioners from demanding higher fees from them. Still, black women discovered ways to work around these challenges. The fact that vendors like Lucinda Meyer and Rosa Tilman operated more than one stall reveals the degree to which black market women might expand their entrepreneurial operations. One black woman in particular stood out in the directory as an owner of her own eating house. Sarah Parry's establishment was located on Louisiana Avenue near Ninth Street West.[45] Black codes restricted black women's access to shop licenses, but by the beginning of the war, and as the example of Parry shows, exceptions could be made. Black women's shops and entrepreneurial ventures originated in the streets where they erected their own stands in the local marketplace.

In the face of economic inequality, black women set in motion improvisational strategies for earning income. Their enterprises positioned them to purchase freedom, earn a livelihood, and survive with a relative degree of independence. While African Americans stood to benefit financially from the collective labor of spouses and kin, entrepreneurship offered a viable economic opportunity for many black women outside patriarchal norms. Even as black women participated in creating their own informal and entrepreneurial economies, they remained subject to lower compensation for goods and services exchanged. Throughout the war, black women decidedly violated the legal and social codes of the city to enter the sex and leisure economy. Many of them tried their hand at washing, cooking, and selling goods, and, for reasons that varied for each of them, they sought income as prostitutes, madams, brothel servants, and owners of gambling dens. The women who worked at these establishments first learned to navigate the streets before entering the discrete enclaves of sex and leisure. Undoubtedly, prostitution increased the likelihood of encounters with sexual violence, exploitation, and venereal disease. These factors also shaped black women's economies more broadly, but the solicitous nature of prostitution meant that black women and white men commodified the blurred lines of interracial sex in complex ways.[46] Nineteenth-century codes of morality dictated strict standards of moral virtue, and society did very little to defend black women, regardless of whether they followed the social mandates of domesticity. More broadly, black women's involvement in sex and leisure enterprises brought their extralegal labor, and its racial implications, to the forefront of the streets.

In wartime Washington, prostitutes and their clients did not fit in neatly segregated racial and gender categories. Moreover, same-sex encounters did not appear in the sources, though I did search for them, but it is likely that these relationships occurred during the war. For instance, pornographic literature featuring sexual encounters between women appeared in popular stories that men, and soldiers in particular, consumed.[47] Sources are impressionistic regarding whether women acted on these images, but language and metaphors used to sensationalize, and underscore, perceived aberrant sexual relationships indicate that same-sex encounters existed in the wartime sex economy.[48] News reports and police records directly disclosed encounters between women and men, along with their racial status. The clientele primarily included white men and immigrant and free black laborers who could afford the services of more inexpensive prostitutes and bawdy houses. White madams who earned higher wages obtained the property and material goods that came with higher-end, parlor-style bawdy houses. Such houses resembled the parlors of elite women, channeling a nineteenth-century decorum of domesticity while catering to the sexual fantasies of elite men.[49] White madams ranked at the top of the sex economy in antebellum Washington, and many earned a reputation for unquestionable material success during the Civil War. The criminal record reveals that black women could be found in bawdy houses managed by white women, confirming that such houses were sites of interracial sexual leisure. As white men were the highest-paying clients, ideas of black women's racial inferiority factored into compensation. Furthermore, white men's racial fantasies about black women's sexuality shaped their expectations and encounters.[50]

Black women in the District participated in the local sex economy as madams, prostitutes, slaves, and servants in bawdy houses. Although madams made the most money and often paid the highest fees in court, it was not uncommon for prostitutes to earn more than wage earners and laborers in other industries. For many prostitutes, the work functioned as a transitory phase shaped by personal circumstances and the dynamics caused by major events like war.[51] Often black women regarded prostitution as a relatively more lucrative enterprise for the material incentives that came with the work, such as food, shelter, and the collective security of working with other women in the same house. Under these conditions, they found work with a modicum of autonomy by inviting clients into a space they inhabited and controlled. Some prostitutes, however, did not work in the organized environments of bawdy houses and rented rooms at houses of assignation or rented apartments alone. This allowed the women to collect more money, but it also made them vulnerable to the exploitation and violence that often came with working independently of communal support.[52]

African American women working in sex and leisure found limited protection beyond their own networks of kin and accomplices in the business. Even so, conflicts among black women working in the local sex economy show a dynamic that appeared either competitive or collaborative depending on the circumstances.[53] One incident involved three black women who worked as prostitutes near Maryland Avenue. Elizabeth Johnson, along with her accomplice, Elizabeth Downs, marched to the home of Rebecca Thomas upon learning that Thomas had become romantically involved with a man whom Johnson claimed as her lover.[54] Johnson confronted Thomas and soon after pulled out a razor with which she proceeded to cut Thomas across her eye and face. Johnson and Downs immediately absconded to the home of another black woman named Rebecca Gant, but two officers soon discovered their whereabouts and arrested them. The judge charged Johnson with assault but dismissed Downs. The women quite possibly interacted with the man at the center of the quarrel on a client basis, making the offense both personal and financial. Black and white women also confronted one another in instances of conflict, but they just as often collaborated as well. The precinct records show instances in which groups of women who were charged with assault of one another were later arrested together in the same bawdy house.[55] Black prostitutes appeared in and out of court and the workhouse for a variety of violations.

As previously mentioned, in the District, prostitution was not illegal, but activities associated with it were. Gambling, disorderly conduct, and selling liquor might all lead to a fine or sentence to the workhouse. Vagrancy charges functioned as the gateway allegation for black women lingering or promenading on major thoroughfares of the District. Historians recognize the ways that police employed vagrancy laws to apprehend prostitutes.[56] The black codes stipulated "that all idle, disorderly, or tumultuous assemblages of negroes, so as to disturb the peace or repose of the citizens, are hereby prohibited."[57] The precise meaning of the phrase "idle, disorderly, or tumultuous" was assigned by the policing officer. The application of vagrancy law in the

District, however, appeared highly racialized and foreseeable in cases involving black women who confronted more limited employment prospects than black men and white women and men. The association of prostitution with vagrancy stems from English Common Law practices that did not directly criminalize prostitution. Courts primarily left assessments of vagrancy to the judgment of the police.[58]

Exercising a copious degree of discretion in the enforcement of laws, police benefited from the fines collected among those arrested for activities associated with vice.[59] The black codes were created on the premise of suspicion and specific ideas about how race, gender, and sex organized the use and access of public and private spaces. The criminalization of black women's participation in vice meant that their lives became public as notices of their whereabouts, arrests, and conflicts appeared in the daily news and police returns.[60] Prostitutes solicited on the streets, approached military camps, and offered experiences in dens located in houses, apartments, and alley neighborhoods. During the war, black women traveled through these spaces under suspicion, as it became increasingly clear that the sex and leisure economy had gained a viable foothold in the capital. The legal scaffolding that supported slavery and black codes in the District also supported the ways that local police and judges presumed the culpability of black women working in sex and leisure spaces. The imperatives of mobilizing an army that defended the Union headquarters meant that how and when black women traveled and entered spaces in the capital mattered. The rhetoric that appeared in the press rang loud and clear—white soldiers and young white women required protection from black women who might lure them into a life of vice.

The height of the nineteenth-century sex economy in the District coincided with the advent of the Civil War as the local demographic and political character of Washington changed. After South Carolina led the fateful defense against Union forces at Fort Sumter, the newly elected president, Abraham Lincoln, was faced with the dual challenge of preserving the Union and defending the nation's capital against a Confederate victory.[61] Indeed, even within the city, southern sentiment dominated politics, as most local leaders owned slaves and expressed support for the South.[62] Thousands of Washingtonians refused to take an oath of allegiance to the Union, while others simply relocated to the South.[63] Others reluctantly remained and even performed reconnaissance work for the Confederacy throughout the remainder of the conflict. War meant that Washington became the headquarters of the Union, and not since the War of 1812 had the capital possessed greater significance to Americans. The conflict also meant that residents were driven out and newcomers appeared in droves, as locals became divided by loyalties to the Union and support for secession. The demographic character of Washington changed, and so too did the racial and gender dynamics of the city.

The war and the imperatives of defending the capital ignited an immediate population shift, and just a year after shots were fired at Fort Sumter, the population of Washington had tripled.[64] During the war, black Washington grew from 14,316 to 38,663 and the overall population increased from approximately 75,000 to 140,000.[65] Over ten thousand men from the capital served as soldiers for the Union, and thousands more, representing the regiments of other loyal states, either passed through or temporarily encamped in the capital.[66] Officials struggled against men's attempts to satisfy their appetites for sex and leisure while away from their respective hometowns, as well as women's willingness to satiate their desires at a profit. Furthermore, the realities of war and the death toll that came with it drove many soldiers to drown their sorrows in libations or look for a diversion in less reputable establishments. This proved particularly distressing for local officials and civilians at a moment when the nation faced a crisis of legitimacy. Leaders struggled to bring southern states back into the fold of the Union, and perceptions of the nation's capital as an immoral and vile city only added to their troubles.[67] With black women's active solicitation of military clientele, the policing of prostitutes reached a pinnacle and the sex economy became more visibly interracial. Furthermore, a life of prostitution clashed with the strictures of moral reform efforts driven by black antislavery activists. The racial and class lines were also blurred in black women's covert efforts to benefit from the sex economy. One article observed, "There are a number of females sailing under false colors afloat here, and who, until they are found out, frequently manage to quarter themselves at respectable boarding houses and hotels."[68] The demographic shifts and the rapid pace at which these transformations occurred created opportunities for obscurity. For black women in the sex and leisure business, the material realities of urban freedom made the market both an attractive and perilous option.[69]

When the war began, prostitution surged in the city, even as a process of wartime emancipation was under way.[70] An article in the *Daily National Republican* lamented, "It is impossible to conceive anything more harrowing to the feeling than the negro breeding State, where boys are reared for the lash, and girls for prostitution."[71] The article captured antislavery anxieties about the sexual immoralities associated with the South and slavery. These sentiments also captured the demographic flux of war, but perhaps inspired more hyperbole than truth. One observer noted that, while the numbers of prostitutes did not quite amount to the sensational estimates of 15,000, they likely swelled closer to nearly half that figure.[72] The editorial identified at least a third of these women as African American and reported that seventh-eighths appeared as a result of the war. Historians estimate that there were approximately 5,000 prostitutes in Washington and 2,500 in Alexandria and Georgetown.[73] Although Alexandria retroceded from the District, the connections to the capital and the vicinity still made prostitution networks within reach to Union soldiers in the capital. Of the overall number of prostitutes in the city, at least a third were characterized as "street walkers of a character of unblushing indecency never before known in Washington."[74] The women arrived in the capital from both southern cities and northern metropoles such as New York, Boston, and Philadelphia. Poverty brought on by the war presented challenges that led women to prostitution. The influx of African Americans meant an inflated job market and a large number of black women desperate to earn a living. Those looking for jobs or simply eager for any source of income, food, and housing looked to the burgeoning sex economy.

The sex and leisure economy of the District converged and clashed with the Union military effort. Police arrested a soldier named Edwin S. Perry for "associating with colored prostitutes" in the Fourth Ward of the city.[75] On September 12, 1862, Mary Ann Jackson, "a colored nymph," was arrested by military authorities and served a brief stint in jail. Jackson and many other black women were arrested particularly for their solicitations of soldiers during the Civil War. These women interacted intimately with members of the military, whether through transactions of sex, the selling of goods such as liquor, acts of theft, or disciplinary policing. In this case, military authorities were charged not only with supervising regiments but also with disciplining both soldiers and prostitutes to maintain order between the army and local civilians. The sex and leisure economy increased black women's interactions with the Union military and local officials as they visibly and boldly solicited clients near the city center.[76]

Black prostitutes repeatedly frequented the jail and court for their disruptive enterprises in the capital. Military encampments afforded black women opportunities to offer commercialized leisure, sex, and goods, or they might help themselves to the supplies and foodstuffs provided by the government. Accusing them of stealing "military goods," police arrested three black prostitutes, Josephine Picton, Elizabeth Wilson, and Sarah Gonefs, together for possessing property belonging to the military. Similarly, police arrested Annie Grant for robbing a drunken soldier of fifty cents. Black women prostitutes seized various opportunities for financial and material gain, capitalizing on the resources of the military and enlisted soldiers. These modes of improvisation meant that some women might resort to theft to avoid sexual encounters or in instances in which clients refused to pay. From police arrests to organized raids, black women emerged as participants in local crime and vice.[77]

At the beginning of the war, the provost marshal recorded 450 registered bawdy houses and the *Evening Star* reported 5,000 prostitutes working in Washington City alone, not including the 2,500 women in Georgetown and Alexandria who worked in the wartime sex economy.[78] A register kept by officials featured twelve "coloured bawdy houses" with addresses that are difficult to decipher because of their location among hidden alley communities.[79] Residential blocks in nineteenth-century Washington typically included streets within the block that formed a T or H shape.[80] More noticeable structures faced outward toward the street, but behind the houses and other buildings, inhabitants, particularly those associated with the "lower" classes, lived and congregated in the smaller configurations of the alleys. The alley streets typically measured thirty feet wide, and structures stood much closer to adjacent buildings.[81] While solicitation occurred near Union military camps and along main thoroughfares with high foot traffic, the quarters in which sex and leisure took place existed beyond the prominent avenues, in the alleys where makeshift structures occupied by black inhabitants remained out of sight. For instance, "Misses Seal and Brown," Theadosia Herbert, Rebecca Gaunt, Sarah Wallace, and Josephine Webster appear in the register with establishments located in alleys.

The record listed the inmates according to a hierarchy of race and status, with 1 being the best and "low" being the worst. Ranked pretty far down on the list of establishments are two houses located in the "rear" of E Street. The "rear" typically indicated that the structures existed closer to the alleys. Although these two houses ranked lower on the scale, a place located in an alley didn't always receive a lower rating. Tin Cup Alley housed many black and white bawdy houses, including those operated by Herbert, Gaunt, and Wallace, who ranked in the first and second tiers. Tin Cup Alley served as a popular site of interracial sex and leisure enterprises that appealed to a broader range of clientele. Seal and Brown, on the other hand, managed their operation, an enterprise regarded as a particularly "low" bawdy house, in Marble Alley. A notorious site for prostitution, Marble Alley was nestled between Pennsylvania and Missouri Avenues within the crime-ridden district popularly known as Murder Bay.[82] Similarly, Webster owned a place that employed twelve prostitutes in Fighting Alley, also known for crime. Webster most likely managed tight quarters that attracted a number of clients. This classification system may also serve as an indicator of the class standing of patrons, but as the locations and rankings of black women's establishments show, facilities, amenities, and the willingness of clients to enter spaces that made them vulnerable to crime determined how clients and officials categorized black-owned sites of sex and leisure.[83]

The marshal's attempts to document the list of bawdy houses reveal the degree to which officials regarded the growth of the sex economy as an unwieldy enterprise to be controlled and surveilled. Even as the number of prostitutes and bawdy houses increased, the establishments appeared more discreet with the use of alley dwellings for such purposes, as well as the anonymity provided by overcrowded conditions. As soldiers and civilians moved in and out of the purview of city streets, officials struggled to keep track of every rendezvous of soldiers and black prostitutes. One feature in the *Daily National Republican* reported, "As houses for illicit and disreputable purposes are on the increase in this city, it has been determined upon by the proper military authorities to close them up."[84] Congress passed a measure to create a new metropolitan police department in the District to respond to disloyal dissenters of the war, as well as the heightened criminal activity that came with the war.[85] Despite efforts to shut down bawdy houses, local police were no match for the persistent efforts of women and men who sought diversions and financial gain from the war. It was noted that "in many instances soldiers are found in these places beasty drunk, when they ought to be with the army."[86] The sex and leisure activities of soldiers and women contrasted with efforts to restore the stability and Christian mores of the Union.

Local religious leaders, particularly preoccupied with the moral state of the capital, immediately expressed concerns over the vices of the District during the war. At the monthly meeting of the Young Men's Christian Association of Washington in the fall of 1862, the members in attendance discussed the "spiritual wants of the soldiers" and the "spiritual and temporal welfare of the soldiers."[87] Indeed, the U.S. Christian Commission, previously the Army Committee of the Young Men's Christian Association of New York, sent packages of wholesome reading to Union soldiers to ward off the temptation of lewd and immoral behavior, particularly consumption of pornographic literature.[88] In his remarks, Reverend Lancey of the army "spoke of the propriety of this association, taking some measures to repress the vices so generally prevalent in Washington at this time, especially the vice of prostitution."[89] Local and national reform organizations eagerly set in motion efforts to stave off the impact of the sex economy, but the local courts gained first-hand exposure to details behind notable wartime cases.

As the war progressed, Washington gained a "reputation of being an un-godly city" that tempted not only soldiers but also officers who frequented the city. One reporter lamented, "Here we behold a young man in the prime of life, with all his hopes before him, and wearing a military uniform and bearing the honored name of an American officer, now the avowed and shameless paramour of a public prostitute."[90] Major Burtenett appeared before the court on charges of keeping a fashionable bawdy house with "wine circulating to keep the blood hot" and "lewd and lascivious women with low-necked dresses on." To make matters worse, the district attorney observed, "It seems that the gallant Major delights in variety. He is one of those lovers who sees 'Helen's beauty in a brow of Egypt.'" The racialized context in which Burtenett's activity was cast points to broader developments in local sex and leisure enticements. Such pursuits appeared increasingly more interracial as notable patrons and witnesses testified before the court. The jury found him guilty, and District Attorney Edward C. Carrington remarked, "Oh! How high and honored that position, but now how degraded his present position."[91]

Court officials echoed the concerns of reformers and called for the organization of a grand jury to address criminal activity in the District. Chief Justice David Kellogg Cartter charged the jury with the task of serving as the "conservators of the moral health of the District." According to an article entitled "The City in Danger of the Fate of Sodom," the presiding justice stated further, "It is your duty to inquire into crime and bring the criminals to punishment." Carter noted that criminal activity in the District was distinctive, arguing that "there are thrown upon the District a vast deal of crime on account of having so many here from all parts of the world." This "distinctiveness" pointed to the racial and ethnic diversity that characterized mid-nineteenth-century Washington and the fear of interracial sexual liaisons that grew more common during the war. Arguing for the threat that prostitution posed, he concluded, "The nymphs of prostitution, with painted effrontery, insult honest women. This is the only glaring, unblushing crime wandering about our streets." As men flocked to the capital for a variety of reasons, mainly as a result of the demands of war, sex commerce emerged as a central feature of Washington's streets.[92]

The presence of women, and the sexualized connotations of women who wandered into military camps, affected the broader war effort across the North and the South. As scholars note, women known as "camp followers" traveled with military camps for a variety of reasons. Refugee black women were included among the majority of "camp followers" in the Union army. Others included the wives and family members of soldiers who desired to remain close to loved ones, nurses, cooks, domestics, and seamstresses. Some women recognized as "camp followers," or "public women," also worked as prostitutes.[93] In Tennessee, prostitution became so rampant during the war that an estimated 1,500 women worked as prostitutes. Union general Stephen A. Hurlbut took matters into his own hands and marched 300 prostitutes from Memphis onto a steamboat to Cairo and threatened them with a term of hard labor on fortifications should they return. Moreover, Provost Marshal George Spalding and General William Rosecrans became preoccupied with halting the proliferation of sexually transmitted diseases such as syphilis and gonorrhea. Overall, more than 180,000 soldiers suffered from venereal disease. Unable to control the sexuality of women and soldiers, officials in the nation's capital struggled to impede the growth of prostitution.[94] Locals in Washington who praised Hurlbut's initiative remarked, "We believe that if our authorities in this city should adopt similar measures they could not only find 300 of these disorderly characters, but 3,900," not including those in Georgetown. According to this article, the efforts of local police were insufficient, and "the few petty arrests which we hear and read of daily are only as a drop in the bucket." The article declared that "a second Sodom is being built" in the capital of the Union.[95]

At the beginning of the war, the provost marshal of the District began an aggressive campaign against prostitution, and Brigadier General Joseph Hooker made plans to geographically contain the sex industry to monitor the whereabouts of Union soldiers. Named after Hooker, Hooker's Division became the cordoned hotbed of sex commerce in the District, located near what is today referred to as the Federal Triangle and the current location of the National Museum of the American Indian. Hooker convinced many managers of bawdy houses to offer their services in a designated location in order to more closely monitor the activities of soldiers during the Civil War. Such efforts did not stave off the prevalence of sex and leisure entertainment among soldiers, but they did create a strategy of surveillance. This approach mirrored similar approaches of legalizing and containing sex commerce in nineteenth-century France.[96] The police department reported that "houses of prostitution are reported to be fearfully on the increase," and too numerous for officials to manage. The superintendent considered possible solutions, "as it is beyond all question that prostitution cannot be eradicated from cities." Police concluded that "the only thing to be done is to throw around the vice proper restraints," and they looked to other examples abroad for models. The report explained, "In foreign countries, brothels are licensed and placed under the strictest surveillance, but this is so repugnant to public sentiment in this country that such a course here is not practicable." The solution mirrored the approach of the provost marshal with a proposed registry and containment of brothels. Such efforts disrupted some of the most successful bawdy houses and placed them under broader public scrutiny.[97]

One incredibly successful white woman loomed particularly large in accounts of wartime prostitution. Mary Ann Hall appeared in the census as early as 1840 as the owner of a bawdy house that included "five white females, one free colored woman, and one colored male slave." Hall's establishment was emblematic of the racial hierarchy of the antebellum and wartime sex economy. To complete her vision for a fashionable enterprise, she employed black servants and hackmen. Despite her exclusion from the realms of elite society, Hall accumulated enough wealth to create a lifestyle of luxury, which included slave ownership. Economically, Hall was just as prosperous as other white elites. A patron of her establishment might be initially welcomed into a well-furnished parlor where black servants offered fine cuisine and expensive libations as meticulously corseted women awaited them. Hall designed a rendezvous that reflected a fantasy of domesticity centered on sex, leisure, and slavery—an experience of quintessentially southern luxury.[98]

Regarded as "well established," by the beginning of the Civil War, Hall's real estate property was appraised at $14,600. The profitability of the establishment positioned Hall to offer competitive wages for black servants, but to also purchase enslaved people. Catering to clientele elite enough to support the finest cuts of meat, bottles of Piper-Heidsieck champagne imported from France, and corsets made by Jean-Paul Gautier, Hall became famous for her expensive taste.[99] Situated conveniently on the National Mall, a few blocks from the Capitol building, Hall's establishment was regarded as the ultimate haven for luxurious leisure for men who could afford to pay. Her parlor featured a lavish display of domesticity, affirming elite men's desires for power and prestige through exclusivity and indulgence, while she capitalized on an opportunity to build real wealth unparalleled by any other brothel in the city. Hall's proximity to political power players, who often seasonally resided in the capital without a companion to accompany them, made her establishment an important feature of elite white men's lives and leisure.[100] Hall's financial success, however, did not shield her from legal troubles.

A local celebrity during the war, Hall was charged for "keeping a bawdy house" as many other women were, but her case gained extensive coverage in the press. When she entered the courtroom, she came with an entourage of supporters and donned "a suit of virtuous black." Hall appeared among the most successful of a group of notorious brothel keepers that included "Ann

Benter of Tin Cup alley, Ellen Bride of Pear Tree alley, and Mary Heissler, better known as 'Dutch Mary,' of Third Street." They were all summoned to court after a ramped-up effort to reduce the growing number of establishments. Hall's establishment, more specifically, thrived for at least two decades without any serious legal trouble. Ultimately, she maintained her business through the war and retired in 1878. By the time of her death in 1888, her estate was worth an estimated $100,000—no small fortune for any woman or man during the nineteenth century. Hall died wealthy, leaving a generous inheritance to her two sisters, with whom she worked. Undoubtedly, black madams and prostitutes also knew of her and the extent of her success and might model their establishments in a similar parlor style if they possessed the resources to do so. Black women and men working as servants in establishments like these could discover the intimate worlds of the city's most powerful patrons.[101]

Black women worked as servants, cooks, and laundresses in bawdy houses, particularly in establishments that experienced some degree of success like Mary Hall and could afford to hire additional labor. These women often received room and board, and comparable wages at a time of overcrowding and rampant poverty. Hall employed black women as servants, and her house offered "material comforts" to those in her employ while also allowing patrons to experience all the trappings of elite domesticity and the racial hierarchies that came with it. Enslaved and free black women who served in these establishments gained enough exposure to the details of operating a prosperous bawdy house to prepare them for entering the industry themselves.[102] However, leading a life as an entrepreneur in the local sex and leisure economy could also lead to unfavorable attention.

Wartime news accounts reported numerous cases involving both white and black prostitutes who worked in the same establishment. On January 26, 1860, Ellen Johnson, a black madam, was put on trial for keeping a bawdy house between F and Twenty-Sixth Streets in the First Ward. One witness testified that he watched "deeply veiled white women go there and go in the gate." He further testified that "men and women of lewd reputation go in there" and that he had "even seen a little girl not above 14 years of age go in there." Another witness stated that when he worked for Johnson, he "once saw a girl go there and a man went upstairs with her." Johnson informed the witness that the girl he saw was "the daughter of a clerk in the Patent Office." The witness also testified that he also saw "a respectable man, an officer in the Marine Corps," take a woman upstairs with him. Most madams typically refuted or denied such allegations offered by the witnesses to avoid workhouse sentences or financial penalties. It is quite possible, however, that Johnson offered a mixed-use space that provided boarding and privacy for a number of clients. Additionally, it was not uncommon for men of respectable standing to patronize spaces that allowed for privacy and anonymity, mainly because they were financially positioned to consistently frequent bawdy houses. The presence of respectable white people, particularly men of standing, reveals that Johnson's establishment likely attracted reputable clients and perhaps offered amenities similar to those provided by Mary Hall. Wartime Washington allowed for a broader range of bawdy houses operated by black women that catered to different men across classes.[103]

Martha Douglass appeared in the news under the headline "Another Fancy House Visited" after a local officer arrested her.[104] The headline, intended to convey the intrigue around this particular African American prostitute, offers insights into Douglass's entrepreneurial self-making, which leveraged ideas about class and the very real incomes of elite clientele that sustained the enterprise. The title reveals that a number of bawdy houses, including African American ones, designed around upper-class notions of domesticity appeared during the war. Douglass repeatedly appeared before the court, and two months later, the same officer arrested her again, though she evaded the workhouse by paying a fine.[105] The fact that the writer characterized the house as "fancy" underscores not only the sense of mockery tied to such claims but also the possibility that Douglass intended to create an experience much like the one that Hall became known for. A couple of weeks before her arrest, Douglass appeared in court for her activity in Prather's Alley. She was arrested, along with two white prostitutes, after complaints from "a number of the respectable citizens residing nearby."[106] Prather's Alley certainly held a reputation for vice, but their activities reverberated beyond the alley and onto visible thoroughfares where respectable citizens, "very much to their disgust," witnessed the interracial melee. Black women's "fancy houses" were created from their economic strategies of self-making and the demands for interracial sex.[107]

The rampant publicity about interracial bawdy houses reflects a broader frustration with the ways that prostitutes, and black women in particular, visibly took up residence in the streets. Police repeatedly arrested a white madam named Mary Ann Burke, who operated a bawdy house on South G Street, between Ninth and Tenth Streets. She was depicted as a nuisance that plagued the neighborhood throughout the course of the war, and the press described her establishment as a "resort of both white and colored prostitutes, and a place of frightful disorder."[108] The proliferation of interracial prostitution enterprises made public a long history of interracial intimacy and desire that existed before the war. White men's sexual relations with black women represented an old idea, but black women's sexual encounters with white men now supported their economic mobility. Furthermore, the Union military salaries that filled the pockets of soldiers regularly ended up in the hands of these women during the war.

Interracial sites of sex and leisure typically ignited public outrage to the extent that the enterprises implicated the moral condition of white men. Editorials and precinct records did not link black men to the arrests of interracial establishments. News commentary emphasized public anxieties about interracial prostitution and concerns about the condition of white men. Reporters explained that such establishments were "continually frequented by soldiers, who get liquor there, and under its influence behave in a way to make themselves the terror of the neighborhood."[109] For instance, Georgianna Pickrell, Sarah Lee, and Sarah Farrity, described as "notorious colored prostitutes," were arrested for "enticing white men."[110] The war had already imposed the mass migration of thousands of soldiers, immigrants, and black refugees, and the presence of lewd activity only exacerbated the tensions of local life in the city. An article with the headline "Black and White in Company" illuminates this point. A local constable arrested a lieutenant named Thomas Black "for being in company with black women."[111] Policing sex did not always translate into a strict interpretation of the law, but rather sometimes reflected an informal set of customs shaped by the discretion of local constables. Black women could certainly be arrested on a disorderly charge, but the law did not explicitly prohibit white men's sexual interactions with black women. Similarly, the court did not prosecute prostitution, but the manner in which the solicitations and transactions occurred justified the decisions of police to arrest them. Well-paid white men were attractive prospects for black women in the business of sex and leisure.

Women of all ages took advantage of these wartime inducements. Even with repeated arrests, sex and leisure commerce positioned women who worked in these establishments to pay the fines. A news report that appeared in *The Evening Star* stated that, "The police have tried many times to correct the evil, but find themselves utterly powerless," since the women would just pay the necessary fees and "start business again."[112] The war created stable employment prospects for men, but young women continued to search for viable work. The profitability of the sex and leisure economy varied depending on the establishment, but even the uncertainty of sex work did not prevent young women from entertaining the possibility of prostitution or some form of sexual relationships that involved compensation. Some of these relationships might involve a patron who subsidized the expenses of a woman exclusively regarded as a "kept woman."[113] Others might occasionally make a foray into the sex economy to temporarily generate income until other employment opportunities materialized. These instances are less documented than the cases involving women with recurring appearances in jail and court. Additionally, employers that hired seamstresses, washerwomen, cooks, and servants might select more experienced women in the local labor economy over younger women.

Black girls were introduced to the sex and leisure economy at a relatively young age during the war. Black girls as young as fifteen years of age appeared in wartime precinct reports as prostitutes.[114] In 1862, a group of four prostitutes was arrested, G. Simms at the age of seventeen; Hester Neil, fifteen; Julia Coley, seventeen; and Jane Washington, eighteen. None of these girls could read or write, indicating that they did not attend the local schools available to free black girls. They probably worked to earn income for their own survival or to contribute to their family households. Police fined each of them $3.94 for disorderly conduct, which they paid to be released from jail. That same year, two "colored servant girls" were arrested and listed as prostitutes at the age of sixteen. The simultaneous listing of the girls as servants and prostitutes quite possibly points to fluctuations and uncertainties that came with wartime employment for black girls. As black women took advantage of wartime emancipation in the District, they also experienced separation from families, left their former masters or employers, and ventured out on their own with the hope of earning a living as free women. For some, prostitution offered a path to self-making that positioned them to pay for basic living expenses in a city overcrowded with recently freed women, men, and children. The bodies of black girls, however, were commodified and sexualized throughout the history of chattel slavery, and the commercialization of wartime sex in the capital mirrored this idea in rather complicated ways.[115] The degree to which black girls made the "choice" to enter into sex commerce was largely shaped by factors such as gender and racial inequality that limited the job prospects available to black women and girls. They learned at an early age the strategies of survival and improvisation.

African American girls appeared in the news as the prey of older black women working in sex and leisure. One such case involved a sixteen-year-old girl from Elmira, New York, who eloped with a soldier. Her mother learned that her daughter lived in Washington, so she sent an inquiry along with a "likeness" to the superintendent of the police department, and the detectives immediately recognized her as the "young girl they had seen at 13th Street between C and D." They searched for the girl and learned that she had sought treatment from a local hospital. After searching "various houses of infamy," the detectives proceeded to a house kept by "a notorious old negro woman" who lived on Third Street between Maryland Avenue and B Street South. Detectives found the girl in an emaciated state seated near a window. As they entered the house, they found "a number of negroes, male and female, and soldiers playing cards upon their knees for lack of a table or spare stool." In addition to the people playing cards, the detectives noticed that "a number of sick prostitutes were lying around." Before the search, police had already arrested the owner of the establishment, Julia Fleet, on other charges, and "an old deformed negro woman was acting in her stead." The woman locked the girl in a room and refused to let the officers take her into custody until they threatened legal action. Officers who returned the girl to her mother reported, "The distress of the mother when the wasted figure of her once beautiful daughter was brought into her presence, was heartrending even to those accustomed to scenes of distress." The girl appeared as a fallen soul who "exhibited much penitence." These reports served as "real life" depictions of the dangers of vice and immorality that appeared in the city, but the story, under the surface, is much more complicated.[116]

After detectives took the girl to the police department, she left on an evening train to return to New York with her mother. Julia Fleet, the "notorious" woman who had lived in Washington "for thirty years past as a prostitute," did not lead her to Washington. The soldier she married persuaded her to follow him, but he soon left for eight months, and with nowhere to go, she sought help from Fleet. The realities of wartime poverty and the way that black women in particular struggled to survive offer insights into how the girl arrived at Fleet's Third Street establishment. Fleet operated a house that likely offered sex, but at the time of the bust, detectives discovered a card game being played by civilians and soldiers, a common form of leisure and socializing. The ailing prostitutes found at Fleet's home affirm another detail of her life. Locals described Fleet as "a sort of doctress for afflicted females of her class."[117] The girl conceivably worked for Fleet, but there's a possibility she sought Fleet for medical care as well. When the detectives initially began their search for her, they learned that she had gone to a local hospital in search of treatment. Locals contracted diseases from the overcrowded and unsanitary conditions of the city. Women and girls in sex commerce were certainly vulnerable to venereal disease. Evidence marginally supports that Fleet lured the girl into her brothel, but the report sheds light on how these establishments served multiple functions, even the purposes of healing. These reports seldom explained details from the perspectives of black women. Indeed, the record does not even provide a name for the girl. Her story reminds us that improvisation meant a distillation of responses to desperate circumstances.

While many young women found their way into the sex economy, some African American girls were entangled in the local sex economy against their will. In Bates Alley, located in the Fourth Ward, Henrietta West was arrested for harboring a thirteen-year-old black girl who resided in the neighborhood. Her mother reported to the local police that West abducted her daughter "for the purposes of putting her to the vilest use." [118] Once the officer arrested West, he discovered that she had transported the girl to Virginia to a bawdy house likely located in Alexandria. If the allegation was true, West's incentive for abduction aligns with the demands of her enterprise since she owned multiple bawdy houses. [119] West appeared in jail a year later after officials descended on her establishment, as well as the houses operated by Gracey West and Susan Bell, but she immediately covered the cost of bail after the bust. Gracey West potentially bears relation to Henrietta West, since a local report noted that "three families lived in the house." The news described her Fourth Ward location as "a common resort of black and white" comprising "four women, mulattoes." [120] Not all of the women associated with the establishment were arrested, and while the rest remained "to be dealt with, as being sick, they were not at trial." The bawdy houses attracted white clientele, but the working conditions were such that Henrietta West faced allegations of abduction and abuse, as some of them appeared ill. Even as black girls were funneled into the local sex economy, anxieties about the vulnerability of young women focused primarily on young white girls in popular wartime discourse.

Reports of young white girls being "enticed" by black women to work as prostitutes also caused local concern. On December 7, 1861, police retrieved a thirteen-year-old white girl from a house of assignation kept by a black woman whom they referred to as "a yellow woman." The feature noted that this was the third instance that week in which the police had responded to "distressed relatives of girls (minors) to recover them from houses of ill fame." Furthermore, the article offered that "there is no law here punishing the keepers of bawdy houses for harboring or enticing away girls under age from their homes." With an emphasis on the disturbing racial dynamic of this particular incident, the writer argued, "The fact that the victims of such villainy are white, will not disqualify them, it is to be hoped, as candidates for redress at the hands of our law-makers." [121] The racial context of the young girl's "rescue" from a black woman underscored the reporter's insinuation that this crime was of particular offense to the "distressed" families of white girls vulnerable to the sex industry.[122] Even single white women working in perfectly respectable jobs were subject to local suspicions of lewd behavior, despite their attempts to advance their own economic and social mobility.[123] Locals already expressed their disgust with illicit sexual encounters between black women and white men, but the idea of black women as facilitators of young white women's involvement with sex commerce was more than they could bear.

To manage the growing presence of vice, police and military officials organized raids at various moments during the war. In 1862, police arrested Hester Chase, Mary Dorsey, Mary Shipley, Mary Fergerson, and Hannah Queen for prostitution, along with five white prostitutes found at the same venue.[124] Later that year, some of the same women reappeared in the record when the *National Republican* reported breaking news of a descent upon a cluster of bawdy houses in the Seventh Ward. About ten "vile characters" were arrested for prostitution, two of whom were black women. Shortly after, another "batch of beauties," including one black prostitute, "graced the magistrate's office." The next group that came before Justice William R. Stratton included eight prostitutes, two of whom were black. At eleven o'clock that same evening, police arrested three more women listed as prostitutes, including two black women, Mary Ward and Mary Brown. The white woman arrested with Ward and Brown paid the highest fine at $20.94 for selling liquor, which may also indicate that she worked as the madam or brothel owner. The paper described the women as representative of "all complexions and degrees of beauty or decay, with mixtures of chalk, paint, tinselry, and ribbons."[125] Initiated by police as a targeted effort, these particular busts disrupted sites of interracial prostitution at a time when these networks were becoming a commonplace feature of urban Washington. While black and white women might have collaborated before the war, strong evidence of this didn't appear until the 1860s—indicating a visible interracial sex economy catalyzed by the Civil War.[126] In the Fourth Ward, at the "notorious den" of Eliza Crittenden in Prather's Alley, five prostitutes were arrested, including Mary and Annie Eaton, who were black. A madam could not afford to employ a prostitute if she did not generate the expected interest from clients. Thus, Mary and Annie possibly catered to returning, possibly white, clients. In the same bust, two black men found in the house were also arrested, but it is unclear whether they were clients or hackmen affiliated with the house. They were immediately released, as "nothing could be proved against them."[127] It was not unusual for black women and men who worked as servants in these establishments to end up in jail as a result of a prostitution bust. At a moment of national crisis, the prostitution enterprises of the District featured more prominently in public discourse than desired, and as a result, all individuals associated with such establishments became increasingly vulnerable to arrest.

Collaborative gatherings that targeted military clientele revealed that prostitutes, madams, and their servants were a key feature of the urban wartime landscape, particularly in the context of opportunities for leisure among soldiers. According to an article titled "A Den of Infamy Broken Up" featured in the *Daily National Republican,* "a most abominable house of prostitution" was broken up by the infantry patrol of the Tenth New Jersey. Ordered by the provost marshal, the detachment went to the house after it had "been complained of as a filthy den, a rendezvous for the assemblage of the vilest characters of both sexes, and of the worst class of soldiers." Those arrested included eight prostitutes, military engineer Sergeant Weyton, nine soldiers, one citizen, and three colored servants. All were taken to the central guardhouse, and the provost marshal gave the women twenty-four hours to leave the city. The soldiers, citizen, and military engineer were not ordered to leave the city. Many of the narratives concerning prostitution busts emphasized the need to monitor the sexual and leisure activities of soldiers—this typically involved getting rid of the women. As indicated by the anxieties expressed by the local Young Men's Christian Association and the justices of the criminal courts, the moral character of Union soldiers was of central concern in wartime Washington, and the virtue of the women appeared unredeemable.[128] These arrests also left black women servants without employment.

Affiliation with bawdy houses meant that black women servants might find it difficult to seek employment after working for establishments that were regarded as disreputable. Among those associated with the "den of infamy," three black servants went to jail for their affiliation with the bawdy house. As a result of the raid, and the subsequent sentence that required the women to leave the city, they lost their jobs. Often exploited by their employers and subject to unfavorable work conditions, some cooks and servants willingly exposed managers of the houses when given the opportunity. One cook testified in court against owners of a bawdy house near D Street. She stated, "Nobody has yet paid me for cooking; I haven't got my pay yet; Miss Roberts was my employer." One keeper of a bawdy house who maintained the house with his wife went to jail for selling liquor without a license. His servant "testified to her own prostitution with the man from whom the house is rented," at the direction of the wife, who also worked as a prostitute. Black women could be exploited and forced to work beyond the terms of the initial employment arrangement—in this case, beyond the typical responsibilities associated with domestic service. Thus, working at a bawdy house quite possibly led to the vulnerability and exploitation that free black women hoped to avoid.[129]

During the war, black women appeared in modest numbers, but more frequently than in the antebellum era, as brothel owners. Both black and white men patronized bawdy houses owned by black women, but white men who frequented the establishments of black women primarily made the headlines. Between 1863 and 1864, police found a black woman named Kate Ford with white men and arrested her for keeping a bawdy house between Eleventh and O Streets. Three additional black prostitutes and two white men discovered at Ford's brothel paid fines for disorderly conduct and intoxication.[130] Despite repeated appearances in jail, black women like Ford typically continued building their respective enterprises. The white men involved were affiliated with the military and represented a broad spectrum of economic and social categories. Upon arrest, the men paid modest fines for the offense and appeared in the daily news not as particularly immoral but rather as victims who surrendered to the temptation of black women. The presence of these men in black women's bawdy houses visibly frustrated the hierarchies of race and gender, but by the end of the war, the interracial sex economy read as seemingly unexceptional.

Branding white men as victims of their "natural" proclivities for lust in some ways excused them from their covert excursions to black-owned bawdy houses. One nineteenth-century writer commented that "men couldn't really be expected to control their sexual appetites." Gendered ideas about white men helplessly surrendering to the sexual appetites of lusty black women underscore prevailing notions about race and sexuality that regarded black women as particularly sexually depraved. Similarly, white slave owners known to have sexual encounters with enslaved women were thought to be momentarily "possessed by evil" or overtaken by "the devil." Such sentiments made white men's sexual violence and escapades a minor offense or even excusable at a time when antimiscegenation framed popular and widely accepted views of interracial sex.[131] While race did not deter white patronage, assumptions about black women's racial inferiority factored into the perceptions of bawdy houses owned by black women. As the war came to a close, many white patrons returned to their respective hometowns, and black enterprises increasingly catered to black clients.[132]

The transformations that came with the war required black women to reconstitute their participation in sex and leisure over time. Black women who leased or owned property shifted the use of that property as demand redirected its uses. Their homes, alleys, and communities were sites of improvisation. Some enterprises thrived throughout the course of the conflict, while the owners of those that were less successful employed tactics to avoid providing sexual services. An article titled "Low Bawdy House" featured an arrest initiated by the Tenth New Jersey on Fifteenth Street near M Street. This house was considered particularly "low" or debased because it involved the common practice of robbery.[133] The guard arrested "the keepers, man and woman, who are charged with robbing money from a colored man who visited the place." The fees acquired at bawdy houses that serviced black men specifically were not always as lucrative as the managers and prostitutes hoped. Consequently, black women occasionally lured men into an establishment under the guise of offering sexual services but decided to rob them instead. The arrests did not deter the keepers from maintaining their operation. The madam served a term in the workhouse, and the establishment was "ordered to be closed several weeks since." The news, however, reported that "they have repeatedly violated the order." Black women involved in sex commerce consistently lived in and out of the workhouse if they were unable to pay the fines. In the First Ward, Maria Payne was arrested and jailed for keeping a bawdy house at the corner of Eighteenth and E Streets. Amanda Mathews also faced jail time for keeping a bawdy house that catered to black men. The duration of the sentence typically ranged from thirty to sixty days in the workhouse, but women who accumulated enough profit left the jail after paying hefty fines for assurance of their good behavior.[134]

Black women and men developed entrepreneurial strategies to maximize the use of the properties they managed. For instance, the multiple designations used to characterize Theodora Herbert's establishment point to the inconsistencies in the charges against her and the testimonies offered in court. While witnesses characterized the people associated with the establishment as "lewd" and lacking good "character," one witness shared a different experience. Laura Thompson, a white woman, testified to her having "lived in the house of defendant as a boarder, and paid the defendant bed money." Thompson further offered that she remembered "respectable persons" visiting the house. Even with testimony that indicated otherwise, the charges of prostitution were upheld, and Herbert was fined the hefty sum of $500. Thompson's account demonstrates that black women used their property for a variety of purposes other than sex work. The same held true for black men in the city who strategized about ways to maximize use of their property. Amos Pratt was charged with keeping a disorderly house on the fourth story of the

Woodward Building. After a round of testimonies, it was clear that Pratt at times "held religious meetings of very respectable colored people" and at other times hosted "assemblages of disorderly, lewd, and drunken colored persons." He also hosted "dances" and at times "made such a noise as to be heard two squares and used profane and indecent language." Pratt argued that his property "was not more disorderly than others in the neighborhood" and that the witness could hear "only 'colored noise' and was deaf to 'white noise.'" Pratt desired the same degree of privacy and autonomy afforded his white neighbors, who made just as much noise as the black residents. The use of such black spaces challenges us to see their flexible utility, as well as the fluidity of their occupants' identities.[135]

Madams and owners of "disorderly houses" that offered liquor, sex, and gambling for black patrons appeared more visibly toward the end of the war as black men became increasingly positioned to participate in these black-owned spaces. Indeed, the presence of black men in local dens of prostitution, gambling, and vice countered reform rhetoric that focused on thrift and frugality.[136] Arrested earlier for her involvement with interracial prostitution networks in 1862, Eliza Crittenden reappeared in the press after the war. In her second appearance in the press, an article titled "Raid on Liza Crittenden's" captured the "descent" upon the bawdy house she operated in Prather's Alley. Of those arrested included "five colored men and three colored women" who were reportedly found "playing cards." Police took them to the Fourth Ward station and charged them with disorderly conduct. The reporter noted that one of the men arrested had a razor in his possession, and informed the reader that a razor was "the favorite negro weapon." The man with the razor was fined ten dollars, and everyone else involved paid a fine of five dollars each. Crittenden was not home at the time of the bust, but she was found the next morning and held in jail for further hearing. When police arrested her in 1862, she went to jail along with the prostitutes she employed and the white male clients who patronized her establishment. The arrest of 1866 shows evidence of a sex and leisure business that increasingly serviced black men.[137]

By the end of the war, the effort to shut down bawdy houses had gained traction, with more targeted raids and mounting fines against both black and white proprietors. A report of the chief of military patrols and detectives, published in the *Daily National Republican*, shows the police force in "very efficient condition," asserting that during the month of March, "their labors were herculean." In one month, twenty-six people went to jail for selling liquor to soldiers, seven for selling liquor without a license, and twelve for selling liquor on Sunday, and a total of ten bawdy houses were broken up. Patrons expected black madams to offer libations, and entrepreneurial black women frequented the local jail because they were not permitted to obtain licenses to sell liquor. Police forced black women to vacate the premises of the ten bawdy houses that were raided, "which were either permanently closed, or turned over to their owners on the promise of renting them to families of respectability." After the war, the local police persistently made efforts to dismantle opportunities for sex and leisure commerce among black entrepreneurs. On April 16, 1866, one writer of the *Evening Star* observed, "The officers of the Seventh Ward seem to be earnestly engaged in rooting out the dens of infamy which have so long disgraced portions of that large ward." The article continued with claims that the Seventh Ward, in particular, had "been a cause of annoyance to the order-loving residents of the Island." Officers reportedly conducted seven more raids, which led to the arrest of a number of women and men associated with bawdy houses. Of those arrested, five of the owners of bawdy houses were white and dismissed, and two, Virginia Magruder and Caroline Adams, were black and held to bail for court. The article concluded that the officers of the Seventh Ward "succeeded in ridding that locality of a great many notorious characters within a few months."[138] The end of the war meant the reconstitution of social order and relationships, and the raids reflected a concerted effort to restore order to the capital.

African American women's enterprises shaped much of their ability to survive and, therefore, improvise during the Civil War. The economic opportunities available to black women in Washington often required them to think creatively and entrepreneurially about how to earn income. Working independently to cook, serve, wash, sew, and sell goods or sex offered a degree of flexibility and opportunities for negotiation. The racial and gender hierarchies of the capital, however, situated black women at the bottom of the labor economy, and thus their vulnerability to exploitation, intimate and public violence, and arrest remained a reality for many. A demand for their labor existed just before the war, but the mobilization of the army and the significance of the capital caused an influx of soldiers, refugees, and laborers that signaled a shift in the local labor economy for black women. Overcrowding led to more competition for limited jobs and an increase in the cost of living. The presence of Union soldiers expanded the demographic of potential patrons in search of a diversion from the demands of war. Their relatively stable salaries fueled the local sex and leisure economy. By the advent of the Civil War, bawdy houses and dens of leisure sparked scrutiny in the local news, which specifically highlighted the increasingly interracial nature of black-owned establishments.

At the end of the war, soldiers who survived returned home, officers retired from duties, and freedpeople relocated to jobs elsewhere or settled in the capital. The restoration of social order became the charge of reformers. It was time to clean up the streets. Local officials and religious leaders offered their support for initiatives to dismantle black, white, and interracial sex enterprises in the city after the war. In an 1866 article titled "Improving," the police reported that "respect for the Sabbath is being restored." Reformers hoped to restore not only the Sabbath but also monogamous marriages, free labor ideology, and honor. The war inspired officials to lead a charge against the presence of prostitutes who "prey upon the army" and made "fortunes from unprincipled men." The mores of white men were at stake, and recovery from the effects of the war required an earnest effort to undermine the sex and leisure economy. The report offered that "where the Sabbath was passed in dancing and drunkenness has suddenly quieted down." The officers were glad to finally "return a 'clean sheet' to the Superintendent" that morning.[139]

The restoration of social order meant that black bawdy houses appeared less interracial than they had during the war. Black women carved out spaces within the city to remain in operation in the absence of soldiers and military officials. Local black and white men continued to frequent the sex and leisure enterprises of black women, but not with the same visibility that had characterized their visits throughout the war. Moreover, at the end of the war, the increase in black patronage cemented sites of black leisure and sex even as many of them remained hidden in the alleys that police targeted in raids. The sex economy offered the incentives of entrepreneurial work and collaboration with other workers but came also with vulnerability to violence, exploitation, criminalization, and venereal disease. Furthermore, many women attempted to undermine other prostitutes when opportunities emerged. In the midst of the instability brought on by the war, and wartime emancipation, sex work in a bawdy house offered a means through which one could obtain food, housing, and income. Participation in the sex economy could provide the financial foundation from which to begin self-making as a free woman. The decision to remain involved in the sex and leisure economy at the risk of recurring arrest shows that some black women found such work viable. The tension in black women's work in criminalized and sexualized enterprises remained in the degree of autonomy afforded in working with relative flexibility, and the subsequent sexual commodification, vulnerability to violence, and exploitation that came with it. As free black women discovered entrepreneurial ways to take advantage of the wartime economy, the social and political transformations of the war led to the demise of slavery in Washington.

The outbreak of war and the mobilization of the military transformed not only the dynamics of the local labor economy but also the Union's commitment to emancipation. Wartime legislation sparked the flight of scores of refugees who journeyed to Union lines. During the war, former bondwomen employed strategic avenues for earning income and navigating life as a free person in the capital. Their experiences shed light on the fact that black women experienced the war very differently depending on their social, legal, and geographic position. While entrepreneurial economies shaped the dynamics of improvisation and self-making of free women working in Washington, that same spirit of improvisation and self-making translated into the efforts of enslaved women who crossed the borders of the District and made direct appeals to the federal government. For bondwomen, emancipation and the prospects of new opportunities for self-making were on the horizon.

CHAPTER SIX

Government

On September 8, 1862, Emeline Wedge filed petitions on behalf of herself, her two children, and her sister Alice Thomas, who were all enslaved on the property belonging to Alexander McCormick. McCormick refused to take advantage of the compensation provision of the new law the year it took effect in Washington, D.C., and Wedge saw an opportunity. He reluctantly appeared before the clerk of the court after receipt of a summons. According to court records, McCormick "denied the Constitutionality of the Emancipation Act, and said that he would bide his time until it was declared unconstitutional." Besides, he was a citizen with rights to property, and why would anyone take seriously claims made by an enslaved woman? Just before his case was decided, McCormick reappeared before the clerk and commissioners of the District and, for the first time, formally contended with the liberty claims of Wedge. In this case, emancipation threatened the property rights of slaveholders and excluded white residents more generally from any democratic processes that decided the fate of slavery in Washington. Ideas about liberty and bondage were inextricably tied to place, and Washington was changing. African American women like Wedge assumed a new role, not completely carved out for them, but with anticipation and even hope of what could be. Throughout the course of wartime emancipation, refugee women and freedwomen navigated the power dynamics that made liberty possible in order to secure it for themselves and their kin. This chapter investigates how former bondwomen employed their knowledge of the geographic and political importance of Washington as they approached officials of the government to make claims to liberty. These experiences were distinctive in how the women transformed their own futures, as well as the significance of the nation's capital as a site of liberty. For these women, liberty was the work of self-making.[1]

Working in Wedge's favor was the fact that Congress abolished slavery in the District of Columbia in 1862. For black Washington, the years of waiting for Congress to exercise such power ended at the beginning of the Civil War in spite of arguments against the constitutionality of local emancipation. With the exodus of a strong contingent of Democrats following Lincoln's election, the Republican-dominated legislative body passed the measure with votes at twenty-nine to thirteen in the Senate and ninety-two to thirty-eight in the House.[2] Although the bill passed by a significant margin, the opposing votes underscore an underlying truth about this era. Historically, white Americans expressed hostility toward the idea of black liberty in both antebellum and wartime shifts toward emancipation. Scholars have pointed to the rehearsals of gradual emancipations in the North and prevailing attitudes against racial equality.[3] While many Americans embraced the prospect of ridding themselves of slavery, the manifestations of black women's self-making in times of emancipation placed them at odds with dissenters who expressed concerns over equality, "amalgamation," and citizenship.[4] This sentiment rang true for white locals in Washington.

The emancipation bill made provisions for compensation to slaveholders to the tune of $300 along with a financial incentive set at $100 for former slaves to relocate to another country. Still, even as some African Americans entertained the possibility of colonization, they decisively charted their course in the Union and remained in the capital.[5] Accordingly, this marked the moment that white locals in Washington dreaded most. It might appear that the struggle for liberty ended with local emancipation, but Washington was the "citadel" of the Union, and what applied to those enslaved in the city in 1862 sent signals to enslaved people and slaveholders alike throughout the region.[6] For most of the country, slavery and the fugitive slave law prevailed, but slaveholders still felt threatened by what they saw happening in Washington. When Congress legally authorized the emancipation of a population of roughly three thousand enslaved people, countless others took advantage of the measure.[7] White Washingtonians braced themselves for a tidal wave of refugees, and black women, both refugees and recently freed, recognized an important opportunity.

Throughout the course of the war, refugee women and freedwomen arrived in the nation's capital with intentions to be free and to define for themselves what life would look like. This was not a new pattern, however, since wars before the Civil War had also inspired flight and claims to liberty.[8] Whereas the incentives for emancipation in previous conflicts emphasized leverage against foreign foes, the legal measures deployed by Republicans were designed to undermine states in rebellion (although Confederate views of themselves as sovereign could mean that they too were foreign). As the war progressed, soldiers, officials, and legislators, empowered by martial law and legislation, helped usher in the process of emancipation.[9] This constituted both a measure of strategic advantage and inconvenience, as they often managed more crowds of refugees than their camps could accommodate.[10] The revolutionary legal transformations of the war marked Union lines, and the capital in particular, as key sites of power and significance. The perilous journeys bondwomen and children made to these sites both inspired and tested the effectiveness of these policies. We learn from them the limits of government, the violence that comes with monumental societal shifts, and the idea of liberty as a powerful motivator for navigating such turbulent terrain.

Refugee women took steps necessary to secure their freedom while prompting a social contract between themselves and the government. This dynamic unfolded even as they navigated conflicting ideas about the status of refugees and the rights of freedpeople in the nation's capital. The navigation strategies of refugee women and freedwomen employed a variety of insights about how to search for family members, how to understand new laws, which soldiers to trust, which hospitals provided care, and how to access provisions. At various moments, they made a series of negotiations with federal officials, and in other instances they took action on their own—they expressed their own understandings of their rights.[11] Furthermore, black women refugees articulated the claims entitled to a free person, and therefore initiated the process through which they transitioned from the status of enslaved to that of American citizen. This process of self-actualization and protest reflected long-held beliefs about liberty among black women in Washington. In their self-making, black women navigated the complex application of emancipation laws as they traveled to or from Washington, Virginia, and Maryland.

Historians have aptly noted that the outcomes of the war were incredibly contingent, and black women's wartime navigations of the shifting policies of the government solidify this point.[12] The case of Emeline Wedge illuminates how black women were critical in initiating the process through which formerly enslaved people realized their freedom. The displacement caused by the war also spurred refugee women to travel to the nation's capital in search of loved ones, shelter, clothing, medical care, and employment. Those who became legally freed by wartime emancipation measures still struggled to realize the rights to their own labor and found conditions in the capital precarious at best. During the Civil War, black women participated in a process of self-making that involved fraught and complex modes of survival, improvisation, and navigation. Historian Chandra Manning refers to this experience as "troubled refuge," and Thavolia Glymph reminds us that we've barely touched the surface in our understanding of the degree of suffering experienced by enslaved women and children.[13] The women in this chapter made claims to liberty in the nation's capital, with all of its power and government, and for better or for worse, Washington became a key site of black women's aspirations for freedom.

The emancipation process in Washington, D.C., involved a series of critical policies instituted under martial law and enacted in Congress, including the First Confiscation Act of 1861, the District of Columbia Emancipation Act of 1862, the elimination of black codes, the Supplemental Act of 1862, the Second Confiscation Act of 1862, the Emancipation Proclamation of 1863, and the repeal of the Fugitive Slave Act in 1864.[14] This complicated sequence of policy changes had varying impacts on the lives of black women, particularly those arriving from neighboring slaveholding states. Wartime policy in the District, nestled between Confederate territory in Virginia and the nebulously loyal slave state of Maryland, created uncertain terms of liberty that black women struggled to decode. Congress introduced emancipation in the capital at the beginning of the war, but women like Wedge made the law a reality.[15]

In the spring of 1862, Congress approved a proposal to free just over three thousand enslaved people in the District. The abolishment of slavery in Washington legally set in motion the emancipation process, making the violation of the Emancipation Act a felony and incentivizing compliance with the new order through compensation for each enslaved person freed.[16] Slaveholders applying for compensation were offered a specific amount of money determined by the assessed value of each slave, which at times exceeded the $300 allotted by the measure. The shift away from chattel slavery and the property disputes that ensued disrupted the social fabric of the District. Black women stood ready for the possibilities, but legislators remained unsure as they cautiously entertained the prospects of emancipation with broader implications in mind.

Refugee women who arrived in the capital during the Civil War did so at their own risk—confronting a system in which their legal status was deeply ambiguous. Refugee and fugitive women took advantage of the geographic and political position of Washington, D.C., particularly in instances in which they arrived from slaveholding states during or after 1862. Many of them traveled to the District from Virginia, a bastion of the Confederacy, or Maryland, a loyal slaveholding state. According to the laws and customs of the Confederacy, black women coming from Virginia were considered fugitives and, depending on one's views, refugees. With Virginia in rebellion, officials might be less sympathetic to Virginia slaveholders, but an enslaved woman could never be sure. The intraregional ties were strong, and locals with southern sympathies likely undermined black women's liberty claims if given the opportunity. Concerned with appeasing loyalists in Maryland, the federal government legally protected the interests of slaveholders in the state by upholding the Fugitive Slave Act of 1850. Depending on whether the laws of the Confederacy or the Union applied, black women traveling from slaveholding states could be considered enslaved even as wartime emancipation took its course. Thus, black women remained in a state of legal limbo as they navigated wartime policy created in the interests of states loyal to the Union and against the interests of the Confederacy.[17]

As emancipation unfolded, white locals resented the blatant absence of any democratic processes with regard to such significant matters and subsequently petitioned in protest.[18] Slaveholders represented a small population of the District, but the loss of property value and the inability to claim the total value associated with enslaved people forced the government to decide whether to prioritize the claims of white slaveholders, the freedom of bondpeople, or strategic advantage in the war. Cheryl Harris arguably offers the most compelling interpretation of the correlation between property and whiteness. With regard to property, American law not only inscribed racial identity on property with the legality of African slavery, but as Harris demonstrates in her important work, whiteness developed into a specific form of property affirmed by the law.[19] In the moment of wartime emancipation, black women with the legal backing of the Union government disrupted this property interest in whiteness even if momentarily diverting a centuries-long pattern of white expectations of power over black Americans. These measures, however, were also about the shifting tides of war and the implications for wartime emancipation more broadly. Thus, the government demanded that white locals take the deal and prioritize the interests of the Union and its military policies regarding enslaved people. Although the bill offered compensation, white residents only begrudgingly conceded to a Union government that violated a long-standing social contract with white men.

Amid protests, as many as 966 slaveholders filed claims for compensation for the enslaved people freed by the emancipation law. The clerk and board of commissioners, along with the secretary of the Treasury, were responsible for assessing the claims, determining the value of slaves, and providing compensation. Commissioner records indicate that the majority of the claims involved smaller slaveholdings, ranging from one to eight slaves. For the value of four slaves—Caroline Lucas, a woman named Rosanna, and Rosanna's children William and Alexa Gordon—the infamous brothel owner Mary Ann Hall requested $3,000. According to Hall, Rosanna alone was valued at

$1,200. White women appeared as frequently as men in seeking compensation for their property. A woman named Harriet White, for instance, requested a little over $6,800 for twenty-four slaves. White's case was one of many filed by white women hoping to profit from the compensation provision of the law, revealing that both white women and men were financially invested in slavery and believed they were entitled to compensation.[20] Some locals possessed holdings as large as, if not larger than, White's. District resident George Washington Young, for instance, boasted holdings of sixty-eight slaves, with an attested compensation value set at over $17,000.[21]

Slaveholders in Washington generally either took advantage of the compensation provision made for emancipation or questioned the constitutionality of the new legal measure altogether. White possession of black people, as they understood the practice, was permitted by the law and protected by the Fifth Amendment.[22] Particularly in a state like Maryland, slaveholders felt entitled to protection of their property rights regardless of how events unfolded in the District.[23] Compensation did not amount to the full value that an enslaved person might command in the antebellum market, and the provision could never replace the power to exercise full discretion over the decision to free them. Slaveholding and nonslaveholding whites feared that the hierarchies that shaped society were being undone by such measures, but this was an assumption that black women could only hope for. The geopolitical borders of the Chesapeake could either undermine or work in favor of black women's navigation of wartime transformations.

The facts of Emeline Wedge's case reveal the unique position of Washington, D.C., and the neighboring Chesapeake counties, as a distinctive geopolitical battleground over liberty during the Civil War. As an enslaved woman, Wedge both challenged the legal validity of her enslavement and forced McCormick to contend with her testimony against him. The Supplemental Act, passed in the summer of 1862, permitted enslaved women in the District of Columbia to testify against white men and women for the first time. Evidence showed that McCormick's farm was located along the border dividing the District from Maryland and that, just one day after the Emancipation Act became law, he instructed the slaves to reside on the Maryland side of his property. According to the records of the board of commissioners, he built a small tenement for them on the Maryland side, while his main living quarters remained in the District, along with the cow pen and other buildings included on the homestead. While McCormick generally prohibited enslaved people from traveling to the District side of the property, it was proved that Alice was "required to drive cattle from the pasture to the cow pen," which was located on the District side. Unidentified witnesses also testified that they had seen the women and children in McCormick's Washington home daily and that, for approximately seven or eight weeks, Wedge and her family had resided in the District with an older man also bearing the last name Wedge, who was identified as the father of Emeline's husband.[24]

The board of commissioners ultimately acknowledged Emeline Wedge's right to claim freedom under the Emancipation Act of 1862. Her case is illuminating because, among other things, Wedge's husband and father-in-law did not file the petition, but she instead took the initiative to make her own liberty claims. But this was not unusual. In her work on gender and the political dynamics of Reconstruction, Laura Edwards argues that "African American and common white women formed a loud, visible, and vigorous public presence both during and after the Civil War."[25] Patriarchy did not always feature prominently in black women's quests for self-making or liberty. To the contrary, freedwomen in the moment of local emancipation filed numerous claims and complaints on behalf of themselves and members of their families, initiating the transition of entire families into liberty rather than waiting on men to do so. Early understandings of citizenship rested largely on the imperatives of the patriarchal head of the household to uphold the rights and obligations of citizenship.[26] Free black men often made the argument that discrimination denied them the recognition necessary to fulfill their duties as heads of their households and as formal political citizens. Indeed, white women and free African Americans found ways to participate in associational and community-centered forms of citizenship in the absence of more formal privileges of citizenship such as the vote.[27] For refugee women, patriarchy at times proved inapplicable or irrelevant, and black women found alternative expressions of their position in society or were not tied to any men at all. Nevertheless, patriarchy factored into outcomes in emancipation petitions depending on the commissioners and bureau agents involved.

Throughout the course of the war, black women litigated, petitioned, and organized in the capital. The legal and extralegal steps they took to realize liberty set in motion an array of claims to their lives and labors that challenged their racial and gendered exclusion. In many cases, officials from the board of commissioners, the Union military, and the Bureau of Refugees, Freedmen, and Abandoned Lands assisted enslaved women in their efforts to be free, find kin, or find employment leads.[28] White locals also deployed a variety of strategies to prevent black women and men from realizing a life of freedom and equality. Former owners like McCormick attempted to evade new emancipation measures by claiming residence in loyal slaveholding states.

Others employed violence or harassment to reinstate control over the lives of black women. Slaveholding and nonslaveholding whites in the District and surrounding Chesapeake counties made it clear that they would not simply acquiesce to the terms of emancipation. In fact, the government still wavered on what life after emancipation might look like for refugees and existing black residents.[29]

After the emancipation bill passed, black residents either remained in the District or left for other cities, but the law also included provisions for a government-subsidized emigration initiative. A longtime proponent of colonization, President Lincoln met with a delegation of black leaders during the summer of 1862 to discuss the possibility of encouraging black people in the District to leave the country. He made a point to express the potential of Liberia and especially Central America as potential sites for relocation. Liberia, founded in 1822 by the American Colonization Society; Haiti; and Chiriqui, a region in New Grenada, were among the places under consideration for black settlements.[30] Founded in 1816, the American Colonization Society held its first meeting in Washington and, over the years, led several initiatives for black immigration to Liberia and Haiti. Moreover, black proponents of emigration also entertained the possibility of colonizing specific locations in Central America as early as 1854. While emigration gained support from a minority of the free black population, enthusiasts continued to fuel ongoing efforts to fund colonization. In fact, in 1862 150 African Americans made plans to board a vessel headed to Haiti from Alexandria, Virginia.[31] Discourses around emigration were certainly not new, and they did not inspire wholesale rejection from black leaders.[32]

The delegation that met with Lincoln included black leaders with established roots and residences in the capital who had founded the District's oldest black churches and intellectual societies. Among them were John F. Cook, John T. Costin, Edward Thomas, Cornelius Clark, and Benjamin McCoy.[33] These men descended from an established tradition of civic, intellectual, religious, and antislavery activism in Washington. They were not the black men who would most likely be directly affected by the emancipation measure, but they could be driven out by colonization. The black leaders, however, possessed the influence to convince black Americans in the District that emigration could represent the beginnings of a promising new era of black liberation. During the meeting, Lincoln remarked that, without the presence of black people, a civil war would be unnecessary. Careful not to overlook the obvious fact that people of African descent had arrived in the country through brutal force, he also acknowledged slavery as "the greatest wrong inflicted on any people."[34] He believed that black people should live where they "are treated best" and argued that it is better for both races "to be separated." Lincoln further stated, "You may believe you can live in Washington or elsewhere in the United States the remainder of your life, perhaps more so than you can in any foreign country, and hence you may come to the conclusion that you have nothing to do with the idea of going to a foreign country. This is (I speak in no unkind sense) an extremely selfish view of the case."[35] Lincoln tried to convince the delegation that the greatest service to black people, particularly those new to freedom, involved relocation to a place free from white prejudice. This was an attempt to appeal to their leadership and influence among black Washingtonians. He further explained the appeal of Chiriqui, a place rich with natural coal deposits that black people could extract to generate profit from exports. He also emphasized the strategic location of the colony and duly noted that Central America was close to the North American mainland, unlike Liberia. With Lincoln's strong endorsement of the scheme, Congress appropriated $600,000 toward colonization. Black leaders such as Henry McNeal Turner, Joseph E. Williams, and delegate Edward Thomas supported the idea and encouraged black people to remain open to the possibility.[36] Such support represented one of many expressions of black desires for independence and self-determination. The majority of black Washingtonians, however, remained hopeful that liberty on American soil might appear on the horizon.[37]

Emancipation symbolized an important victory for black Washington, as well as white abolitionists, but it was clear that Congress and the president encouraged their exodus. Although such colonization efforts had gained some traction before the war, the government could not convince a critical mass to emigrate outside the country after emancipation, nor could it convince white people to affirm the idea of black equality and citizenship on American soil.[38] As historian Martha Jones has argued, African Americans articulated visions of birthright citizenship long before the outbreak of war, and refugee women and freedwomen asserted their right to remain in the District when emancipation took effect.[39] They did not see themselves as citizens of a foreign land. Their labors, struggles, and loyalties had fostered a sense of belonging in North America.

Realizing liberty in the United States, however, was no easy feat for African American women. Legal reform would be necessary for emancipation to be effective in releasing black women, children, and men from the tyranny of slavery.[40] Even with emancipation, black codes still limited the scope of liberty at the beginning of the war. Republican senator Henry Wilson, for instance, understood the legislative loopholes that could keep free black people bound. As former chair of the 1852 Free Soil Convention, and a long-standing proponent of abolitionism, Wilson submitted a proposal, just weeks after the passage of the Emancipation Act of Washington, D.C., to eliminate the black codes. By way of background, Wilson, along with Senator James Grimes and the Committee on the District of Columbia, had produced a report on the conditions of "degradation and inhumanity" that African Americans faced in the Washington jail.[41] The concomitant discussions concerning the abhorrent treatment of enslaved and free black people led to further deliberation over the root of these injustices, which included the black codes and the Fugitive Slave Act of 1850. Wilson then submitted a proposal on May 22, 1862, stating, among other things, that "all persons of color . . . shall be subject and amenable to the same laws and ordinances to which free white persons are."[42] The subsequent repeal of the black codes ended a system of surveillance and control that had circumscribed the lives of African Americans since the inception of the nation's capital.[43] The measure served a vital function in the emancipation process—but white locals would not relent so easily.

The actions of African American women catalyzed the social transformation that came with the war, particularly when wartime policies proved difficult to realize.[44] Indeed, emancipation exposed the remaining strength of the multilayered regime of slavery and the correlating racial hierarchy. Evidence of defiant slaveholders who resisted their former slaves' claims to legal freedom shows that white contempt stifled the emancipation process initiated by enslaved people and the government. The value of whiteness as a social category and race as a mechanism for labor organization raised the stakes for white locals, slaveholders and nonslaveholders alike.[45] During the Civil War, reports surfaced of white hostility, abuse, manipulation, and disregard for the law.

Navigation was complicated by what the legislation left unclear. How could enslaved women appeal to the court or testify against slaveholders under this new regime? The logistical issues presented by resistance to the Emancipation Act led to the Supplemental Act of July 12, 1862, which set forth the terms under which enslaved women claimed free status even in instances in which a former owner refused to apply for compensation. The Supplemental Act stated, moreover, "in all judicial proceedings in the District of Columbia there shall be no exclusion of any witness on account of color."[46] This stipulation, which permitted enslaved people and refugees to testify against white people, was the distinctive feature of the Supplemental Act. Slave testimony would be critical in the efforts of black women and men to counter white arguments that they were not residents of the District, or that they had unlawfully claimed entitlement to the terms of the act. For the first time in the history of the nation's capital, enslaved women could exert individual legal agency in their own self-defense—they could testify against white men and women.[47] The testimony of enslaved women offered a critical avenue to freedom and also provided them expanded possibilities of self-making. Navigation of the laws of the District could now include their own voices. These new legal measures, however, clashed with existing laws in surrounding counties.

The Fugitive Slave Act of 1850 complicated the emancipation process, particularly for enslaved women who were hired out in the District by Maryland planters or for those who escaped from loyal slaveholding states. The law stipulated that fugitives must be returned and that penalties should be imposed on officials and locals who refused to return them. Therefore, while thousands of enslaved women made their way to the District from loyal slaveholding states like Maryland and Delaware, they claimed freedom illegally. Even after local emancipation and the abolishment of the black codes, the courts in Washington, D.C., enforced fugitive slave laws on behalf of owners residing in states that professed loyalty to the Union.[48] White supremacy was not antithetical to the aims of the Union—secession was. Competing legal priorities made navigation complicated for enslaved women.

Some women managed to evade fugitive slave laws with the assistance of military officials acting pursuant to the Second Confiscation Act of 1862. The Second Confiscation Act freed rebel-owned enslaved people as an "act to suppress insurrection, to punish Treason and Rebellion, to seize and confiscate the Property of Rebels."[49] Essentially, while the First Confiscation Act had only freed those employed to assist with the Confederate effort, the Second Confiscation Act freed the enslaved people of all disloyal slaveholders.[50] These wartime measures brought nearly forty thousand refugees into the nation's capital.[51] Although the acts affected the economic and labor productivity of the Confederacy, particularly as refugees arrived from the states closest to battle lines, they did not legalize the freedom of those who traveled from loyal slaveholding states, where a number of enslaved women came from.

Just as the system of racial slavery was built on a multifaceted legal framework, emancipation was multilayered. Family networks figured prominently in recorded appeals for freedom in Washington as black women and men sought to locate and reunite themselves with missing or abducted relatives.[52] When the superintendent of contrabands at Camp Barker gave testimony before the American Freedmen's Inquiry Commission, he stated that, as a general rule, refugees "wish and seek to preserve family ties renewing again their relations as parents, children, husband and wife whenever they are able."[53] These family ties were threatened not only by the system of slavery but also by the war itself. Many women were left alone with as many as seven children to clothe and feed while their husbands worked for the military or federal government. While most of these women sought employment to support their families, they wrestled with starvation, inclement weather, and disease. Indeed, when their husbands were not paid adequate wages or died during the war, women and children were subject to the most abject living conditions of the city.[54] The labor arrangements proved the most threatening to white economic interests. Enslaved and free women persistently submitted their grievances, complaining of legal entanglements with manipulative white locals who attempted to evade the terms of emancipation.

On March 28, 1862, Emeline Brown, a free black woman, submitted a petition for a writ of habeas corpus to the Circuit of Court of the District of Columbia, asserting that her daughter, Lucy Brown, was "uniquely and illegally detained and held in custody and keeping by one Benjamin J. Hunt of Georgetown."[55] Twelve-year-old Lucy was "hired out" to Hunt before the petition, but Emeline argued that "said child Lucy is maltreated." Emeline requested that the court grant her a habeas petition "directed to and commanding the said Benjamin J. Hunt, to be and appear" before the court. Her petition, however, was denied—the court did not order Hunt's appearance or Lucy's release. As a result, Lucy continued working for Hunt without the protection of the law to shield her from his abuse. Eight months later, after the passage of the Emancipation Act of April 1862, Lucy's father, John Brown, a newly freed man, submitted a petition arguing that he was her "natural guardian and protector." This petition was deemed valid and Hunt was mandated to release and return Lucy to her parents.

Emeline's appeal to free her child from Benjamin Hunt's cruelty was one of many cases involving the legally sanctioned mistreatment of free black women and girls in wartime Washington. Emeline's free status could do little to save her daughter from abuse, but with the help of the Emancipation Act of 1862, and the petition initiated by Lucy's father, the parents secured Lucy's release. Liberty during the era of emancipation often demanded that African Americans subscribe to patriarchal familial arrangements. Indeed, this structure, in some instances, legitimized their legal claims.[56] Emeline Brown initiated the case, which might offer insights into whether their family structure reflected these norms, but the petition of the father secured Lucy's release. Moreover, the parents' case quite possibly gained traction because of the

Emancipation Act. Nevertheless, legal transformations and the patriarchal authority of freedmen quite possibly factored into the decision in any given instance. These factors were not fixed but applied to the degree that authorities were compelled to observe them. Localized law or customs often prevailed in favor of white interests, but in this instance the persistence of the petitioners and the mounting pressure of wartime emancipation led to Lucy's release.[57]

The blurred boundaries of the District and the complex ties locals held with the surrounding Chesapeake states surfaced in another petition. On May 29, 1862, just after the passage of the Emancipation Act, an enslaved girl named Maria Diggs submitted a petition for her freedom. Although the slaveholder had applied for compensation for Diggs's mother and father, who resided with him in the District, he declared that Diggs was "not freed by the act." He argued that because Diggs had been hired out to a man just outside the District, the new law did not apply to her. While scholars have argued that the hiring-out system of enslavement undermined slavery, in this case, it preserved the institution by drawing on its Chesapeake origins. The commissioners opined that "all who were out of the District when the bill was approved, do not come within its provisions—are consequently slaves still." Thus, Diggs was not as fortunate as Emeline Wedge. Because of the hiring-out system, Diggs's owner not only received compensation for her parents but also found a way to invalidate her claims to freedom. The former slaveholder still held the reins— his property rights were protected accordingly.[58]

While over nine hundred slaveholders received compensation for local emancipation, this incentive only applied to those who resided in the District. The Emancipation Proclamation, issued on January 1, 1863, declared that all slaves within the Confederacy "are, and henceforward shall be free."[59] The proclamation notably authorized the enlistment of black soldiers, a measure the government hoped would enhance the prospects for liberty for them and their families. Military service provided a regular, albeit unfair, salary that could help support women and children back home. Women too served the Union army as camp laborers, nurses, cooks, and seamstresses.[60] For those slave owners in the surrounding counties who were subsequently forced to release their slaves in accordance with the Emancipation Proclamation, no analogous provision for compensation existed. Thus, resistance appeared more pronounced as enslaved women fled the homes and plantations of slaveholders. Unwilling to surrender the people who augmented their labor force in a war-ravaged landscape, slaveholders defiantly resisted these new laws and the ways they empowered enslaved women to take their families and leave. In-

deed, slaveholders of the seceded states did not see themselves as account-
able to these laws; instead, they believed they were only governed by the laws
of the Confederacy, which affirmed their right to slave ownership and referred to slaves behind Union lines as "runaways." Black women, however,
fought tirelessly to release themselves and their relatives from the strangle-
hold of slavery.

Emancipation-era self-making could not completely erase the racial and
gendered injustices that prevailed throughout the Civil War, nor the rampant
effects of poverty that kept freedwomen subject to hunger, disease, and inad-
equate living conditions. Childcare posed tremendous challenges to black
women's efforts to secure employment. Furthermore, black women earned
the lowest wages and often found themselves in dire circumstances as they
tried to feed and clothe their children.[61] Josephine Griffing, an agent of the
National Freedman's Relief Association, wrote to the secretary of war about
her encounters with the deplorable condition in which black women and
children lived in the District. After delivering wood to "over one hundred families," she discovered that many families composed of women and children
were "without food of any description." Griffing was confounded when she
saw mothers "confined with infants with four, six, and seven children in their
care—their Husbands either in Gov't Service or dead."[62] Facing limited flexibility in terms of childcare, coupled with the low probability of making enough
income, freedwomen attempting to survive in the nation's capital had tremendous odds stacked against them.[63]

Some freedwomen traveled to "contraband camps" to navigate the trials of
free life and the demands of survival. Camps appeared at Duff Green's Row
right near the Capitol, and Mason's Island or Analostan Island (currently
Roosevelt Island), where the First U.S. Colored Troops trained in 1863. Freedman's Village on Robert E. Lee's confiscated estate in Arlington, Virginia,
housed approximately 1,500 former slaves in one hundred family homes. The
village was known for the rather large population of women, children, and el-
ders frequently depicted as "dependents" and not citizens of the government.[64]
Dependence, as a term, carried connotations that were antithetical to ideas
about liberty and citizenship, and refugees were regarded as a burden despite
the circumstances in which they became free. The community's members,
however, cultivated gardens, earned wages, built homes, sewed clothing, and
built a school for children.[65] When offered a refuge from violence and exploitation, many freedpeople made plans to work and develop land for themselves
and their families. Government officials envisioned the camp as a temporary
community and hoped to make employment arrangements with white

families in need of additional labor in the North. Residents in the village, by contrast, felt that they had created sustainable living conditions that allowed them to experience the privileges of citizenship. Just across the Potomac between Twelfth and Q Streets, Camp Barker appeared comparatively different from Freedman's Village; it looked more like a "tent city," and it had higher mortality rates and unsanitary living conditions. In 1864, when officials decided to move residents of Camp Barker to Freedman's Village, only 120 agreed to move, while the remaining 685 refused to set foot on the slaveholding territory.[66]

Charged anywhere between five and eight dollars per month for damp and cold shacks exposed to the inclement winters in the District, black women during the war found it difficult to earn a sufficient living and keep themselves and their families healthy. Many black children lost both parents during the war and were forced to rely on overcrowded orphanages or their closest relatives as they fought to survive. Their struggle for survival often ended in death. In 1864, as officials evicted freedpeople from Camp Barker, one grandmother was forced to leave the premises as her grandson was dying beside her. According to reports, "The grandmother who had taken care of it [the grandson] since its mothers death begged leave to stay until the child died, but she was refused."[67] Camp Barker—a "contraband" camp organized by the government to house and employ refugees who escaped from Confederate territory—thus served as an outpost not only of freedom but also of frailty. For instance, Georgiana Willets, a missionary who worked at Camp Barker, observed in 1864, "There is now some suffering but it is chiefly amongst the women who have small children—These can barely obtain the necessaries of life."[68] The traumas of war exposed black women, in particular, to precarious conditions as many of them were charged with caring for young and elderly kin. As in many wars, women in poverty and particularly black women were also vulnerable to sexual violence. Their treatment at times reflected the views shaped by a country that rendered black women's bodies as chattel, degraded, and disposable.[69] In the aftermath of wartime emancipation policies, refugees flocked to Union lines searching for asylum and opportunities to reclaim families and find work in sustainable communities built by freedmen and freedwomen. Contraband camps functioned as military intermediaries of the Union government that provided much-needed assistance but also subjected refugee women to conditions similar to those of slavery. Contraband camps could be saturated with habits and customs that merely reminded black women that, for the moment, emancipation remained incomplete. The story of one black woman, Lucy Ellen Johnson, is illuminating.

Upon her arrival at Camp Barker, Johnson understood that she was sup-posed to work in the camp and "earn [her] food and clothing like other con-trabands." She moved into the camp with her mother while her husband worked for the Union army. In fact, before her arrival, she worked as a cham-bermaid on the steamboat *Zephyr*, showing a history of and eagerness to work. Shortly after arriving at Camp Barker, however, Johnson became ill and was unable to perform her duties. When she asked for rations, a blanket, and clothing, she was interrogated by Mr. Nichols, the official at Camp Barker who distributed supplies. Nichols could not understand why Johnson's hus-band had not provided for her, but Johnson pleaded, "I am here to earn my board and the same clothes that others have." She offered to request money from her husband so that she could pay for the needed items, but Nichols re-sponded, "You can't buy them from me—you can't have anything." Nichols clearly despised Johnson and resented what he perceived as her "dependence" on the government. Johnson argued that if her arrangements at the camp were problematic, then Nichols should have spoken to her husband about the matter so that she could find work elsewhere. Nichols became angry and ordered Johnson to a room where she was pinned down and harassed by a corporal, a sergeant, and soldiers. The gang of men took her to a tent, where they kicked her and grabbed her by the throat. She reported, "They fastened a rope round my two thumbs and passing it over the limb of a tree raised me from the ground so that my weight was suspended by the thumbs." To pro-long the torture, they adjusted the rope and hung her by her wrists. "In this position," Johnson recalled, "one kicked me—another choked my throat—another stuffed dirty wool in my mouth." After a half hour of torture, she was finally released.[70]

According to one assessment, fifty people filed testimonies regarding the abusive treatment of freedpeople at Camp Barker.[71] Stories like those of Johnson are vivid reminders of the violent undercurrents of white contempt during the moment of legal emancipation. This contempt for refugee women who migrated to the nation's capital manifested itself in a variety of forms, ranging from abuse in contraband camps to local mob violence in the city.[72] The laws that abolished slavery and black codes inspired galvanized resis-tance from slaveholders and soldiers in both the Union and the Confederacy. The possibilities for violence and hostility were not foreclosed by the mere fact of the existence of contraband camps or the legal transformations initi-ated by the government. And the fact that refugee women made it to Union lines did not guarantee support from military and government officials. Many of their experiences were informed by the temperament and attitudes of those in a position to wield the power of the federal government. As Johnson's story tells us, legislation alone could not secure liberty and protection for African American women.

Reaching Union lines came with its own challenges, and refugee women who escaped Confederate territory did not simply do so because the Emancipation Proclamation allowed it. Instead, they charted hazardous terrain, evaded detection by Confederate troops, and fought nearby residents willing to expose them.[73] Wartime emancipation sparked a violent backlash across regional boundaries from those who maintained the view that African Americans burdened the nation and should by every means be returned to slavery or relegated to second-class citizenship. During the war and toward its end, Maryland remained a point of contention for refugee women and slaveholders, even after the state adopted a new constitution banning the practice of slavery.

On November 14, 1864, just days before Article 24 of Maryland's new constitution, which made slavery illegal, took effect, Harriet Anne Maria Banks sent a letter testifying, "[Dr. S. S. Hughes, her owner] treated me badly & this was my principal object in leaving they informed me that Abraham Lincoln could not free me that he had no right to do so."[74] Along with slavery, much of the Maryland black codes were no longer in effect, but the constitution did make leaving an employer a punishable crime for black Marylanders alone.[75] Formerly enslaved women struggled against planter resistance to realize liberty not only for themselves but for their children as well. Countless cases of child abduction emerged after the war as southerners made efforts to reconstitute their labor force. Thus, a provision intended to inaugurate a free labor system in Maryland actually catalyzed a corrupt system of child abduction, labor exploitation, and rejection of the parental rights of black mothers and fathers.

The apprenticeship system in Maryland arose as a convoluted collaboration between former slave owners and local justices committed to the order of the old South. The provost marshal of the District of Maryland, Andrew Stafford, observed that, just four days after the adoption of the new constitution, "a rush was made to the Orphan's Court of this County, for the purpose of having all children under twenty-one years of age, bound to their former owners, under the apprentice law of the State."[76] These apprenticeship arrangements were validated by local judges, who typically decided in favor of the former master and determined that black parents were unfit to financially provide for their child, particularly when the father was away at work or war and could not claim the child's labor. In Maryland, decisions of the court reflected a racial and gendered hierarchy that prioritized the interests of whites first, then occasionally, if at all, black men as the head of the household, before those of black mothers.[77] Reminiscent of the plantation, the courts too often reinforced white power and paternalism to decide the fate of black families.

In the absence of testimony from parents and guardians, orphans' courts enacted judgments that supported apprenticeship. The judges administered parental authority as parents searched for children, attempted to claim guardianship rights, or faced threats and intimidation from former owners. Although the labors of all household members were critical to the subsistence of families during the nineteenth century, local justices in the orphans' court often refused to acknowledge the rights of black parents to protect the labor of their children. In many instances, slaveholders hoped to entice parents to remain on farms by withholding children. As a result, black women sometimes took matters into their own hands in order to retrieve their children from the grips of planter exploitation and create a life where their families could enjoy the fruits of their own labors. Jane Kamper, a former bondwoman who belonged to William Townsend of Talbot County, Maryland, reportedly told Townsend that she had become free, and she testified, "[I] desired my master to give my children and my bedclothes he told me that I was free but that my Children Should be bound to me [him]." She testified further, "He locked my Children up so that I could not find them. I afterwards got my children by stealth & brought them to Baltimore." Kamper, like many other freedwomen, risked her life to save her children "by stealth" from unconsented apprenticeship. She concluded her statement by saying, "My Master pursued me to the Boat to get possession of my children but I hid them on the boat."[78] As Kamper's story reveals, the Union government made the freedom of black women and children lawful, but not always tangible. Even upon assuming freedom rights gained from the war, black women continued the work of resituating their relationship with the government and the communities in which they lived.

Freedwomen navigated the geopolitical terrain as strategically as possible to avoid any manipulative slaveholders or even exploitative work conditions in the North. The path to liberty and self-making could be isolating in the absence of trustworthy allies. In the capital, the assistance of kin and exposure to community resources found in churches, schools, and relief organizations supported the transition from slavery. For countless others, however, the District was a strange, overcrowded place that paled in view of their expectations of freedom and government support. Founded in 1865, the Bureau of Refugees, Freedmen, and Abandoned Lands, known as the Freedmen's Bureau, employed commissioners who commenced the complicated work of connecting bondpeople to family members, jobs, and homes, in the case of orphans. John Eaton worked as the assistant commissioner for the District of Columbia.[79] In a letter sent to a military captain, Eaton instructed him to visit freedpeople "for the purpose of ascertaining the condition of labor, finding where more laborers are demanded and giving those now idle about this city an opportunity to support themselves, free from the vices and diseases which are likely to arise from inhabiting abodes of filth and spending their time in idleness."[80] The bureau divided the capital into districts led by a corps of northern volunteers composed mostly of women and bureau agents working for the commissioner. Their duties required them to "investigate all cases of destitution" and to provide "food, clothing, medicines, and medical attention."[81] The bureau sent three investigators to Georgetown and fourteen were placed in Washington. In addition to visiting the families in the city, the bureau arranged for roughly 150 women to attend industrial schools throughout the country for work and education.[82] General Oliver Otis Howard, commissioner of the Freedmen's Bureau, charged Eaton, and other assistant commissioners appointed to posts throughout the South, with the tremendous task of serving as a liaison between the federal government and the people. In fact, what makes this moment in the history of the nation's capital so exceptional is the direct involvement of the federal government in the affairs of former bondpeople and slaveholders, and the role of black women in this process.[83]

Assistant commissioners carried out a number of orders that often varied on a case-by-case basis. Black women at times corresponded with sympathetic bureau officials and at times dealt with those less helpful and even resentful.[84] Among many responsibilities, agents mediated conflicts, answered letters of inquiries about family members, addressed labor disputes, and supervised the placement of refugee women in jobs and homes. Eaton sent agents into local counties to secure employment prospects for freedwomen and girls. Black girls were particularly in demand for jobs as domestic servants, where duties included cooking, cleaning, washing, nursing, and serving as an attendant for women and children.[85] For black women unfamiliar with the interregional communities and urban enclaves of the capital, Eaton functioned as a key correspondent who attempted to search for answers to their queries. A large part of Eaton's job involved overseeing the expenditures and development of freedmen's camps in the District.

By the end of the war, refugees in contraband camps were either placed in jobs or relocated to Freedman's Village in Arlington and Barry Farms near

Anacostia. At Freedman's Village, former fugitive and abolitionist Harriet Jacobs supported the refugees in their transition to freedom and established a school. She wrote and published her own account of life as "a slave girl" and now she remarked, "The good God has prepared me for this work." In an article, she recounted that she discovered "men, women and children all huddled together, without any distinction or regard to age or sex. Some of them were in the most pitiable condition."[86] Refugee women found a capital rife with poor living conditions, limited access to food, and diseases that abounded in the enclaves they inhabited. Jacobs explained that "many were sick with measles, diphtheria, scarlet and typhoid fever," and some only had "filthy rags to lie on; others had nothing but the bare floor for a couch." After refugee women made the onerous trek to the capital, liberty came with its own bleak realities upon their arrival to the city. Locals feared that Washington would become an "asylum" for formerly enslaved people, but over time, their growing presence became a regular feature of wartime Washington. Jacobs noted that "each day brings its fresh additions of the hungry, naked, and sick," and "there they lie, in the filthy rags they wore from the plantation. Nobody seems to give it a thought. It is an everyday occurrence, and the scenes have become familiar." The aged and infirm were moved to the hospital and the government-subsidized land made available to freedpeople in Freedman's Village.

Residents paid a percentage of rent and raised funds to build a community school. Named after Harriet Jacobs, the building of the Jacobs School was a tremendous feat given the extreme conditions of poverty the freedpeople were subjected to. To capture their progress, Jacobs arranged for a photograph to be taken in front of the school. The *Freedmen's Record* observed, "It is delightful to see this group of neatly dressed children, of all ages, and with faces of every variety of the African and mixed type, all intelligent, eager, and happy."[87] Northern reformers described school operations as "diligent and efficient," a place of black improvement. Why did Jacobs arrange this photo shoot? The transition from slavery involved a new way of socializing children and a sense of self-making shaped by the norms of freedpeople's new wartime and postwar communities. Jacobs, having experienced a similar transition, understood this and addressed the kinds of assumptions people made about former slaves. The photograph served as an emblem of the ways that black women activists and teachers institutionalized self-making in the era of emancipation. Jacobs explained, "Some of them have been so degraded by slavery that they do not know the usages of civilized life."[88] Forced to labor and live according to the interests of slaveholders, she cautioned northerners, "Have patience with them. You have helped to make them what they are;

teach them civilization. You owe it to them, and you will find them as apt to learn as any other people that come to you stupid from oppression." The tinge of condescension in her statement appears in the reflections of other prominent black women at the time. Elizabeth Keckly, a former bondwoman who became a prominent seamstress for Mary Todd Lincoln, echoed similar sentiments. In her observations, she noted that "dependence had become a part of their second nature, and independence brought with it the cares and vexations of poverty."[89] Interestingly, the autobiographies of black women emphasized their own rise to prominence through self-making but never characterized the transition from slavery as one imbued with ignorance or dependence. Perhaps the stark contrasts made in these statements, or even the photograph, served to emphasize the tremendous odds over which children such as those in the photograph prevailed. The image portrayed the future of "worthy black citizens" who embodied order, intelligence, and self-determination. These characteristics underscored nineteenth-century ideas about civic virtue that offered a contrast with Jacobs's earlier findings about life as a "contraband." Having understood this, however, Jacobs used this photograph to deploy a visual articulation of the potential for full black inclusion into American society.[90] These children represented the beginnings of emancipatory self-making. Such images inspired hope in the midst of the displacement, poverty, and desperation that shaped the experiences of those struggling in the capital. These were complicated transitions made even more difficult in the absence of loved ones.

Agents of the Freedmen's Bureau assisted with locating information about the whereabouts and welfare of family members.[91] For black women, correspondence with John Eaton could provide much-needed answers concerning the whereabouts of kin. During the war, Lieutenant Colonel Elias M. Green, the chief quartermaster of the Department of Washington, secured employment for refugees arriving in the capital. This task often involved placing children in the homes of strangers. Freedom proved to be an isolating experience for young black girls and boys after the war. Those who made it to the capital were either hired out nearby or sent from Washington to cities such as Baltimore, Philadelphia, and New York. Eaton wrote to a woman who hired a young girl named Isabella. Isabella's relatives contacted the assistant commissioner to learn of her residence and to reach her at her new place of employment.[92] In another letter addressed to a lawyer in Philadelphia, Eaton inquired about a young girl named Cornelia Robertson who had been hired to work for him. Eaton noted that her family expressed concern about her where-

abouts and wanted to make contact with her.[93] The bureau made arrangements to send black girls, in particular, to northern cities to work as domestic
servants. In many cases, they were preferable to immigrant laborers and were
regarded as more appealing sources of labor.[94] The idea of black women and
girls as choice labor for domestic work found its origins in the perceptions of
southern wealth and class. The bureau agents saw an opportunity in sending
girls to the North, and many willingly employed them despite objections
from parents. The letters went beyond inquiries; in many instances, mothers
and fathers hoped to use the correspondence to authorize the retrieval of
children.

Liberty for freedwomen meant recognition of their legal guardianship
over their children—a novel concept after years of chattel slavery. By the end
of the war, children found themselves separated from loved ones and familiar
surroundings and thrown into labor arrangements without the consent of
parents. White locals as well as agents at times questioned the parenting abilities of black mothers, which further complicated their efforts to claim their
children.[95] Catherine Green's children James and Charlotte worked on separate farms in southeast Virginia.[96] She requested that Eaton write to the
people who hired them and demonstrate that she possessed the legal authority to secure her children. Similarly, Susannah Johnson reached Eaton in
search of her ten-year-old daughter, Phillis. In a letter to Betty DeVaughn, Eaton stipulated that, since Phillis was not legally bound with the consent of her
mother, in a possible case of "violence or resistance," "Susannah Johnson is
authorized to call upon the nearest military authorities for assistance."[97] Just
a few days later, Eaton sent another letter to DeVaughn, requesting the release
of a seven-year-old boy named Jackson. Jackson's mother, Adeline, had asked
Eaton for assistance in securing her son from DeVaughn's home.[98] Women
like DeVaughn, however, did not relent so easily to the requests of the assistant commissioners.[99] The following month, Eaton sent another letter with
the same request, stating, "We deem it our duty to do all that we can legally to
reunite families, that were separated under the old system of slavery."[100]

The customs of the "old system of slavery" proved hard to break in the region.
Even with assistance from the Freedmen's Bureau, the resistance of former slaveholders appeared regularly in correspondence. Patsey Berlin attempted to recover her mother and her four sisters from a Mr. Garnett near Fredericksburg,
Virginia. Berlin noted that Garnett starved them and that "they are working for
this Garnett, their former owner without compensation."[101] Eaton sent correspondence to Fredericksburg stating, "I would respectfully recommend

that this statement, as made by the colored woman, be referred to the Officer in charge of the district for investigation for the correction of any abuses."[102] While the treatment of former slaveholders remained unchanged, the assistant commissioner's willingness to intervene and prioritize the testimony of a black woman demonstrates that freedwomen initiated a transformation in their relationship with the government. In order for liberty to translate in the lives of freedwomen, they had to articulate their preferred terms of labor for themselves and their families and wield authorization given by officials like Eaton. They were engaged in both personal and political processes of self-making.

The black women who sent letters to Eaton applied gender norms in their appeals to the federal government. For them, liberty implied the obligations of the government to the citizens, and particularly those who subscribed to acceptable gender norms to secure that liberty. Black women entreated officials to intervene when the realities of their lives and their loved ones conflicted with the tenets of liberty and the entitlements of independent households. One woman, Mary, requested that Eaton write on her behalf as she retrieved her daughter Mary Agnes from Maryland. In the letter, he stipulated, "She acts with the advise [sic] and consent of her husband, the father of the said Mary Agnes, and so has full authority to bring her daughter home. No person or persons will interfere with her lawful acts for this purpose, and any Officers of the army she may be so situated as to aid her."[103] Agnes called on the hierarchies of patriarchy to reinforce her claims to her daughter, since Eaton made reference to the consent of her husband to authorize the retrieval. Furthermore, the presence of the military provided another motivation to enforce compliance with the order.

Black women in the capital approached Eaton with an expectation of advocacy and endorsement in the event of disputes. Amelia Hanson contacted the bureau to seek help retrieving her two sons, Charles and Israel. Should the former slaveholder resist her claims to her children, Eaton indicated that "Amelia is authorized to call upon the nearest military authorities for assistance."[104] In another case, Sophia Smith requested assistance with securing her children from a Mrs. Lucinda Dodson. Eaton wrote to Dodson that because she refused "to allow them to come to her [Smith]," "said Sophia Smith is authorized to call upon the nearest military authority for assistance."[105] Similarly, Mary Queen, grandmother to twelve-year-old Kitty, complained that Charles Mills "refused to give the child up to her." Eaton made clear that he recognized Queen as the "rightful protector, as the father and

mother of the child are both dead."[106] Bureau and military officials functioned as federal liaisons in the transition to freedom as black women called
on their authority to recover loved ones from the grips of bondage. The correspondence reminds us that not every orphan was truly an orphan. Even as
children lost their parents, guardians and kin appealed to the bureau to intervene on their behalf.

Black women not only attempted to seek the release of loved ones from
planters who exploited the labors of kin; they also sought the discharge of
loved ones confined in jails and slave pens during the war.[107] Such a release
could take up to a year or two after the war ended. Dola Ann Jones petitioned
on behalf of John Jones, Richard Coats, and Caleb Day, black men who had
received convictions for aiding slaves in an escape that took place in 1863, the
same year that President Lincoln issued the Emancipation Proclamation.[108]
At the time, slavery still prevailed in the Union and free and enslaved black
people continued to disentangle themselves from the old legal regime. The
refugees likely came from Union territory, perhaps Maryland or Delaware,
since the police regularly housed fugitives in the city jail. Sentenced to eleven
years in prison, Dola Ann Jones, kin to John Jones, hoped to appeal to the
bureau for their release. Well after states legally recognized emancipation, the
convicted men had already served two years when Jones submitted the inquiry in 1865.

Eaton realized that these previous verdicts based on slave laws and black
codes posed a problem at the end of the war when slavery became illegal, except in instances of criminal convictions. He pleaded with the governors of
Maryland and Virginia to ensure that those confined for violation of the fugitive slave laws or any slave codes be granted pardon.[109] In the capital, he
wrote to President Andrew Johnson requesting a pardon for a thirteen-year-
old boy named Beverly McCall. McCall's mother, who "appears like an industrious intelligent colored woman of good character worthy and competent to
provide for her son," made Eaton aware of the two-year sentence in the peni-
tentiary.[110] The court had charged McCall with theft. Eaton learned that the
Union army had brought him to the capital from nearby Fredericksburg. In
his possession, McCall had held a breast pin valued at forty dollars. He was
condemned and "confined with hardened criminals," and the mother now
pleaded for her son's release. Eaton informed the president that he believed
McCall's mother could "train him to virtue and usefulness as a Citizen." Young
boys and girls, and women and men who ran into legal trouble throughout the
war, found themselves not only in the city jails but also in workhouses serving

long sentences or slave pens as late as the winter of 1866.[111] Black women in the region struggled to disentangle themselves and their kin from the racial oppression that slavery inspired well after emancipation.

Life in the capital presented an array of social and economic hurdles that underscored the barriers that freedwomen confronted in the era of emancipation. To begin, those new to the city struggled to secure employment free of exploitation. One report appeared of a man named Cissel who regularly approached freedpeople for the purpose of hiring them out to farms in Maryland. Described as an older man of medium size with gray hair, he was paid a hefty commission by planters for securing laborers in the neighboring counties. The planters deducted the commission from the wages the freedmen earned, leaving them little to nothing for their hard work. The bureau investigated this scheme and discovered the whole operation based at 501 New Jersey Avenue.[112] Freedpeople in the District faced vulnerabilities to exploitative work conditions, but the destitution that drove refugees into such labor arrangements proved even more menacing.

Countless letters arrived in local bureau offices reporting scores of families plagued with poverty, starvation, and disease. One bureau agent reported that several groups of refugees hired out to labor for wages arrived at the farms infected with smallpox and other infectious diseases.[113] Volunteers from the bureau set out to provide rations and investigate their condition further. Agents made their way to D, L, and U Streets, where black families had erected shanties between Tenth and Eleventh Streets.[114] The cramped makeshift homes proved far from sufficient in providing adequate shelter in the bitter cold of February in 1866. Communities of black families cramped in the alleys and rear of main thoroughfares experienced harsh conditions even as agents provided these neighborhoods with relief when provisions became available. Similarly, the Kyle family, huddled on Virginia Avenue between First and Second Streets, was found in destitute condition at the beginning of winter.[115] Even those who resided in the District before the war found their resources depleted by wartime conditions. Mary Johnson, born a free black woman in the capital, lived on F Street.[116] Bureau agents found her living in destitution despite the fact that her husband worked for the Union military. In this particular instance, they set out to secure employment for her.

Without the assistance of local black activists, and black women in particular; northern philanthropy; and the intervention of the federal government, resources proved scarce in addressing poverty after the war. Reverend Henry McNeal Turner of Israel African Methodist Episcopal Church acknowledged, "It is female assistance which has given impetus to all reforming enterprises, and redeeming deeds."[117] The mayor of Washington reportedly made no organized effort to address poverty in the city, and as a result, "the different churches are dispensing from voluntary contributions, necessary aid, in all cases brought to their notice."[118] Black institutions such as churches and relief societies generated the momentum necessary for raising funds and collecting material goods that black families needed in the District. Black women founded a number of organizations available to refugee women.

Elizabeth Keckly organized the Contraband Relief Association with black women who attended Fifteenth Street Presbyterian Church. She felt inspired to take action upon "seeing and hearing of the sufferings of the contrabands who are sent to Washington," and she subsequently "proposed to some of her lady friends when returning from church one Sabbath day, the necessity of a contraband relief association."[119] Keckly explained, "The Contraband Relief Association was formed for the purpose, not only of relieving the wants of the destitute people, but also to sympathize with, and advise them." She made appeals in the black press and explained, "We need for them food, clothing, and money. We have now several invalid families of women and children under our care, for whose house-rent, fuel and medical attendance, we are obliged to expend money."[120] With the assistance of northern benefactors and prominent women such as Mary Todd Lincoln, Keckly reported, "We have visited and counseled them, and we have, as far as we have the ability, relieved their wants by giving them food, clothing, and medicine." There were a number of societies devoted to the aid and relief of refugees and freedpeople, many specifically devoted to women and girls.

The financial contributions of northern philanthropists made transportation and admission into industrial schools possible for young black girls. Congress approved the incorporation of the National Association for the Relief of Destitute Colored Women and Children. According to Eaton, they emphasized the "training for virtuous citizenship many outcast children."[121] The association focused on raising funds and providing basic necessities and instruction in moral improvement. Even as the government shut down bureau operations in 1872 and withdrew military support in former slaveholding states in the late 1870s, the National Association for the Relief of Destitute Colored Women and Children continued operations into the twentieth century. By the late nineteenth century, during the nadir of antiblack violence and repression, a vibrant social and political movement of black women's activism had appeared at the forefront of the nation's capital.[122] This activist tradition among black women in the District originated with the claims that enslaved and free black women made much earlier at the conception of the nation's capital.

Photograph of Elizabeth Keckly. Prints and Photographs, Moorland-Spingarn Research Center, Howard University.

From the very beginning, the processes of self-making led black women to imagine and, at various intervals, realize visions for liberty. Black women continued, well after the Civil War, to forge a social contract with the federal government.

The Union government altered the possibilities for liberty through legislation, but the refugee women in this chapter put those policies to the test before, during, and after the Civil War. The chances of becoming free were greater where the Union wielded authority and corresponding officials acted in accordance with the legal measures, but even under these circumstances, refugee and fugitive women were not shielded from abuse and violent backlash. Black women and men, as well as government officials, employed the term *citizen* to describe free African Americans and refugees at the moment of wartime emancipation.[123] Overstating this fact, however, wrongly suggests that all white Unionists extended to refugees an invitation to share equally in the rights of American citizenship. Republican support and military authorization of emancipation did not always translate in the lives of black women. White acceptance of emancipation was shaped by place, borders, and factors tied to local customs. Moreover, while some locals rejected slavery, they also resisted the notion of black equality just the same. Liberty came with a set of expectations articulated by freedwomen who made claims to their lives, labors, and families in ways that made them equal contenders for the legal protections afforded by the Union government. Thus, white Americans no longer possessed sole access to legal recourse and rights. The imperatives of liberty, for both black and white people, were at odds in that the property rights of one violated the liberty rights of another. Government officials too struggled with the adjustment that wartime policies called for. Just as lawmakers within the halls of Congress and the soldiers at Union camps observed the new radical measures that came with emancipation, they also employed terms such as *contraband* and *dependent* to describe the refugees they encountered—terms rhetorically antithetical to nineteenth-century ideas about citizenship.

The emphasis on the actions of Union authorities often obscures freedwomen's struggles to define the terms of their inclusion. The process of realizing and navigating liberty was more collaborative than patronizing. This doesn't mean that freedwomen didn't appeal to soldiers or federal authorities or even call on nineteenth-century gender norms. They strategically navigated a changing government and society to help make legislation a reality for themselves. Black women challenged the notion that liberty stopped at legal emancipation. Using tactics such as flight and appeals and petitions to the government, black women found kin, shelter, food, jobs, and support for survival. These were the strategies deployed to set up the foundations for self-making.

The actions of refugee women set in motion a dynamic that positioned black women to confront white resistance and appropriate various channels of recourse recognized by the government. While she initially lost her case, Emeline Brown petitioned the courts—months before the Emancipation Act passed—and ultimately saw her daughter freed with the help of her husband. Emeline Wedge, however, took her former owner to court less than six months after the Supplemental Act was passed and won her case on behalf of herself and her family. These cases reveal that enslaved women were central to their communities of kin in that they defended the rights of their loved ones even as they struggled for their own freedom. They created an ethos of redress by engaging rituals of liberty that became a feature of black women's wartime self-making. Jane Kamper, for instance, evaded the law and, "by stealth," fled from the grips of slave owners with children in tow. Just as lawmakers enacted important emancipation legislation, black women and men decided for themselves their own future in the country where they toiled, fought, and lived. The conditions of the war presented opportunities for refugee women to both imagine and act on new visions of themselves. This process was multilayered and complex, and it would take time for white residents of Washington, D.C., to be persuaded to treat black women fairly and humanely. The legalization of emancipation did not foreclose antiblack resistance, nor did it offer consistent recognition of liberty and rights. Emancipation was the culmination of a hope long deferred, and the beginning of an arduous path toward self-making in the face of countless obstacles. In Washington, black women discovered a government sorting out its commitment to liberty, and they decided for themselves and the ones closest to them that they would have a say in what it looked like.

Conclusion

Our lofty notions of democracy, egalitarianism, and individual freedom were articulated by the Founders, but they were consecrated by the thousands of slaves fleeing to Union lines.

—Ta-Nehisi Coates

We stumble upon her in exorbitant circumstances that yield no picture of the everyday life, no pathway to her thoughts, no glimpse of the vulnerability of her face or of what looking at such a face might demand.

—Saidiya Hartman

The stories of the women in this book do not fit into neat historiographical themes but show the rather complicated and unanticipated directions in which their lives took shape. This history of black women does not frame American liberty in exceptional terms but instead tells a story about the obstacles that come with the ways that slavery, race, and gender posed barriers to liberty and the manner in which black women in Washington responded. Self-making offers an interesting framework for exploring the lives of these women, not for reasons that emphasize triumph but rather for the ways they help us understand just how someone begins to live through slavery, the nation's founding, antebellum political upheaval, and wartime emancipation. Navigation for black women, then, hinged not on a desired end but rather on a continuum of decisions and efforts to sustain their imagined selves. Throughout this book, the impulse of readers might be for each woman to become completely free, and self-making offers an appealing framework from which to make a deterministic claim about liberty. But the reality is that these women learned to shape and reconstitute their ideas about liberty in ways that were constrained by the obstacles of their time and, for the historian, constrained by an imperfect archive. As Saidiya Hartman argues, the idea of self-making as a key feature of "democratic individuality" and the illusion of promises that come with being self-made in America are based on the fundamental premise of fairness in the structure of America's brand of democracy. She argues, "It was easier to recognize and correct the exclusion and inferiority written into slave law through formal measures like the Thirteenth Amendment than it was to remedy the disparities and inequalities that were the consequence of this former condition."[1] In other words, for these women, the abolishment of slavery from the nation's capital did not create a clean slate from which equality and self-making automatically emerged. And so, in this book, I have explored the lives of enslaved, manumitted, fugitive, free, and refugee women to show the foreclosures, fits and starts, and iterations of liberty from which black women imagined, survived, and gave meaning to life in nineteenth-century America.

These women, who included cooks, spiritual exhorters, enslaved laborers, teachers, and prostitutes, stole moments of joy, experienced their share of hardships and disappointments, and lived through the tumultuous events of the nineteenth century. The District of Columbia became a city where slaveholders hired, sold, and occasionally freed enslaved women, but it also became the place where African American women patronized religious institutions, built schools, cooked in homes, and launched their own businesses. They discovered ways of knowing and seeing themselves that appeared in what we know about their lives. For instance, Sukey Dean reconstituted her name and labor to discover a life outside Thomas Tingey's household. The Sukey who worked in Dolley Madison's house did not escape, but she reminded the first lady that she understood the value she added to the presidential household and expressed her frustrations when she reached her limits. Jane Johnson testified that she always wished to be free and, on a fateful evening in Philadelphia, found a way to defy the fugitive slave law. Mina Queen did not win her freedom suit, but her case reveals her knowledge of the legal loopholes that made the admissibility of hearsay evidence possible, as well as her own genealogical memory of her ancestry, a powerful archive of self-making through the generations. Eliza Crittenden ran a bawdy house while also providing a space of leisure for black women and men to play cards, drink libations, and socialize with discretion. Such black-owned enterprises were spaces of respite with radical implications in a city rife with slavery and black codes. Emeline Wedge made claims to freedom based on wartime emancipation laws in the District, becoming the first to successfully challenge her former owner in court on behalf of herself and members of her family. As Mary Brent, a student at the Miner School, reminds us, "Though men enslaved the body they cannot enslave the mind and prevent it from thinking."[2] These stories give us glimpses of women's imagined selves and help us understand how their presence shaped the history of the nation's capital.

From the onset, enslaved women worked intimately in the households and farms of white families in a city where enslaved people outnumbered free black people. After the revolution, a wave of manumissions shifted the demographic portrait of the Chesapeake to show growing numbers of free African Americans. The growth of the domestic slave trade funneled enslaved people out of the region, and the enslaved women who remained in the area were hired throughout the city. Some enslaved women were permitted to earn additional money selling goods and produce from their small gardens and assumed additional labor responsibilities through the hire system. Enslaved women used surplus earnings to purchase their freedom and even pay the purchase price of family members. In the first decades of the nineteenth century, slavery remained intact in the capital. When freedom suits were neither effective nor within reach, enslaved women escaped within the region into free communities of African Americans just as Sukey Dean did at the beginning of this book.

Fugitive women escaped intraregionally as well as beyond the region into the northern reaches of North America as far as Canada. While women were typically the least likely to escape, often because of familial obligations, enslaved women in Washington made attempts at flight both with and without kin. They employed networks composed of enslaved and free African Americans, churches, white allies, and vigilance networks outside the District to become free. In addition to these networks, these escapes reveal that black women acted on knowledge about geography, laws, and social customs in the region. Not all women successfully fled, nor did the majority of women escape, but their stories shed light on the ways that black women imagined themselves and their lives beyond slavery. The pathways to freedom were not linear and, for some, not within reach at all. The legal and extralegal activities associated with becoming free reveal the constraints and opportunities of pursuing liberty in the nation's capital.

Enslaved and free black women appeared before the local courts for a number of reasons that shed light on the strategies of self-making and improvisation that they employed. Women who filed suits against slave owners argued that they were unlawfully held in bondage. Some women landed in jail and court after an attempt to take their lives or the lives of loved ones upon learning that they were being sold farther south. Others petitioned the courts with freedom claims based on maternal lineage, but after the first decade of the nineteenth century, courts applied a stricter interpretation of hearsay evidence to verify the genealogy of black women. Once freed, some women barely found means to survive and stood before the courts on charges of theft and prostitution. Thus, even as black women became legally free, many of their challenges remained unmitigated without institutions built by African Americans to provide initial support and connections to job and housing prospects. Black residents established businesses, founded churches, and cultivated schools that became the center of black intellectual life in Washington.

By the 1850s, Washington boasted a rich tradition of literacy and education with the creation of schools that admitted black students. These schools were available to African American girls who gained the training necessary to establish their own institutions. As pupils, the black girls were engaged in intellectual, political, and spiritual processes of self-making. When they attended these schools, white mobs harassed and threatened them with physical violence and arson. The city's mayor published a tirade proposing that municipal officials take the necessary steps to close the schools for girls. Moreover, he argued that such schools posed a threat to the Union since they encouraged equality among the races and migration of free African Americans to the capital. The girls understood the implications of their education and what it might mean to be groomed to establish and lead future institutions. Their experiences underscore ways that schools for black girls institutionalized self-making through learning and the advancement of political ideas that prepared them for a life of uplift. Not all free black girls, however, were afforded an education, despite the efforts of educators who aimed to make schools available to as many as possible.

Survival in the capital meant that most black women and girls performed various types of labor that helped them cover the costs of food, housing, and clothing. These jobs brought them out into the streets as they searched for work as washerwomen, servants, cooks, seamstresses, nurses, and peddlers. The nexus between self-making and survival often meant juggling more than one job or creatively negotiating for better work conditions. Some women worked in the marketplace as entrepreneurs, selling goods, renting space, or selling sex in their efforts to pursue independent avenues for income. Women in the sex and leisure economy of the city capitalized on the mobilization of Washington's defenses and the federal employees drawn to the city for new jobs. The influx of soldiers, federal employees, and refugees raised the cost of living and contributed to the overcrowding and poverty that plagued the capital. Men earned relatively stable salaries away from home, and those funds went to prostitutes, proprietors of leisure, and the police for payment of services and fines. Black madams and prostitutes worked with white women and catered to white clients during the war. The sex and leisure economy became characteristically interracial until the end of the war, when efforts to restore order demanded adherence to racial and gender distinctions and order. Black women improvised in their use of space, with whom they chose to work, and in the changing racial dynamics of the wartime sex and leisure economy. The war marked an era when the racial and legal lines of demarcation for black women were temporarily blurred and yet profitable at a moment of tremendous transformation.

During the war, refugee women reached the boundaries of the District to claim kin, find jobs, and validate their new legal identities as free women. As legislators worked on a series of wartime measures to undo the legal framework of slavery and black codes, black women were also in search of opportunities to ensure that they became free. They petitioned local commissioners, appeared before the courts, and fled to contraband camps to separate themselves from slavery. In addition to realizing freedom, they hoped to authorize the release of their loved ones as area slaveholders adamantly refused to observe the new laws. Refugee women struggled to realize emancipation in their confrontations with slave owners who abducted family members, relocated to Maryland or Virginia, or contested the validity of emancipation and compensation all together. Throughout the course of the war, black women forged a dynamic relationship with the government as they combated both white resistance and violence and searched for family, housing, and jobs. Liberty remained a work in progress.

The experiences of African American women complicate Thomas Jefferson's definition of "rightful liberty," which allowed "unobstructed action according to our will within its limits drawn around us by the equal rights of others."[3] They wanted to be included among those who determined those limits, since Jefferson admittedly acknowledged, "I do not add 'within the limits of the law' because law is often but the tyrant's will, and always so when it violates the rights of the individual." African American women were well aware of the "tyrant's will," just as much as they were aware of liberty. The weight of the racial and gender framework of chattel slavery in early nineteenth-century life illumined the value and significance of liberty. When it appeared within the realm of possibility, they were reminded of it and all of their hopes for it even if they did not dare to dream that they'd ever see it. When African American women realized for themselves the new laws of freedom, they participated in the process of defining a new era of liberty. Liberty emerged somewhat within reach, however imperfect and unfinished the process. From the beginning of Washington history, black women actively sought liberty as they pursued the possibilities and impossibilities of self-making.

The experiences of black women offer insights into the ways that our assumptions prevent us from fully understanding the scope of liberty's reach and deficiencies. We risk forgetting that these women thought about this idea repeatedly even as they imagined, washed, cried, ironed, hummed, cooked, laughed, nursed, killed, and suffered. For centuries, a liberation struggle, spanning generations and reaching back before the country's founding, shaped the black American experience. The contagious yearning for liberty that shaped the hopes of millions did not simply appear because a government or society allowed it to. The tensions created by those deprived of it play an equally important role in manifestations of liberty. I started this book with the hopes of writing about black women and the Civil War. I looked at Freedmen's Bureau records, mined criminal and police records to locate extralegal activity, and kept reaching back further. Ultimately, the stories of these women helped me understand that the wartime moment was an important development along a broader continuum of liberty struggles. I knew this from my training in African American studies, but to see it unfold in the archive yielded more scholarly lessons. As historian Thavolia Glymph tells us, such an undertaking requires us to "rethink and rewrite the story of the price paid for Union, freedom, and citizenship."[4] We haven't fully comprehended the depths of black women's experiences and the stakes of producing knowledge about their lives. Such an undertaking requires new questions and frameworks, and a willingness to tell their histories.

Toward the end of my research, I began assembling a working list of illustrations I might include in the book. I came upon a stunning rendering of Alethia Browning Tanner. Breathless, I just stared at her portrait. She wore a dress with a neckline adorned in lace, and her hair was partially pinned up, with tendrils framing her face and cascading over her shoulder. She gazed outward with upright posture and her eyes looking ahead. Only rarely do those who research African American women from this period get to visualize the people they've spent years trying to understand. In that moment, I thought of all of the names included in this book and was reminded that I've only touched the surface of all there is to know about them. If the viewer did not know her story, she could appear as any elite woman in the early nineteenth century. Behind the moment in which she posed for that portrait lies a history of chattel slavery, a young woman with an enterprising ethos of independence who embodied the kind of generosity that made her one of the great benefactors of her time in the most symbolic city of the nation. I wondered if she ever looked at the likeness and whether she had always envisioned herself in this way in her imaginings of liberty. On the cover of this book is a photograph of Elizabeth Keckly, a formerly enslaved woman who purchased her freedom by designing gowns for elite white women. A young Keckly poses in a beautifully detailed and modestly cut gown with an ornate brooch pinned at the higher neckline of her dress. Her hair is parted down the middle and draped past her ears in the style that many elite women wore to showcase dangling earrings and a slender neck. She stands at a decorated chair partially covered in heavy drapery and her gaze is both direct and fierce. Keckly is a survivor who lived to tell the story of her self-imaginings. She moved to Washington, D.C., to begin a sewing school for black women and girls and opened her business preparing what designers today might refer to as couture, custom formal wear that involves painstaking detail and precision. She brought this knowledge of design and artistry that she cultivated over the years of her life to curate a reputation known throughout the nation's capital and throughout powerful political circles. She wrote a telling memoir of her experience, "Behind the Scenes," of life in the White House during the most tumultuous conflict in the nation's history.[5] But she was far from "behind" the scenes. This book allowed me to use the skills of a historian to place African American women at the forefront of our conversations about the history of the nation's capital. I've offered a starting point, but as the pictures of Tanner and Keckly remind us, much remains beneath the surface.

Notes

Introduction

1. Thomas Tingey, "Slave Owner Navy Yard Washington Reward [Runaway Slave]," *Daily National Intelligencer* (Washington, DC), August 16, 1821.

2. Margaret Tingey to Thomas Tingey, January 25, 1800, Commodore Thomas Tingey Research Collection, Historical Society of Washington, D.C.

3. Robinson, *Black Marxism*, xiii, 2, 9; Baptist, *Half Has Never*; Daina Ramey Berry, *Price for Their Pound*; Walter Johnson, *Soul by Soul*; Joshua D. Rothman, *Flush Times*; Schermerhorn, *Business of Slavery*.

4. Hartman, *Scenes of Subjection*, 152. See also Sharpe, *In the Wake*.

5. Costanzo, *George Washington's Washington*, 150, 186; Harrison, *Washington during Civil War*, 2–3.

6. James C. Scott, *Domination*, 200; Robin D. G. Kelley, *Race Rebels*, 6–7.

7. Here, freedom is treated as a legal status.

8. Berlin, *Slaves without Masters*, 86, 199.

9. Jennifer L. Morgan, *Laboring Women*, 10.

10. He subtitled his book, *The Underground Railroad, A Record of Facts, Authentic Narratives, Letters, &c., Narrating the Hardships, Hair-Breadth Escapes and Death Struggles of the Slaves in Their Efforts for Freedom, as Related by Themselves and Others, or Witnessed by the Author; Together with Sketches of Some of the Largest Stakeholders, and Most Liberal Aiders and Advisers of the Road*. For more on centering black abolitionists, see Jackson, *Force and Freedom*, 9.

11. Masur, *Example*; Harrison, *Washington during Civil War*; Ferguson, *Freedom Rising*; Asch and Musgrove, *Chocolate City*; Harrold, *Subversives*.

12. Constance McLaughlin Green, *Secret City*; Letitia Woods Brown, *Free Negroes*.

13. Takagi, *Rearing Wolves*; Rockman, *Scraping By*; Wade, *Slavery in the Cities*.

14. Baptist, *Half Has Never*; Daina Ramey Berry, *Price for Their Pound*; Walter Johnson, *Soul by Soul*.

15. Daina Ramey Berry, *Price for Their Pound*, 15.

16. Historians such as Daina Ramey Berry challenge us to rethink what we consider "skilled" and "unskilled" labor among enslaved women in particular. The gendered assessment of women's labor mirrored the patriarchal values of nineteenth-century society. See Berry, *"Swing the Sickle"*; and Jennifer L. Morgan, *Laboring Women*.

17. Alexander, *Ambiguous Lives*; Camp, *Closer to Freedom*; Glymph, *Out of the House*; Hine, *Hine Sight*; Hunter, *To 'Joy My Freedom*; Martha S. Jones, *All Bound Up Together*; Wilma King, *Essence of Liberty*; Lebsock, *Free Women of Petersburg*; Lindsey, *Colored No More*; Amrita Chakrabarti Myers, *Forging Freedom*; Schwalm, *Hard Fight for We*; Frankel, *Freedom's Women*.

18. Camp, *Closer to Freedom*; Glymph, *"Rose's War."*

19. Evelyn Brooks Higginbotham encourages us to look beyond singularity to the array of black women's experiences across class. See Higginbotham, "African-American Women's History," 255.

20. Hartman, "Venus in Two Acts," 11; Fuentes, *Dispossessed Lives*, 2, 16, 48.

21. Gordon-Reed, *Hemingses at Monticello*, 31. See also Fuentes, *Dispossessed Lives*, 144–46.

22. Baptist, *Half Has Never*; Daina Ramey Berry, *Price for Their Pound*; Pargas, *Quarters*.

23. Franklin and Schweninger, *Runaway Slaves*; Kaye, *Joining Places*, 147.

24. Letitia Woods Brown, *Free Negroes*, 14; Provine, "Economic Position."

25. Farmer-Kaiser, *Freedwomen*; Zip, *Labor of Innocents*.

26. Chandra Manning, "Emancipation as State Building from the Inside Out," in Blight and Downs, *Beyond Freedom*, 61–62; Edwards, "Epilogue: Emancipation and the Nation," in Link and Broomall, *Rethinking American Emancipation*.

27. Glymph, *Out of the House*, 100, 102, 146–48.

Chapter One

1. Daina Ramey Berry, *Price for Their Pound*; Jones-Rogers, "'[S]he Could'"; Camp, *Closer to Freedom*, 31–32; Amrita Chakrabarti Myers, *Forging Freedom*, 75, 85; Deborah Gray White, *Ar'n't I a Woman?*, 67, 113–14, 121.

2. Edmund S. Morgan, *American Slavery, American Freedom*.

3. Baptist, *Half Has Never*, xxii; Sven Beckert and Seth Rockman, introduction to Beckert and Rockman, *Slavery's Capitalism*, 6; Robinson, *Black Marxism*, 187; Jennifer L. Morgan, *Laboring Women*, 167; Schermerhorn, *Unrequited Toil*, 10; Eric Eustace Williams, *Capitalism and Slavery*, 210; Wright, *Slavery*, 30.

4. *Second Census of the United States, 1800*, M32 microfilm, National Archives and Records Administration, Washington, DC; An Act concerning the Territory of Columbia and the City of Washington, November 1791, chap. 45, 22; Wade, *Slavery in the Cities*, 119–24; Dunaway, *African-American Family*, 123.

5. Corrigan, "'Whether They Be,'" 170.

6. Corrigan, "Making the Most," 92, 99; Corrigan, "'Whether They Be,'" 173, 189.

7. Corrigan, "Making the Most," 92; Corrigan, "'Whether They Be,'" 170, 186.

8. Gordon-Reed, *Hemingses of Monticello*, 564.

9. Gordon-Reed, 569.

10. Gordon-Reed, 570.

11. Gordon-Reed, 572–73.

12. Gordon-Reed, 574.

13. Dickens, *American Notes*, 282.

14. Baptist, *Half Has Never*, 153; Daina Ramey Berry, *Price for Their Pound*, 12; Rashauna Johnson, *Slavery's Metropolis*, 56; Walter Johnson, *Soul by Soul*, 25; Joshua D. Rothman, *Flush Times*, 10; Schermerhorn, *Business of Slavery*, 36.

15. *National Intelligencer and Washington Advertiser*, June 24, 1803.

16. Arnebeck, *Slave Labor*, 42; Lusane, *Black History*, 106.

17. Felicia Bell, "'The Negroes Alone Work': Enslaved Craftsmen, the Building Trades, and the Construction of the United States Capitol, 1790–1800" (PhD diss., Howard University, 2009, ProQuest Dissertations Publishing, 3387195).

18. Asch and Musgrove, *Chocolate City*, 24; Holland, *Black Men Built the Capitol*, 58.

19. Corrigan, "Imaginary Cruelties?," 7; Hine, *Hine Sight*, 4–5.

20. *National Intelligencer and Washington Advertiser*, February 4, 1805.

21. *National Intelligencer and Washington Advertiser*, May 5, 1802.

22. Walter Johnson, *Soul by Soul*, 29.

23. Edmund S. Morgan, *American Slavery, American Freedom*, x.

24. Allgor, *Parlor Politics*, 6, 134, 138.

25. Margaret Bayard Smith, *First Forty Years*, 45.

26. Walter Johnson, *Soul by Soul*, 21.

27. Jones-Rogers, *They Were Her Property*, 68, 101–2.

28. Schermerhorn, *Business of Slavery*, 39.

29. *National Intelligencer and Washington Advertiser*, April 5, 1802.

30. *National Intelligencer and Washington Advertiser*, May 20, 1801.

31. *National Intelligencer and Washington Advertiser*, February 4, 1807.

32. Walter Johnson, *Soul by Soul*, 185.

33. *National Intelligencer and Washington Advertiser*, October 18, 1804.

34. Deyle, *Carry Me Back*, 167–71, 249.

35. *National Intelligencer and Washington Advertiser*, January 22, 1808.

36. *National Intelligencer and Washington Advertiser*, January 22, 1808.

37. Pargas, *Slavery and Forced Migration in the Antebellum South*, 106; McInnis, *Slaves Waiting for Sale*, 138–39, 197.

38. Walter Johnson, *Soul by Soul*, 138–40, 151.

39. Corrigan, "'Whether They Be,'" 170–71.

40. Deyle, *Carry Me Back*, 144–45, 157, 161–62, 166, 249.

41. *National Intelligencer and Washington Advertiser*, March 5, 1802.

42. Forret, *Williams' Gang*, 209.

43. Bowling, *Creation of Washington, D.C.*, 231.

44. *National Intelligencer and Washington Advertiser*, May 20, 1801.

45. *National Intelligencer and Washington Advertiser*, January 9, 1801.

46. *National Intelligencer and Washington Advertiser*, July 6, 1804.

47. Partridge, "L'Enfant's Methods," 27; Pamela Scott, "L'Enfant's Washington Described."

48. *National Intelligencer and Washington Advertiser*, October 21, 1808.

49. *National Intelligencer and Washington Advertiser*, January 30, 1805.

50. *National Intelligencer and Washington Advertiser*, December 24, 1806.

51. Corrigan, "'Whether They Be,'" 182.

52. Bonnie Martin, "Neighbor-to-Neighbor Capitalism: Local Credit Networks and the Mortgaging of Slaves," in Beckert and Rockman, *Slavery's Capitalism*, 108.

53. Baptist, *Half Has Never*, 179; Schermerhorn, *Business of Slavery*, 42, 127.

54. Deyle, *Carry Me Back*, 166.

55. *National Intelligencer and Washington Advertiser*, December 1, 1806.

56. *National Intelligencer and Washington Advertiser*, February 22, 1805.

57. *National Intelligencer and Washington Advertiser*, September 23, 1805.

58. Holmes, "City Tavern"; Bryan, "Hotels of Washington," 81.

59. Jones-Rogers, "'[S]he Could'"; Walter Johnson, *Soul by Soul*, 143; Wilson, *Freedom at Risk*, 27; Pease and Pease, *They Who Would Be Free*; Whitman, *Price of Freedom*, 82.

60. Baptist, *Half Has Never*, 247–48; Daina Ramey Berry, *Price for Their Pound*, 137; Martin, "Neighbor-to-Neighbor Capitalism," 110–11.

61. Certificate of slavery, November 25, 1820, in Rogers, *Freedom and Slavery Documents*, 113.

62. Bill of sale, November 10, 1820, in Rogers, 112.

63. Bill of sale, November 22, 1820, in Rogers, 112.

64. Hunter, *Bound in Wedlock*, 54, 59.

65. Milly and Cely (or Celia) and their children, July 21, 1818, in Rogers, *Freedom and Slavery Documents*, 126.

66. Eliza, bond, October 3, 1818, in Rogers, 127.

67. Term slavery is also discussed by Seth Rockman in *Scraping By*, 113.

68. Emma, bill of sale, August 11, 1821, in Rogers, *Freedom and Slavery Documents*, 148.

69. Adrienne Davis, "'Don't Let Nobody,'" 119.

70. Deyle, *Carry Me Back*, 35, 39; Jones-Rogers, *They Were Her Property*, 39.

71. Bill of sale [and chattel mortgage], January 22, 1821, in Rogers, *Freedom and Slavery Documents*, 116.

72. Eliza, Matilda, and Sandy, deed of trust, April 9, 1822, in Rogers, 123.

73. Henny and her children, bill of sale, November 16, 1821, in Rogers, 122.

74. Louisa and Mary, bill of sale, January 3, 1822, in Rogers, 118.

75. Fanny and Henry, bill of sale, November 12, 1822, in Rogers, 120–21.

76. Ariela J. Gross, *Double Character*, 42; Kilbourne, *Debt, Investment, Slaves*; Ransom, *Conflict and Compromise*, 145; Wright, *Old South, New South*, 87.

77. Nelly (or Nelsy), Charlotte, and John, bill of sale, July 31, 1821, in Rogers, *Freedom and Slavery Documents*, 149.

78. David, Jenny, Jane, and Francis, bill of sale, September 11, 1821, in Rogers, 149.

79. Jack, Patrick, Salley, Katey, and Sophia, deed of trust, February 12, 1822, in Rogers, 155–56.

80. Maria, Cloe, and Her Children Westly, Caroline, John, and Nance, chattel deed, January 3, 1820, in Rogers, 160.

81. Wilma King, *Stolen Childhood*, 102–9.

82. Milly, bill of sale, June 18, 1819, in Rogers, *Freedom and Slavery Documents*, 197.

83. Bill of sale, May 22, 1821, in Rogers, 115.

84. Bill of sale, January 9, 1821, in Rogers, 116.

85. Jemima, bill of sale, January 24, 1821, in Rogers, 116.

86. Fanny, bill of sale, December 4, 1817, in Rogers, 142.

87. Priscilla (or Priss), bill of sale, January 28, 1817, in Rogers, 124.

88. Kate, bill of sale, July 18, 1822, in Rogers, 120.

89. Mary and Louisa, mortgage, December 12, 1821, in Rogers, 140.

90. Polly, bill of sale, April 29, 1818, in Rogers, 143.

91. Gracy and her children Esther, Edwin, and Marshall, deed [bill of sale], February 4, 1819, in Rogers, 144.

92. Molly and son Sanford and daughter Mary, bill of sale, June 25, 1819, in Rogers, 145.

93. Milly and her children Charity, Henry, and Annette, bill of sale, October 9, 1821, in Rogers, 148–49.

94. Walter Johnson, *Soul by Soul*, 162; Daina Ramey Berry, "'We'm Fus' Rate Bargain': Value, Labor, and Price in a Georgia Slave Community," in Walter Johnson, *Chattel Principle*, 55.

95. Baptist, *Half Has Never*, 26.

96. *National Intelligencer and Washington Advertiser*, December 1, 1806.

97. An Act concerning the District of Columbia, February 27, 1801, Sixth Congress, Second Session, Library of Congress, 103.

98. Bruch, *Digest of the Laws*; District of Columbia, Maryland, Virginia, and the United States, *Slavery Code*.

99. Bowling, *Creation of Washington, D.C.*, 65, 68–69.

100. As early as 1795, Georgetown passed ordinances that empowered local constables to "seize and apprehend" black inhabitants who violated the laws that governed enslaved persons in the District. According to the law, slaves could not assemble in groups, escape bondage, commit acts of theft, drink "spirituous liquors," sell goods to local merchants, or drive carriages over brick-paved footways. Once the seat of the government moved to the Potomac, the slave laws and black codes that existed in Georgetown and Alexandria applied to black inhabitants in the capital. The law permitted slavery and the exchange of enslaved persons. These codes also prohibited black people from activities such as playing games and appearing in the city after ten o'clock at night. Countless enslaved and free black women were funneled in and out of the city jails, courthouses, and workhouses as they attempted to survive a repressive code that only applied to them.

101. Abbott, *Political Terrain*, 33, 64, 181; Eltis, *Economic Growth*, 54; Lightner, *Slavery*, 18–23; Mason, "Slavery Overshadowed."

102. Baptist, *Half Has Never*, 180.

103. Daina Ramey Berry, *Price for Their Pound*, 14.

104. Takagi, *Rearing Wolves*; Wade, *Slavery in the Cities*.

105. Forret, *Williams' Gang*, 217.

106. Jesse Torrey, *Portraiture of Domestic Slavery*, 41.

107. Jesse Torrey, 41.

108. Dickens, *American Notes*, 2:294.

109. Jesse Torrey, 41.

110. Williams H. Williams, *Slavery and Freedom*.

111. Jesse Torrey, *Portraiture of Domestic Slavery*, 48–49.

112. Torrey, 58.

113. Berlin, *Slaves without Masters*, 161.

114. Letitia Woods Brown, *Free Negroes*, 14, 31, 38; Constance McLaughlin Green, *Washington: Village and Capital*, 13.

115. Takagi, *Rearing Wolves*; Wade, *Slavery in the Cities*.

116. Kaye, *Joining Places*, 85.

117. Kaye, 129. See also West, *Family or Freedom*, for analysis of free blacks who sold themselves into slavery to remain connected to family.

118. Kaye, *Joining Places*, 87–88.

119. Allgor, *Perfect Union*, 250.

120. Allgor, *Parlor Politics*, 95–96.

121. Schwartz, *Ties That Bound*, 278.

122. Elizabeth Downing Taylor, *Slave in the White House*, xvi, 28.
123. Alan Taylor, *Internal Enemy*, 3.
124. Schwartz, *Ties That Bound*, 288.
125. Schwartz, 269.
126. Madison to Anna Cutts, July 23, 1818, in *Selected Letters*, 231.
127. Madison to Anna Cutts, July 23, 1818, in *Selected Letters*, 231.
128. Jones-Rogers, *They Were Her Property*, 142.
129. Jones-Rogers, 318.
130. Jennings, *Colored Man's Reminiscences*, v–vi.
131. Madison to Richard Cutts, August 11, 1833, in *Selected Letters*, 300.
132. Allgor, *Parlor Politics*, 1–2.
133. "Notice," *National Intelligencer* (Washington, DC), November 28, 1817.
134. "Treasurer's Office, Washington City," *National Intelligencer and Washington Advertiser*, July 13, 1808.
135. Kaye, *Joining Places*, 85.
136. Still, *Underground Rail Road*, 264–68.
137. Still, 267.

Chapter Two

1. Still, *Underground Rail Road*, 50.
2. Franklin and Schweninger, *Runaway Slaves*, 237, 239–40; Glymph, *Out of the House*, 30, 68; Camp, *Closer to Freedom*, 141; Deborah Gray White, *Ar'n't I a Woman?*, 79; Fox-Genovese, *Within the Plantation Household*, 320; Stevenson, "Gender Conventions, Ideals, and Identity among Antebellum Virginia Slave Women," 174–75, 180.
3. Deborah Gray White, *Ar'n't I a Woman?*, 70.
4. Franklin and Schweninger, *Runaway Slaves*, 210.
5. Blackett, *Captive's Quest for Freedom*, 148.
6. Hine, *Hine Sight*, 28–34; Scott, *Weapons of the Weak*, 329.
7. Camp, *Closer to Freedom*, 42, 58.
8. Forret, *Williams' Gang*, 45–48; McInnis, *Slaves Waiting for Sale*, 93.
9. "Proceedings and Debates of the House of Representatives of the United States at the Second Session of Second Congress, Begun at the City of Philadelphia, November 5, 1792," in *Annals of Congress, 2nd Congress, 2nd Session (November 5, 1792 to March 2, 1793)*, 1414–15.
10. Ames, "National Intelligencer," 72.
11. Corrigan, "Imaginary Cruelties?," 10.
12. Browne, *Dark Matters*, 53–54.
13. "Appropriations and Expenditures," 121.
14. Jesse Torrey, *Portraiture of Domestic Slavery*, 42.
15. Julia King, *George Hadfield*, 103–6.
16. *National Intelligencer and Washington Advertiser*, June 28, 1802.
17. Manion, *Liberty's Prisoners*, 25–27, 138.
18. *National Intelligencer and Washington Advertiser*, March 24, 1802.
19. *National Intelligencer and Washington Advertiser*, March 8, 1802.

20. *National Intelligencer and Washington Advertiser*, March 8, 1802.

21. *National Intelligencer and Washington Advertiser*, May 26, 1802.

22. *National Intelligencer and Washington Advertiser*, August 31, 1804.

23. *National Intelligencer and Washington Advertiser*, March 19, 1806.

24. *National Intelligencer and Washington Advertiser*, February 27, 1805.

25. *National Intelligencer and Washington Advertiser*, February 10, 1806.

26. *National Intelligencer and Washington Advertiser*, July 23, 1804.

27. Stevenson, *Life in Black and White*, 172, 254, 327.

28. *National Intelligencer* (Washington, DC), May 11, 1803.

29. *National Intelligencer*, September 18, 1805.

30. *National Intelligencer and Washington Advertiser*, February 20, 1805.

31. Ibid.

32. Jesse Torrey, *Portraiture of Domestic Slavery*, 41–43; Wilhelmus B. Bryan, "A Fire in an Old Time F Street Tavern and What It Revealed," Records of the Columbia Historical Society, Washington, D.C. 9 (1906): 200.

33. Michael Burton, Kwakiutl L. Dreher, William G. Thomas III, dirs., *Anna* (Lincoln, NE: Salt Marsh Productions, 2018).

34. Baptist, *Half Has Never*, 27–28.

35. Baptist, 25–27.

36. "Ann Williams, Maria Williams, Tobias Williams, & John Williams v. George Miller & George Miller, Jr.," O Say Can You See: Early Washington, D.C., Law & Family, ed. William G. Thomas III et al., University of Nebraska–Lincoln, accessed June 13, 2019, http://earlywashingtondc.org/cases/oscys.caseid.0105; Leepson, *What So Proudly*, 74, 82.

37. Asch and Musgrove, *Chocolate City*, 54–55.

38. Schweninger, *Appealing for Liberty*, 9; Forret, *Williams' Gang*, 131–33.

39. Andrews, *Slavery*, 128–29; Bryan, "Fire," 201; Leepson, *What So Proudly*, 108.

40. McGraw, *African Republic*, 32, 96; Jesse Torrey, *Portraiture of Domestic Slavery*, 85–86. The American Colonization Society promoted the emancipation of slaves on the condition that they relocate to a separate country.

41. Delbanco, *War before the War*, 113–15; Gudmestad, *Troublesome Commerce*, 1–4.

42. "WANTED, a Servant Woman," *Daily Union* (Washington, DC), November 9, 1846.

43. Deyle, *Carry Me Back*, 98.

44. Abdy, *Journal of a Residence*, 382.

45. "SHIP NEWS," *Alexandria Gazette*, December 7, 1836; Forret, *Williams' Gang*, 48.

46. "Alexandria and New Orleans Packets," *Alexandria Gazette*, January 27, 1836.

47. "Alexandria and New Orleans Packets," *Alexandria Gazette*, September 4, 1834.

48. "CASH for 400 Negroes," *Alexandria Gazette*, January 22, 1835.

49. "Southern Hotel," *Phoenix Gazette*, January 23, 1826.

50. Bancroft, *Slave-Trading*, 53–56; Winkle, *Lincoln's Citadel*; "For Sale at Auction," *Alexandria Gazette*, June 20, 1846; "United States Hotel," *Whig Standard*, Washington, DC, November 11, 1844.

51. Snethen, *Black Code*, 28–30.

52. Tomlins, *Cambridge History of Law*, 136.

53. Camp, *Closer to Freedom*, 44.

54. Kaye, *Joining Places*, 136.

55. "Negro Stealing," *Daily Evening Star*, Washington, DC, June 3, 1854; Still, *Underground Rail Road*.

56. Still, *Underground Rail Road*.

57. *National Intelligencer*, December 27, 1823.

58. *National Intelligencer*, October 11, 1823.

59. *National Intelligencer*, September 26, 1828.

60. *National Intelligencer*, August 22, 1826.

61. *National Intelligencer*, April 4, 1820.

62. *National Intelligencer*, March 21, 1829.

63. Constance McLaughlin Green, *Washington: Village and Capital*, 20–21.

64. Kaye, *Joining Places*, 51.

65. Jacob C. White Jr., "Minute Book of the Vigilant Committee of Philadelphia, 1839–1844," n.d., Leon F. Gardiner Collection, Historical Society of Pennsylvania.

66. Harrold, *Subversives*, 66–67; Harrold, *Abolitionists and the South*, 154; E. Fuller Torrey, *Martyrdom*, 80–81.

67. Smallwood, *Narrative*, 32–34.

68. Smallwood, 22–23.

69. Smallwood, 22–23.

70. Smallwood, 22–23.

71. Smallwood, 21.

72. Smallwood, 21.

73. "Ran Away from Subscriber," *Daily National Intelligencer* (Washington, DC), September 2, 1842.

74. Blackett, *Captive's Quest for Freedom*, 6, 21.

75. Margaret Morgan, Fled from Slavery, Hartford County, 1832, SC 5496-8784, Archives of Maryland Biographical Series, Maryland State Archives (hereafter MSA); Finkelman, *Supreme Injustice*, 140–47; Finkelman, "*Prigg v. Pennsylvania*"; Finkelman, "Sorting Out *Prigg v. Pennsylvania*."

76. Lubet, *Fugitive Justice*, 30–32, 308.

77. Still, *Underground Rail Road*, 302.

78. Still, 302.

79. Still, 302–3; Harriet Shepherd, Fled from Slavery, Kent County, Maryland, 1855, SC 5496-51333, Archives of Maryland Biographical Series, MSA.

80. Deyle, *Carry Me Back*, 28, 258.

81. Still, *Underground Rail Road*, 157.

82. Still, 38.

83. Still, 37.

84. Still, *Underground Rail Road*, 501; Harriet Fuller, Fled from Slavery, Kent County, Maryland, 1859, SC 5496-8649, Archives of Maryland Biographical Series, MSA.

85. Still, 501.

86. "Negro Stealing," *Daily Evening Star*, June 3, 1854.

87. Lawson, *Bound for the Promise Land*, 79.

88. May, "Under-theorized and Under-taught," 37, 43.

89. Still, *Underground Rail Road*; Elizabeth Varon, "'Beautiful Providences': William Still, the Vigilance Committee, and Aboliltionists in the Age of Sectionalism," Newman and

Mueller, *Antislavery and Abolition*, 236–42; Lawson, *Bound for the Promised Land*; Sernett, *Harriet Tubman*.

90. Still, *Underground Rail Road*, 10.

91. *Antislavery Reporter* London, March 16, 1853; Still, *Underground Rail Road*, 177–78; Harrold, *Subversives*, 203–4.

92. Still, *Underground Rail Road*, 180–85; Russell, *Operation of the Underground Railroad*, 3:18–21. Also see McCaskill, *Love*, 38–39.

93. Still, *Underground Rail Road*, 180–84.

94. *Baltimore Sun*, September 27–October 26, 1855.

95. Still, *Underground Rail Road*, 156–57.

96. Still, 41.

97. Still, 40.

98. Still, 44.

99. Franklin and Schweninger, *Runaway Slaves*, 43, 216–18.

100. Deyle, *Carry Me Back*, 263–64; Johnson, *Soul by Soul*, 146, 161.

101. "$50 Reward," *The Maryland Journal* Rockville, MD, July 16, 1845, 3; Franklin and Schweninger, *Runaway Slaves*; Meaders, *Advertisements for Runaway Slaves*; Da Costa, *Manual of Modern Surgery*; U.S. Census Bureau, Census Record, MD, for Rachel Davis, 1880, Montgomery County, Sandy Spring, District 119, SM61-324, M 4748-2, p. 3, line 39, MSA; U.S. Census Bureau, Census Record, MD, for Rachel Davis, 1900, Montgomery County, Wheaton, District 65, SM61-416, M 2386-2, p. 2, line 57, MSA.

102. "Six Hundred Dollars Reward," *Baltimore Sun*, February 19, 1851; "$50 Reward," *Baltimore Sun*, August 21, 1851.

103. "Old Waring Homestead Burned," *Baltimore Sun*, April 14, 1896; U.S. Census Bureau, Census Record, MD, for Anna M. Waring, Slaves, 1860, Montgomery County, Clarksburg District, SM61-239, M 7230-2, p. 3, line 19, MSA; *Waring v. Waring*, Montgomery County, Circuit Court, Equity Papers, 1858–1859, T415-22, MSA; Henry B. Waring to Lemuel Clements, Montgomery County Court, Land Records, Liber BS 12, fol. 338, 1843–1845, CE 148-38, MSA; "50 Dollars Reward," *Maryland Gazette and Political Intelligencer* Annapolis, MD, April 27, 1815; "Twenty Dollars Reward," *Daily National Intelligencer*, September 19, 1816; "One Hundred Dollars Reward," *Daily National Intelligencer*, October 28, 1839; "One Hundred Dollars Reward," *Daily National Intelligencer*, April 11, 1842.

104. Angela Davis, "Reflections," 7.

105. Berlin, *Slaves without Masters*, 209.

106. *Daily Union*, August 23, 1847.

Chapter Three

1. *National Intelligencer* (Washington, DC), July 14, 1812.

2. "Susan Bordley v. Anne Tilley," O Say Can You See: Early Washington, D.C., Law & Family, ed. William G. Thomas III et al., University of Nebraska–Lincoln, accessed June 10, 2019, http://earlywashingtondc.org/cases/oscys.caseid.0016.003.

3. Snethen, *Black Code*, 34.

4. Weld, *Power of Congress*, 13. Lord Mansfield argued in the English courts in *Somerset v. Stewart* that "the State of slavery is such a nature, that it is incapable of being introduced, on

any reasons moral or political, but only by positive law." An Act for Establishing the Temporary and Permanent Seat of the Government of the United States, Statutes at Large, 1st Congress, 2nd Session, 1791, Library of Congress, 130; *Howell's State Trials*, 1816, vol. 20, cols. 1–6, 79–82.

5. An act of July 16, 1790, authorized presidential discretion in the location and establishment of the capitol, and Congress to assume residence in the capitol with Maryland and Virginia law prevailing in the respective territories given by each state. Clephane, "Local Aspects of Slavery," 225; District of Columbia and United States, *Slave-Code for the District of Columbia* (1860), LOC.; *Annals of Congress*, Twelfth Congress, First Session, p. 2325; *The Laws of Maryland Made and Passed at a Session of Assembly Begun and Held at the City of Annapolis on Monday the Seventh of November, in the Year of Our Lord One Thousand Seven Hundred and Ninety-Six* (Annapolis, MD: Frederick Green Printer, 1796); Shepherd, *Statutes at Large of Virginia*.

6. Snethen, *Black Code*, 38–39.

7. Snethen, 40–41.

8. Joseph Gales Jr., mayor of Washington, "An Act: Concerning the Negroes, Mulattoes, and Slaves," city ordinance, May 31, 1827, Historical Society of Washington, D.C.; Committee of the District of Columbia, "Free Negroes—District of Columbia," H.R., 19th Cong., 2nd Sess., rep. no. 48, 1–2.

9. Gales, "Act."

10. Gales; Powell, "Statistical Profile."

11. Letitia Woods Brown, *Free Negroes*, 87; Amrita Chakrabarti Myers, *Forging Freedom*, 203.

12. *Georgetown Ordinances of the Corporation of Georgetown* (Georgetown: J. N. Rind, 1834); Georgetown, D.C. Ordinances, etc., *Ordinances of the Corporation of Georgetown: With an Appendix, Containing the Law for Laying Out the Town, the Original and Supplementary Charters, the Act of Cession, and Such Other Laws of Maryland as Relate Immediately to the Town: And Sundry Acts of Congress Relating to the Town and District Generally* (Georgetown, 1821), 31.

13. Cranch, *Code of Laws*, 149, 430; Cranch, *Reports of Cases*, 180–85.

14. An Act concerning the District of Columbia, February 27, 1801, secs. 3, 4, 5.

15. Sean Condon, "The Slave Owner's Family and Manumission in the Post-Revolutionary Chesapeake Tidewater: Evidence from Anne Arundel County Wills, 1790–1820," in Brana-Shute and Sparks, *Paths to Freedom*, eds. Rosemary Brana-Shute and Randy J. Sparks, 336.

16. Schweninger, *Appealing for Liberty*, 211, 288–89; Berlin, *Slaves without Masters*, 33; Letitia Woods Brown, *Free Negroes*, 107–8; Whitman, *Price of Freedom*, 63–67; Grivno, *Gleanings of Freedom*, 38–39, 45.

17. Jennifer L. Morgan, "Partus sequitur ventrem."

18. Millward, *Finding Charity's Folk*, 27.

19. Berlin, *Slaves without Masters*, 79; von Daacke, *Freedom Has a Face*, 75–76; Schweninger, *Appealing for Liberty*, 11.

20. See Letitia Woods Brown, *Free Negroes*, 65, 75–76, 97–98.

21. "Priscilla Queen v. Francis Neale," O Say Can You See: Early Washington, D.C., Law & Family, ed. William G. Thomas III et al., University of Nebraska–Lincoln, accessed June 13, 2019, http://earlywashingtondc.org/cases/oscys.caseid.0025; "Mima Queen & Louisa

Queen v. John Hepburn," O Say Can You See: Early Washington, D.C., Law & Family, ed. William G. Thomas III et al., University of Nebraska–Lincoln, accessed June 13, 2019, http://earlywashingtondc.org/cases/oscys.caseid.0011.

22. Asch and Musgrove, *Chocolate City*, 65; Corrigan, "Making the Most," 94.

23. Schweninger, *Appealing for Liberty*, 67; "Mima Queen."

24. Curtis, *Reports of the Decisions*, 535–36.

25. Leepson, *What So Proudly*, 26–27.

26. Schweninger, *Appealing for Liberty*, 23–24.

27. Mima Queen and Child, Petitioners for Freedom, v. Hepburn, 11 U.S. (7 Cranch) 290, 295 (1813); Newmyer, *John Marshall*, 426.

28. *Mima Queen and Child*, 11 U.S. (7 Cranch) at 296.

29. Schweninger, *Appealing for Liberty*, 11, 67, 125.

30. *Mima Queen and Child*, 11 U.S. (7 Cranch) at 296.

31. Letitia Woods Brown, *Free Negroes*, 65–73; Millward, *Finding Charity's Folk*, 32.

32. Finkelman, *Supreme Injustice*, 114.

33. *Mima Queen and Child*, 11 U.S. (7 Cranch) at 298.

34. *Mima Queen and Child*, 11 U.S. (7 Cranch) at 298.

35. For more information about freedom suits and the Queen family, see "Priscilla Queen v. Francis Neale," O Say Can You See: Early Washington, D.C., Law & Family, ed. William G. Thomas III et al., University of Nebraska–Lincoln, accessed June 13, 2019, http://earlywash ingtondc.org/cases/oscys.caseid.0025; and "Mima Queen." See also Nicholls, "'Squint of Freedom'"; Judith Schaefer, *Becoming Free, Remaining Free*; and Twitty, *Before Dred Scott*, 101.

36. Letitia Woods Brown, *Free Negroes*, 97–98; Amrita Chakrabarti Myers, *Forging Freedom*, 52–53; Condon, "Significance of Group Manumissions"; Gillmer, "Suing for Freedom"; Millward, "'That All Her Increase'"; Walsh, "Rural African Americans"; Calderhead, "Slavery in Maryland."

37. "Mima Queen."

38. Schweninger, *Appealing for Liberty*, 10, 18.

39. Jessica Marie Johnson, "Death Rites as Birthrights," 237.

40. William Thomas III, *Out of the Vineyard*.

41. Schweninger, "Freedom Suits," 37.

42. Jessica Marie Johnson, "Death Rites as Birthrights," 247.

43. Millward, *Finding Charity's Folk*, 36.

44. William G. Thomas III, "The Timing of *Queen v. Hepburn*: An Exploration of African American Networks in the Early Republic," O Say Can You See: Early Washington, D.C., Law & Family, ed. William G. Thomas III et al., University of Nebraska–Lincoln, August 2015, http://earlywashingtondc.org/stories/queen_v_hepburn; Schweninger, *Appealing for Liberty*, 121–25.

45. Berlin, *Slaves without Masters*, 92, 97; von Daacke, *Freedom Has a Face*, 4–7.

46. Dickens, *American Notes*, 62.

47. Cromwell, "First Negro Churches," 65.

48. Asch and Musgrove, *Chocolate City*, 60.

49. John Francis, Cook, Church Records of Union Bethel African Methodist Episcopal Church, July 6, 1838, Box 20-1, Folder 12, Cook Family Papers, Manuscript Division, Moorland Spingarn Research Center, Howard University.

50. Asch and Musgrove, *Chocolate City*, 60.

51. John Francis Cook, History of the Founding of Union Bethel Church, July 6, 1838, Box 20-1, Folders 12 and 13, Cook Family Papers, Manuscript Division, Moorland Spingarn Research Center, Howard University.

52. John Francis Cook, History of the Founding of Union Bethel Church, July 6, 1838, Box 20-1, Folders 12 and 13, Cook Family Papers, Manuscript Division, Moorland Spingarn Research Center, Howard University.

53. John Francis Cook, History of the Founding of Union Bethel Church, July 6, 1838, Box 20-1, Folders 12 and 13, Cook Family Papers, Manuscript Division, Moorland Spingarn Research Center, Howard University.

54. John Francis Cook, History of the Founding of Union Bethel Church, July 6, 1838, Box 20-1, Folders 12 and 13, Cook Family Papers, Manuscript Division, Moorland Spingarn Research Center, Howard University.

55. Greene, "Mount Zion," 65.

56. Greene, 65.

57. *United States v. Dorcas Allen*, Arlington County Judgments, October term 1837, Library of Virginia, Richmond, VA; *Alexandria Gazette*, August 24, 1837; Mann, "'Horrible Barbarity'"; Wilson, *Freedom at Risk*, 12–14, 19, 20, 115; Pease and Pease, *They Who Would Be Free*. Witnesses testified to Dorcas living as a free woman, but her original owner only made a verbal agreement and failed to secure the legal documentation before he died.

58. Deyle, *Carry Me Back*, 110.

59. Deyle, 100.

60. Mary E. Frederickson and Walters, *Gendered Resistance*, 66–67; Hartman, "Seduction"; McLaurin, *Celia, a Slave*; Nikki Marie Taylor, *Driven toward Madness*, chap. 5.

61. Snyder, *Power to Die*, 33; Forret, *Williams' Gang*, 198–99.

62. Mann, "'Horrible Barbarity,'" 8.

63. *United States v. Dorcas Allen*; "United States v. Dorcas Allen," *Alexandria Gazette*, October 13, 1837.

64. Mann, "'Horrible Barbarity,'" 10.

65. Mann, 10.

66. Forret, *Williams' Gang*, 34–35.

67. Lewis, "The Edmondson Family," in *Friends' Review*, 61.

68. For more on self-purchase, see Bernier, "'Never Be Free'"; Whitman, *Price of Freedom*.

69. Emily Edmonson, Fled from Slavery, Washington, District of Columbia, 1848, SC 5496-15206, Archives of Maryland Biographical Series, MSA; Mary Edmonson, Fled from Slavery, Washington, District of Columbia, 1848, SC 5496-15207, Archives of Maryland Biographical Series, MSA; Pacheco, *Pearl*, 131–36; Harrold, *Subversives*, 116–18; Ricks, *Escape on the Pearl*.

70. Pacheco, *Pearl*, 122, 125; Baptist, "'Cuffy'"; Baptist, *Half Has Never*, 242–43; Tadman, *Speculators and Slaves*.

71. "An Appeal for Justice: The Undersigned, a Committee Appointed," *North Star* (Rochester, NY), December 8, 1848.

72. Harrold, *Subversives*, 1, 12.

73. Harrold; "From the Philadelphia North American: The Washington Riot," *National Era* (Washington, DC), April 27, 1848.

74. "The Pearl," June 1848, Criminal Cases of the District of Columbia, Box 20, Record Group 21, National Archives and Records Administration (hereafter NARA).

75. Pacheco, *Pearl*, 236; "From the Philadelphia North American"; Risley, *Abolition and the Press*, 108.

76. Bancroft, "New Orleans," 77; Baptist, *Half Has Never*, 242–43; Walter Johnson, *Soul by Soul*, 113; Tadman, *Speculators and Slaves*.

77. Pacheco, *Pearl*, 136–37.

78. Fletcher, *History of Oberlin College*, vol. 2, 532.

79. Paynter, "Fugitives of the Pearl," 264; Pacheco, *Pearl*, 130–39; Ricks, *Escape on the Pearl*.

80. "The Pearl," June 1848, Criminal Cases of the District of Columbia, Box 20, Record Group 21, NARA; Elizabeth Downing Taylor, *Slave in the White House*, 162–65.

81. Dolley Madison to John Payne Todd, April [24], 1848, in *Selected Letters*, 387.

82. Elizabeth Downing Taylor, *Slave in the White House*, 174–76.

83. Taylor, 148.

84. Taylor, 174–76.

85. Bernier, "'Never Be Free.'"

86. Brandt and Brandt, *In the Shadow*, 51, 59.

87. *National Anti-slavery Standard*, September 8, 1855.

88. Still, *Underground Rail Road*, 261–62.

89. Still, 91.

90. Still, 89.

91. Still, 95.

92. Still, 95.

93. Williamson, *Case of Passmore Williamson*, 22.

94. Brandt and Brandt, *In the Shadow*, 87.

95. Brandt and Brandt, 132, 142.

96. "Opinion of Judge Kane, United States of America, ex Relation *Wheeler vs. Williamson*," *American Law Register* 4 (November 1855): 19.

97. Still, *Underground Rail Road*, 95.

98. Still, 232, 241.

99. *United States vs. Eliza and Henry Butler*, March 1836, and *United States vs. Eliza Butler*, April 15, 1836, Criminal Cases of the District of Columbia, Record Group 21, NARA.

100. *United States vs. Eliza and Henry Butler*, April 15, 1836, Criminal Cases of the District of Columbia, Record Group 21, NARA.

101. All of the prostitution cases in Record Group 21 use a standardized form that includes this language. Criminal Cases of the District of Columbia, Record Group 21, NARA.

102. *United States vs. Ann Simms, Mrs. Wurtz, and Mary Wurtz*, September 1833, Criminal Cases of the District of Columbia, Record Group 21, NARA; Mary Jane Dowd, comp., *Records of the Office of Public Buildings and Public Parks of the National Capital—Record Group 42, Inventory No. 16* (Washington, DC: NARA, 1992); Furgurson, *Freedom Rising*, 13.

103. *United States vs. Ann Simms, Mrs. Wurtz, and Mary Wurtz*, September 1833, Criminal Cases of the District of Columbia, Record Group 21, NARA.

104. *United States vs. Eliza Warner & Eliza Warner the Younger*, November 1833, Criminal Cases of the District of Columbia, Record Group 21, NARA.

105. *United States vs. Ann Johnson and Hannah Contee*, November 1833, and *United States vs. Sally McDaniel, Patty Pallison, and Kell Simpson*, November 1833, Criminal Cases of the District of Columbia, Record Group 21, NARA.

106. *United States vs. Susan Ross*, June 1850, Criminal Cases of the District of Columbia, Record Group 21, NARA.

107. Ball, *To Live an Antislavery Life*, 88.

108. *United States vs. George W. Gray & Celia Gray*, September 1833, and *United States vs. Eliza & Henry Butler*, March 1836, Criminal Cases of the District of Columbia, Record Group 21, NARA.

109. Blair, *I've Got to Make*, 81–82, 90.

110. *United States v. Jane White*, December 1841, Criminal Cases of the District of Columbia, Record Group 21, NARA.

111. *United States v. Ann Joyce*, December 1841, Criminal Cases of the District of Columbia, Record Group 21, NARA.

112. *United States v. Ann Joice*, May 1843, Criminal Cases of the District of Columbia, Record Group 21, NARA.

113. *United States v. Cossa Ducas*, September 1844, Criminal Cases of the District of Columbia, Record Group 21, NARA.

114. *United States v. Jane Holly alias Hanson*, November 1844, Criminal Cases of the District of Columbia, Record Group 21, NARA.

115. *United States v. Ellen Lindsley*, September 1844, Criminal Cases of the District of Columbia, Record Group 21, NARA.

116. "Ellen Lindsley," *American Republican and Baltimore Daily Clipper*, February 7, 1845.

117. *United States v. Ellen Lindsley*, February 1845, Criminal Cases of the District of Columbia, Record Group 21, NARA.

118. Asch and Musgrove, *Chocolate City*, 98.

Chapter Four

1. Sadiq, *Black Girlhood in the Nineteenth Century*, 61–62.

2. Martha S. Jones, *All Bound Up Together*, 32; Cooper, *Beyond Respectability*, 132.

3. Farnham, *Education of the Southern Belle*, 64, 118.

4. For more on the "woman question" and black women in public culture, see Martha S. Jones, *All Bound Up Together*, 5–7.

5. Field, *Struggle for Equal Adulthood*.

6. Preston, "Development of Negro Education," 189; Cornelius, *When I Can Read*, 19; Kammerer, "Uplift in Schools," 309.

7. Department of Education, *Special Report*, 195.

8. Keckly, *Behind the Scenes*, 25; Smallwood, *Narrative*, 14.

9. Cornelius, *When I Can Read*, 31, 34.

10. Douglass, *Narrative*, 82.

11. District of Columbia, Maryland, Virginia, and United States, *Slavery Code*; Snethen, *Black Code*.

12. Biographical details for Harriet Beecher Stowe, n.d. (ca. 1852), Myrtilla Miner Papers, 1825–1950, Manuscript Division, LOC, Reel 2.

13. Cornelius, *When I Can Read*, 62.

14. Snethen, *Black Code*, 40, 55.

15. Dunbar, *Fragile Freedom*, 57.

16. Cornelius, *When I Can Read*, 79.

17. Asch and Musgrove, *Chocolate City*, 44.

18. Preston, "Development of Negro Education," 190–91.

19. Department of Education, *Special Report*, 196.

20. Provine, *District of Columbia*, 154.

21. Department of Education, *Special Report*, 197.

22. Department of Education, 198.

23. Department of Education, 199.

24. Department of Education, 199–200.

25. Jessie Carney Smith, *Notable Black American Women*, 624–25.

26. Asch and Musgrove, *Chocolate City*, 78; Moss, "Education's Inequity," 17, 18, 34; Preston, "Development of Negro Education," 194.

27. Constance McLaughlin Green, *Washington: Village and Capital*, 142–45; "Snow's Epicurean Eating House," advertisement, *National Intelligencer* (Washington, DC), October 26, 1832; entry 47, vol. 16, 1832 tax book, Third and Fourth Wards, Record Group 351, National Archives and Records Administration (hereafter NARA); entry 47, vol. 22, 1834 tax book, Third and Fourth Wards, Record Group 351, NARA; Morley, *Snow-Storm in August*.

28. "Report by A.W. Newton, Supt. Of Colored Schools, Washington, D.C. July 8, 1868," Folder 38, Cook Family Papers, Moorland-Spingarn Research Center, Howard University, Washington, DC; Porter, "Organized Educational Activities," 555–56.

29. Michael Shiner, diary, Michael Shiner Papers, Manuscript/Mixed Material, Reel 1, Library of Congress, 60–61.

30. Shiner, 60–61; "Washington," *Richmond Enquirer*, Richmond, VA, August 18, 1835, LOC.

31. "A Verdict of Guilty," *Alexandria Gazette*, December 14, 1835; entry 6, Case Papers, Box 545, November Term 1835, Record Group 21, NARA; Washington City Dispatch, *Richmond Enquirer*, August 1835; "Mob Violence," *National Intelligencer*, August 14, 1835; Richards, *"Gentlemen of Property and Standing,"* 12.

32. Department of Education, *Special Report*, 212.

33. "The State of the City," *National Intelligencer*, August 14, 1835; Morley, *Snow-Storm in August*.

34. Department of Education, *Special Report*, 201.

35. "Juvenile Plug Uglies," *Evening Star* (Washington, DC), November 12, 1857.

36. Department of Education, *Special Report*, 202.

37. Department of Education, 204.

38. Department of Education, 205.

39. Cyprian Davis, "Black Catholics," 4.

40. Department of Education, *Special Report*, 205.

41. Ball, *To Live an Antislavery Life*, 10, 40, 103.

42. Department of Education, *Special Report*, 205.

43. Harrold, "On the Borders"; Dillon, *Slavery Attacked*; Dorsey, "Gendered History"; Staudenraus, *African Colonization Movement*.

44. Department of Education, *Special Report*, 195.

45. Martha S. Jones, *All Bound Up Together*, 8–10; Higginbotham, *Righteous Discontent*; Dunbar, *Fragile Freedom*.

46. Bay, *White Image*, 42; George M. Frederickson, *Black Image*, 35, 70.

47. Frederick Douglass, "Free Negroes in Virginia," *North Star* (Rochester, NY), 1849.

48. Harrold, *Subversives*, 14–15; Stewart, *Holy Warriors*, 14, 49; Hutton, "Social Morality."

49. Rebecca Moore, "An Essay on Goodness and Sobriety," *Christian Recorder* (Philadelphia), Washington Correspondence, September 12, 1863.

50. For analysis of embodied discourse and the intellectual and activist underpinnings of self-making, see also Cooper, *Beyond Respectability*, 14; and Lindsey, *Colored No More*, chap. 3.

51. Dunbar, *Fragile Freedom*; Ball, *To Live an Antislavery Life*; Sadiq, Black Girlhood in the Nineteenth Century, 52; Harrold, *Subversives*.

52. Moore, "Essay on Goodness and Sobriety."

53. Lasser, "Gender," 336.

54. Welter, "Cult of True Womanhood"; Cott, *Bonds of Womanhood*, 1.

55. Ball, *To Live an Antislavery Life*, 8.

56. For more discussion of advice literature for raising black girls see, Sadiq, *Black Girlhood in the Nineteenth Century*, chap. 3.

57. Dunbar, *Fragile Freedom*, 129–30.

58. Haynes, *Riotous Flesh*, 70.

59. Haynes, 156.

60. Cooper, *Beyond Respectability*, 3; Higginbotham, *Righteous Discontent*; Camp, "Making Racial Beauty in the United States: Toward a History of Black Beauty," in Brier, Downs, and Morgan, *Connexions*, 117.

61. Haynes, *Riotous Flesh*, 158.

62. Nieves, *Architecture of Education*, 11; Karen A. Johnson, *Uplifting the Women*, 164; Graves, *Nannie Helen Burroughs*; McCluskey, *Forgotten Sisterhood*, 6.

63. Farnham, *Education of the Southern Belle*, 60–6; Sadiq, *Black Girlhood in the Nineteenth Century*, 45–46.

64. Jabour, "'Grown Girls, Highly Cultivated,'" 35.

65. Mary Kelley, *Learning to Stand and Speak*, 54.

66. Vinovskis and Bernard, "Beyond Catharine Beecher," 858–59.

67. Baumgartner, "Love and Justice."

68. Null, "Myrtilla Miner's," 256.

69. Farnham, *Education of the Southern Belle*, 113.

70. Charles Grandison Finney, Memoirs of Charles G. Finney (Westwood, NJ: Fleming H. Revell Co., 1908), 78.

71. Myrtilla Miner to Dr. Pharis, July 26, 1847, Myrtilla Miner Papers, 1825–1950, Manuscript Division, Library of Congress, Reel 1.

72. Miner to Pharis.

73. O'Connor, *Myrtilla Miner*, 20; Philip Sheldon Foner and Pacheco, *Three Who Dared*, 146.

74. "A Leaf from History," *Elevator* (San Francisco), September 13, 1873.

75. Biographical details for Harriet Beecher Stow, n.d. (ca. 1852), Myrtilla Miner Papers, 1825–1950, Manuscript Division, LOC, Reel 2.

76. Null, "Myrtilla Miner's," 262.

77. *National Intelligencer*, May 6, 1857.

78. *Daily National Whig*, Washington, DC, April 24, 1849.

79. Provine, "Economic Position," 68.

80. O'Connor, *Myrtilla Miner*, 21.

81. O'Connor, 39.

82. O'Connor, 81; Philip Sheldon Foner and Pacheco, *Three Who Dared*, 137.

83. Philip Sheldon Foner and Pacheco, *Three Who Dared*, 47.

84. O'Connor, *Myrtilla Miner*, 24.

85. O'Connor, 49.

86. Philip Sheldon Foner and Pacheco, *Three Who Dared*, 125.

87. O'Connor, *Myrtilla Miner*, 80; Miner, *School for Colored Girls*, 11.

88. Myrtilla Miner to Newton Miner, March 15, 1852, Papers of Myrtilla Miner, 1825–1950, Manuscript Division, Library of Congress, Reel 1.

89. Mary Thomas to Myrtilla Miner, April 6, 1853, Papers of Myrtilla Miner, 1825–1950, Manuscript Division, Library of Congress, Reel 2.

90. Mary Thomas to Myrtilla Miner, May 11, 1853, Papers of Myrtilla Miner, 1825–1950, Manuscript Division, Library of Congress, Reel 2.

91. Mary Brent to Myrtilla Miner, May 12, 1853, Papers of Myrtilla Miner, 1825–1950, Manuscript Division, Library of Congress, Reel 2.

92. Asch and Musgrove, *Chocolate City*, 101.

93. Kelley, *Learning to Stand and Speak*, 34.

94. Beckett to Myrtilla Miner, July 15, 1854, Papers of Myrtilla Miner, 1825–1950, Manuscript Division, Library of Congress, Reel 2.

95. J. A. Shorter to Myrtilla Miner, May 12, 1853, Papers of Myrtilla Miner, 1825–1950, Manuscript Division, Library of Congress, Reel 2.

96. Marietta Hill to Myrtilla Miner, July 5, 1854, Papers of Myrtilla Miner, 1825–1950, Manuscript Division, Library of Congress, Reel 2.

97. Matilda Jones, "The Widow and Her Children," March 15, 1854, Papers of Myrtilla Miner, 1825–1950, Manuscript Division, Library of Congress, Reel 2.

98. Halttunen, *Confidence Men and Painted Women*, 10.

99. Sarah Shorter to Myrtilla Miner, January 26, 1853, Papers of Myrtilla Miner, 1825–1950, Manuscript Division, Library of Congress, Reel 2.

100. Mary to Myrtilla Miner, February 1, 1853, Papers of Myrtilla Miner, 1825–1950, Manuscript Division, Library of Congress, Reel 2.

101. M. A. Jones, "The Two Little Girls," April 19, 1854, Papers of Myrtilla Miner, 1825–1950, Manuscript Division, Library of Congress, Reel 2.

102. Caroline Elizabeth Brent to Myrtilla Miner, January 12, 1853, Papers of Myrtilla Miner, 1825–1950, Manuscript Division, Library of Congress, Reel 2.

103. Catherine to Myrtilla Miner, January 12, 1853, Papers of Myrtilla Miner, 1825–1950, Manuscript Division, Library of Congress, Reel 2.

104. M. A. to Myrtilla Miner, January 12, 1853, Papers of Myrtilla Miner, 1825–1950, Manuscript Division, Library of Congress, Reel 2.

105. Farnham, *Education of the Southern Belle*, 110.

106. Martha Jane to Myrtilla Miner, January 12, 1853, Papers of Myrtilla Miner, 1825–1950, Manuscript Division, Library of Congress, Reel 2.

107. Varon, *Disunion!*, 297–98.

108. O'Connor, *Myrtilla Miner*, 32.

109. Harrold, *Subversives*, 188; O'Connor, *Myrtilla Miner*, 50.

110. Daniel, "Myrtilla Miner," 41; Wells, "Myrtilla Miner," 368; Mildred Myers, *Miss Emily*, 32–43.

111. O'Connor, *Myrtilla Miner*, 51.

112. O'Connor, *Myrtilla Miner*, 51; See also Jackson, *Force and Freedom*.

113. O'Connor, *Myrtilla Miner*, 55.

114. Philip Sheldon Foner and Pacheco, *Three Who Dared*, 158.

115. Circular prepared by William H. Beecher, December 1856, Papers of Myrtilla Miner, 1825–1950, Manuscript Division, Library of Congress, Reel 2; O'Connor, *Myrtilla Miner*, 62.

116. Philip Sheldon Foner and Pacheco, *Three Who Dared*, 160.

117. Asch and Musgrove, *Chocolate City*, 97.

118. Walter Lenox, editorial, *National Intelligencer*, May 6, 1857.

119. Lenox.

120. Lenox.

121. Asch and Musgrove, *Chocolate City*, 97.

122. Lenox, editorial.

123. Lenox, editorial.

124. Biographical details for Stowe, Papers of Myrtilla Miner, 1825–1950, Manuscript Division, Library of Congress, Reel 2.

125. Hine, Hine Sight, 37; Sadiq, Black Girlhood in the Nineteenth Century, 123–25.

126. Lizzy Snowden to Myrtilla Miner, April 12, 1853, Papers of Myrtilla Miner, 1825–1950, Manuscript Division, Library of Congress, Reel 2.

127. Letter from E. N. Horsford, Cambridge, December 28, 1853, published in *North Star*, January 12, 1855.

128. Mary Thomas to Myrtilla Miner, April 6, 1853, Papers of Myrtilla Miner, 1825–1950, Manuscript Division, Library of Congress, Reel 2.

129. Letter from E. N. Horsford, Cambridge, December 28, 1853, published in *North Star*, January 12, 1855.

130. Thomas to Miner.

131. Farnham, *Education of the Southern Belle*, 3, 28, 64.

132. Jabour, "'Grown Girls, Highly Cultivated,'" 26.

133. Washington Female Institute, in *Boyd's Washington*, 9.

134. Letter from W. H. Channing, Washington, DC, January 7, 1854, published in *North Star*, January 12, 1855.

135. Matilda Jones to Miss Dewey, June 25, 1855, Papers of Myrtilla Miner, 1825–1950, Manuscript Division, Library of Congress, Reel 2.

136. Letter from George W. Sampson, Washington, DC, January 7, 1854, published in *North Star*, January 12, 1855.

137. Department of Education, *Special Report*, 211.

138. Department of Education, *Special Report*, 211.

139. Philip Sheldon Foner and Pacheco, *Three Who Dared*, 189–90.

140. Emma V. Brown to Myrtilla Miner, February 8, 1858, Papers of Myrtilla Miner, 1825–1950, Manuscript Division, Library of Congress, Reel 2.

141. "Colored Schools," *The National Republican*, Washington, DC, May 23, 1862, LOC.

142. Matilda Jones to Myrtilla Miner, April 30, 1858, Papers of Myrtilla Miner, 1825–1950, Manuscript Division, Library of Congress, Reel 2.

143. Jones to Miner.

144. Department of Education, *Special Report*, 216.

145. Du Bois, "How Negroes," 126; for twentieth century treatment of black girlhood, see Marcia Chatelain, *South Side Girls: Growing up in the Great Migration* (Durham: Duke University Press, 2015).

146. Tikia K. Hamilton, "Making a 'Model' System: Race, Education and Politics in the Nation's Capital before *Brown*, 1930–1950" (PhD diss., Princeton University, 2015, ProQuest Dissertations and Theses, 1707675543).

147. Asch and Musgrove, *Chocolate City*, 90.

148. Masur, *Example*, 9–10.

149. "Report on the use of taxes for Colored Primary Schools," n.d. Folder 39, Cook Family Papers, Moorland-Spingarn Research Center, Howard University; Melvin R. Williams, "Blueprint for Change," 376.

150. Daniel, "Myrtilla Miner," 44.

Chapter Five

1. Harrison, *Washington during Civil War*, 24.

2. Von Daacke, *Freedom Has a Face*, 211; Berlin, *Slaves without Masters*, 229.

3. Jessica Marie Johnson and Lindsey, "Searching for Climax," 176, 179.

4. Manion, *Liberty's Prisoners*, 139–40.

5. Clinton, *Public Women*, 10.

6. Hobson, *Uneasy Virtue*, 52.

7. Bynum, *Unruly Women*, 79.

8. *Evening Star* (Washington, DC), March 5, 1862.

9. *Evening Star*, August 25, 1862.

10. Harrison, *Washington during Civil War*, 28. For a discussion of earlier multidirectional commercial networks and mobility among enslaved people during periods of political transformation, see Rashauna Johnson, *Slavery's Metropolis*, 57.

11. Asch and Musgrove, *Chocolate City*, 123.

12. Giesberg, *Sex and the Civil War*, 29; Moulton, *Fight for Interracial Marriage*, 119.

13. Clinton, *Public Women*, 18; Schaefer, *Brothels*, 36–38.

14. Hobson, *Uneasy Virtue*, 16, 29; Harrison, *Washington during Civil War*, 24.

15. Von Daacke, *Freedom Has a Face*, 149; Berlin, *Slave without Masters*, 261–62, 266–67; Hodes, *White Women, Black Men*, 147.

16. Hodes, *White Women, Black Men*, 97.

17. Clinton, *Public Women*, 14, 17.

18. Jacqueline Jones, *Labor of Love*, 30, 38.

19. Letitia Woods Brown, *Free Negroes*, 133–35; Provine, "Economic Position," 63.

20. For histories of early twentieth-century black women's domestic work in Washington, see Clark-Lewis, *Living In, Living Out*; and Elizabeth Clark-Lewis, "Duty and 'Fast Living': The Diary of Mary Johnson Sprow, Domestic Worker," *Washington History* 5, no. 1 (Spring–Summer 1993): 46–65.

21. *Boyd's Directory*, 271.

22. *Boyd's Directory*, 314, 316, 256, 263, 244.

23. Jacqueline Jones, *Labor of Love*, 38, 123, 124.

24. Jones, 51, 273; Keckly, *Behind the Scenes*, 133.

25. Ziparo, *This Grand Experiment*, 31.

26. Ziparo, 29–32, 96, 107, 162.

27. *Boyd's Directory*, 43, 51, 110, 131, 161, 162.

28. Wilma King, *Essence of Liberty*, 77–81.

29. Owens, *Medical Bondage*, 59, 62, 68; Schwartz, *Birthing a Slave*, 57, 312–13.

30. *Boyd's Directory*, 55, 92, 100, 125, 163, 28, 299, 330.

31. Powell, "Statistical Profile," 278; Wilma King, *Essence of Liberty*, 67. For more on nineteenth-century washerwomen, see Hunter, *To 'Joy My Freedom*, chap. 4; and Jacqueline Jones, *Labor of Love*, 104, 128, 142.

32. *Boyd's Directory*, 369–70; Powell, "Statistical Profile," 278.

33. *Evening Star*, June 4, 1861.

34. *Evening Star*, June 4, 1861.

35. *Boyd's Directory*, 148, 300, 321.

36. *Boyd's Directory*, 92.

37. *Boyd's Directory*, 137, 150.

38. *Boyd's Directory*, 186.

39. *Boyd's Directory*, 214.

40. *Boyd's Directory*, 302.

41. Webb, *Laws of the Corporation*, 257. Although this digest was published in 1868, it includes the 1858 Market Ordinances.

42. For Charleston examples, see Marshall, "'They Are Supposed,'" 198–200.

43. *Boyd's Directory*, 259.

44. Morley, *Snow-Storm in August*, 174.

45. *Boyd's Directory*, 239.

46. Kali Gross, *Colored Amazons*, 118.

47. Giesberg, *Sex and the Civil War*, 34.

48. Jim Downs, "With Only a Trace: Same-Sex Sexual Desire and Violence on Slave Plantations, 1607–1865," in Brier, Downs, and Morgan, *Connexions*, 17; Kali Gross, *Colored Amazons*, 84.

49. For examples of African American women's parlor-style houses, see Blair, *I've Got to Make*, 81–82.

50. Criminal Cases of the District of Columbia, Record Group 21, National Archives and Records Administration (hereafter NARA); Mary Jane Dowd, comp., *Records of the Office of Public Buildings and Public Parks of the National Capital—Record Group 42, Inventory No. 16* (Washington, DC: NARA, 1992).

51. Hobson, *Uneasy Virtue*, xiv, 30, 86–87.

52. *United States vs. Eliza Butler,* April 15, 1836, Criminal Cases of the District of Columbia, Record Group 21, NARA.

53. Bynum, *Unruly Women,* 94.

54. *Evening Star,* May 26, 1864.

55. PI 186, Entry 125, Daily Returns of Precincts, 1861–1878, Records of the Metropolitan Police, Records of Washington and D.C., Record Group 351, NARA.

56. Constance McLaughlin Green, *Secret City,* 48–49; Manion, *Liberty's Prisoners,* 86, 99; Wilma King, *Essence of Liberty,* 84.

57. Snethen, *The Black Code of the District of Columbia,* 40.

58. Hobson, *Uneasy Virtue,* 32.

59. Alfers, *Law and Order,* 6–9.

60. PI 186, Entry 125, Daily Returns of Precincts, 1861–1878, Records of the Metropolitan Police, Records of Washington and D.C., Record Group 351, NARA.

61. Winkle, *Lincoln's Citadel,* xii.

62. Asch and Musgrove, *Chocolate City,* 105.

63. Harrison, *Washington during Civil War,* 21–23.

64. Harrison, xiv.

65. Asch and Musgrove, *Chocolate City,* 98, 109, 123 170; Constance McLaughlin Green, *Secret City,* 75; Harrison, *Washington during Civil War,* 28.

66. Constance McLaughlin Green, *Secret City,* 71; Winkle, *Lincoln's Citadel,* 165; Harrison, *Washington during Civil War,* 23.

67. Harrison, *Washington during Civil War,* 309; Furgurson, *Freedom Rising,* 19, 85.

68. "Vice in Washington," *Evening Star,* November 12, 1863.

69. "Prostitution," *National Republican,* Washington, DC, September 12, 1862.

70. Prostitution was obviously not a unique feature of the South but rather was prevalent across the continent, as employment opportunities were limited.

71. "England and Slavery," *Daily National Republican,* December 10, 1860.

72. "Vice in Washington," *Evening Star,* November 12, 1863.

73. Lowry, *Story,* 68, 73–75.

74. "Vice in Washington," *Evening Star,* November 12, 1863.

75. *Evening Star,* September 2, 1864.

76. *National Republican,* September 12, 1862.

77. PI 186, Entry 125, Daily Returns of Precincts, 1861–1878, Records of the Metropolitan Police, Records of Washington and D.C., Record Group 351, NARA.

78. Constance McLaughlin Green, *Washington: Village and Capital,* 259.

79. "Bawdy Houses," report of the Provost Marshal, 22nd Army Corps, District of Columbia, vol. 298, Record Group 393, NARA; Lowry, *Story,* 29.

80. Borchert, *Alley Life in Washington,* 103.

81. Borchert, 5–6, 17.

82. Furgurson, *Freedom Rising,* 14.

83. "Bawdy Houses," report of the Provost Marshal, 22nd Army Corps, District of Columbia, vol. 298, Record Group 393, NARA.

84. "Houses of Ill Fame Closed," *Daily National Republican,* Washington, DC, June 24, 1863, LOC.

85. Harrison, *Washington during Civil War*, 25.

86. Provost Marshal, 22nd Army Corps, District of Columbia, vol. 298, Record Group 393, NARA.

87. "Regular Monthly Meeting of the Young Men's Christian Association of Washington," *National Republican*, October 27, 1862.

88. Giesberg, *Sex and the Civil War*, 4.

89. Regular Monthly Meeting of the Young Men's Christian Association of Washington," *National Republican*, October 27, 1862.

90. "The Trial of Major Burtenett," *Evening Star*, November 7, 1863.

91. "The Trial of Major Burtenett," *Evening Star*, November 7, 1863.

92. "District Criminal Court: Charge of Chief Justice Cartter to the Grand Jury—He Calls Their Attention to the Social Vices of the District—the City in Danger of the Fate of Sodom," *National Republican*, June 20, 1864.

93. Clinton, *Public Women*, 16–20.

94. Clinton, *Public Women and Sexual Politics during the American Civil War*, 14–22; Harper, *Women during the Civil War*, 308; Lowry, *Story*, 29; Massey, *Women in the Civil War*, 73, 77–78.

95. "Local Affairs," *Daily National Republican*, April 20, 1864.

96. Corbin, *Women for Hire*, 9–11, 22–27.

97. Furgurson, *Freedom Rising*, 207; Lowry, *Story*, 64.

98. M704, Sixth Census of the United States, 1840, Roll 35, United States Bureau of the Census 1840, NARA; Corporation of the City of Washington, D.C., Officer of the Register, 1825–1856, RG 351, Records of the Government of the District of Columbia, 1791–1978, NARA; Prints relating to the Estate of Mary Ann Hall, General Photograph Collection, Historical Society of Washington, D.C., Archives, Washington, DC; "The Estate of Mary Ann Hall," *Evening Star*, February 11, 1886.

99. Seifert and Balicki, "Mary Ann Hall's House."

100. Seifert and Balicki; "The Farm of Mary Hall in Alexandria Co.," *Evening Star*, October 21, 1886; "Locals," *Evening Star*, September 20, 1872.

101. "Cyprian Affinities," *Evening Star*, March 13, 1863; "Heavy Raid upon the Fancy, the Big Establishments Attended to Mary Ann Hall and Others of the Elite Marched up to the City Hall," *Evening Star*, January 15, 1864; "Bawdy House Case—Trial of Mary Ann Hall," *Evening Star*, February 19, 1864; *Evening Star*, February 20, 1864; "Criminal Court—Trial of Mary Ann Hall on Charge of Keeping a Bawdy House," *Evening Star*, February 22, 1864; *Evening Star*, March 9, 1864.

102. "Bawdy House Case."

103. *Evening Star*, January 26, 1860.

104. "Another Fancy House Visited," *National Republican*, August 22, 1862.

105. *Daily National Republican*, November 17, 1862.

106. "Prather's Alley," *Evening Star*, Washington, DC, August 5, 1862.

107. "Prather's Alley," *Evening Star*, Washington, DC, August 5, 1862, LOC.

108. *Evening Star*, July 23, 1864.

109. *Evening Star*, July 23, 1864.

110. *National Republican*, September 19, 1862.

111. "Black and White in Company," *National Republican*, September 19, 1862.

112. "Needs Attention," *Evening Star*, Washington, DC, July 23, 1864, LOC.

113. Clinton, *Public Women*, 9–10.

114. Daily Returns of Precincts, PI 186, Entry 125, 1861–1878, Records of the Metropolitan Police, Records of Washington and D.C., Record Group 351, NARA.

115. For a discussion about age and prostitution in other southern cities, see Schaefer, *Brothels*, 48.

116. "A Sad Case of Degradation," *Evening Star*, June 15, 1865.

117. "A Sad Case of Degradation," *Evening Star*, June 15, 1865.

118. "A Fluttering among the Black Ducks," *Evening Star*, October 24, 1863.

119. *National Republican*, July 11, 1862.

120. "Descent upon a den of infamy," *Evening Star*, April 9, 1863.

121. "Rescued," *Evening Star*, December 7, 1861.

122. For examples of this pattern in New Orleans, see Schaefer, *Brothels*, 51.

123. Ziparo, *This Grand Experiment*, 111, 116–17.

124. Daily Returns of Precincts, PI 186, Entry 125, 1861–1878, Records of the Metropolitan Police, Records of Washington and D.C., Record Group 351, NARA.

125. "Breaking Up the Bawdy Houses," *National Republican*, September 22, 1862.

126. Daily Returns of Precincts, PI 186, Entry 125, 1861–1878, Records of the Metropolitan Police, Records of Washington and D.C., Record Group 351, NARA.

127. "Breaking Up."

128. "A Den of Infamy Broken Up," *Daily National Republican*, December 19, 1862.

129. "The Trial of Major Burdenette," *National Republican*, November 5, 1863.

130. PI 186, Entry 125, Daily Returns of Precincts, 1863–1864, District of Columbia Metropolitan Police Force, 1861–1968, Record Group 351, NARA; "Fifth Precinct," *Daily National Republican*, October 21, 1864.

131. For the erasure of white male accountability in illicit sex, see Kali Gross, *Colored Amazons*, 101; and Hodes, *White Women, Black Men*, 145.

132. Beul, *Mysteries and Miseries*.

133. Also known as the "badger game" or "panel game." See Kali Gross, *Colored Amazons*, 72; and Blair, *I've Got to Make*, 74.

134. "Low Bawdy House," *National Republican*, October 9, 1862; "Committed for Court," *Evening Star*, March 27, 1867; "Criminal Court, Judge Fisher Presiding," *National Republican*, December 27, 1866.

135. "United States Cases," *Evening Star*, June 11, 1860; "Given Up," *Evening Star*, June 22, 1860.

136. Fabian, *Card Sharps*, 130–32.

137. "Raid on Liza Crittenden's," *Evening Star*, September 10, 1866; "Breaking Up the Bawdy Houses," *National Republican*, September 22, 1862.

138. "Report of the Chief of Military Patrols and Detectives," *Daily National Republican*, April 5, 1864; "In Earnest," *Evening Star*, April 16, 1866.

139. "Improving," *Evening Star*, January 29, 1866.

Chapter Six

1. Petition of Emeline Wedge, Martha Ann Elizabeth Wedge, George Washington Wedge, and Alice Virginia Thomas, September 8, 1862, United States District Circuit Court for the District of Columbia Relating to Slaves, 1851–1863, Record Group 21, Microfilm M433,

roll 3, National Archives and Records Administration (hereafter NARA); Gates et al., *Oxford Handbook*; Glenn, *Unequal Freedom*.

2. Harrison, *Washington during Civil War*, 116–17.

3. Glymph, *Women's Fight*, chap. 3; Richard Newman, "The Grammar of Emancipation: Putting Final Freedom in Context," in Blight and Downs, *Beyond Freedom*, 13, 17.

4. Kantrowitz, *More Than Freedom*, 389; Moulton, *Fight for Interracial Marriage*, 21.

5. Winkle, *Lincoln's Citadel*, 255–57, 261; Masur, *Example*, 37.

6. Winkle, *Lincoln's Citadel*, xii.

7. Asch and Musgrove, *Chocolate City*, 98.

8. Jasanoff, *Liberty's Exiles*; Alan Taylor, *Internal Enemy*.

9. Downs, *Declarations of Dependence*, 17; Glymph, *Women's Fight*, 106; Varon, *Armies of Deliverance*, 71, 187.

10. Manning, *Troubled Refuge*, 162, 203.

11. Martha S. Jones, *Birthright Citizens*, 37–38, 95. For contextualization of the rights of enslaved women, see Glymph, *Women's Fight*, 9–10.

12. Glymph, *Women's Fight*, 107–8; Amy Murrell Taylor, *Embattled Freedom*, 11.

13. Downs, *Declarations of Dependence*, 114; Manning, *Troubled Refuge*, 32; Thavolia Glymph, "Black Women and Children in the Civil War: Archive Notes," in Blight and Downs, *Beyond Freedom*, 123.

14. Oakes, *Freedom National*, 225–30, 428, 174–77.

15. Petition of Emeline Wedge, Martha Ann Elizabeth Wedge, George Washington Wedge, and Alice Virginia Thomas, December 30, 1862, United States District Circuit Court for the District of Columbia Relating to Slaves, 1851–1863, Record Group 21, Microfilm M433, roll 3, NARA; Edwards, *Legal History*, 83; Oakes, *Freedom National*, 90; Garfield Randall, *Constitutional Problems under Lincoln* (New York: D. Appleton, 1926); Siddali, *From Property to Person*, 37, 175, 233, 259.

16. Act of April 16, 1862 [for the Release of Certain Persons Held to Service or Labor in the District of Columbia], General Records of the United States Government, Record Group 11, NARA.

17. Emancipation Proclamation, January 1, 1863, Presidential Proclamations, 1791–1991, General Records of the United States Government, Record Group 11, NARA.

18. Asch and Musgrove, *Chocolate City*, 114.

19. Cheryl Harris, "Whiteness as Property," 1707, 1714–16. Also see David R. Roediger, "The Pursuit of Whiteness: Property, Terror, and Expansion, 1790–1860," in Morrison and Stewart, *Race and the Early Republic*, 12–13, for precedents in serving the property interests of whites in emancipation.

20. Jones-Rogers, *They Were Her Property*, 164.

21. Petition of Mary Ann Hall, May 7, 1862, Records of the Accounting Officers of the Department of the Treasury, 1775–1978, Record Group 217.6.5, Microfilm 520, Reel 2, NARA; Petition of Harriet White, May 28, 1862, Records of the Accounting Officers of the Department of the Treasury, 1775–1978, Record Group 217.6.5, Microfilm 520, Reel 4, NARA; Petition of George Washington Young, May 21, 1862, Records of the Accounting Officers of the Department of the Treasury, 1775–1978, Records Group 217.6.5, Microfilm 520, Reel 3, NARA.

22. Finkelman, "The Civil War, Emancipation, and the Thirteenth Amendment," 44.

23. Manning, *Troubled Refuge*, 205; Glymph, *Women's Fight*, 97.

24. Records of the Board of Commissioners for the Emancipation of Slaves in the District of Columbia, 1862–1863, Microfilm M520, roll 1, NARA.

25. Edwards, *Gendered Strife and Confusion*, 16.

26. Manning, *Troubled Refuge*, 166–67; Chandra Manning, "Emancipation as State Building from the Inside Out," in Blight and Downs, *Beyond Freedom*, 61–62; Stanley, *From Bondage to Contract*, 140.

27. Elsa Barkley Brown, "Negotiating and Transforming"; Martha S. Jones, *Birthright Citizens*, 11, 152; Pryor, *Colored Travelers*, 72; Isenberg, *Sex and Citizenship*, 71, 94; Kantrowitz, *More Than Freedom*, 5, 63, 188.

28. Downs, *Declarations of Dependence*, 75; Harrison, *Washington during Civil War*, 91–95.

29. Furgurson, *Freedom Rising*, 347; Penningroth, *Claims of Kinfolk*, 120.

30. Masur, *Example*, 36–38.

31. Masur, "African American Delegation," 123.

32. Masur, "African American Delegation," 144; Hahn, *Nation under Our Feet*, 322, 318.

33. Masur, "African American Delegation," 144.

34. Abraham Lincoln, "Address on Colonization to a Deputation of Negroes," in *Collected Works*, 371–73.

35. Lincoln, 371–73.

36. *Christian Recorder*, May 17, 1862; *Christian Recorder*, July 18, 1862; *Washington National Republican*, April 19, 1862; *Washington National Republican*, April 20, 1862; *Washington National Republican*, April 23, 1862.

37. "Colored Men Petitioning to Be Colonized," *Douglass' Monthly*, May 1862, 642.

38. Masur, *Example*, 37.

39. Martha S. Jones, *Birthright Citizens*, 34, 41–45; Constance McLaughlin Green, *Secret City*, 59; Oakes, *Freedom National*, 279.

40. Laura F. Edwards, "Epilogue: Emancipation and the Nation," in Link and Broomall, *Rethinking American Emancipation*, 262–63.

41. Winkle, *Lincoln's Citadel*, 241.

42. Records of the Metropolitan Police Department of the District of Columbia, 1862, Record Group 351, NARA; Harrison, *Washington during Civil War*, 59, 117; John L. Myers, *Senator Henry Wilson*; An Act Providing for the Education of Colored Children in the Cities of Washington and Georgetown, District of Columbia, and for Other Purposes, 12 Stat. 407 (1862); Senate Re. Com. No. 60, 37th Congress, 2nd Session, 1–7, 27, 33–37; Congressional Globe, 37th Congress, 2nd Session, 311 (1862); *Washington National Republican*, January 16, February 14, 1862.

43. Harrison, *Washington during Civil War*, 109.

44. Glymph, "Rose's War"; Susan O'Donovan, "Writing Slavery into Freedom's Stories," in Blight and Downs, *Beyond Freedom*, 32.

45. McCurry, *Confederate Reckoning*, 29.

46. Records of the U.S. District Court for the District of Columbia Relating to Slaves, 1851–1863, section 1, Microfilm M433, roll 1, NARA. Although slaves submitted petitions for manumission certificates in civil suits well before emancipation, the Supplemental Act of July 12, 1862, allowed slaves to secure their freedom upon the refusal of their owners to do so.

47. For exceptions in Maryland for a brief period, see Schweninger, *Appealing for Liberty*, 24.

48. Winkle, *Lincoln's Citadel*, 237.

49. Second Confiscation Act, 12 Stat. 589 (1863).

50. For debates on confiscation acts, see Oakes, *Freedom National*, 118, 133, 226; and Siddali, *From Property to Person*, 132–39.

51. Winkle, *Lincoln's Citadel*, 409.

52. Winkle, 303; Clark-Lewis, *First Freed*, 83; Heather Andrea Williams, *Help Me*, 13, 159; Stanley, "Instead of Waiting."

53. "Liberal Donations for the Contrabands: A Card," *Daily National Republican*, Washington, DC, July 30, 1862.

54. Glymph, "'This Species of Property'"; Masur, *Example*, 63; Manning, "Working for Citizenship"; Downs, *Sick from Freedom*, 132.

55. Petition of Emeline Brown, March 28, 1862, Habeas Corpus Case Records, 1820–1863, of the U.S. District Court for the District of Columbia, Microfilm M434, roll 2, Record Group 21, NARA.

56. Farmer-Kaiser, *Freedwomen*, 29, 93, 170; Frankel, *Freedom's Women*, 74–75, 127–35; Petition of John Brown, November 10, 1862, Habeas Corpus Case Records, 1820–1863, of the U.S. District Court for the District of Columbia, Microfilm M434, roll 2, Record Group 21, NARA..

57. Habeas Corpus Case Records, 1820–1863, of the U.S. District Court for the District of Columbia, Microfilm M434, roll 2, Record Group 21, NARA.

58. "A Case before the Emancipation Commissioners," *National Republican* (Washington, DC), May 29, 1862; Fields, *Slavery and Freedom*, 157–58, 160–61; Takagi, *Rearing Wolves*, 129.

59. Emancipation Proclamation, January 1, 1863, Presidential Proclamations, 1791–1991, General Records of the United States Government, Record Group 11, NARA.

60. Frankel, *Freedom's Women*, 34; Manning, "Emancipation as State Building," 62.

61. Winkle, *Lincoln's Citadel*, 346; Masur, *Example*, 51.

62. Josephine Griffing to Hon. E. M. Staunton, December 27, 1864, in Berlin et al., *Freedom*, 356.

63. Glymph, "Black Women and Children," 124.

64. Harrison, *Washington during Civil War*, 81; Asch and Musgrove, *Chocolate City*, 126–27; Amy Murrell Taylor, *Embattled Freedom*, 115; Downs, *Sick from Freedom*, 162. Edwards, *Gendered Strife and Confusion*, 78.

65. Amy Murrell Taylor, *Embattled Freedom*, 166.

66. Blight, *Slave No More*, 41–43.

67. Testimony of Mrs. Louisa Jane Barker in case of Lucy Ellen Johnson, January 14, 1864, in Berlin et al., *Freedom*, 308.

68. Testimony of Georgiana Willets, January n.d. 1864 in Berlin et al., *Freedom*, 330.

69. Amy Murrell Taylor, *Embattled Freedom*, 128.

70. Testimony of Mrs. Louisa Jane Barker in case of Lucy Ellen Johnson, January 14, 1864, in Berlin et al., *Freedom*, 308–11.

71. Testimony of Georgiana Willets, January n.d. 1864, in Berlin et al., *Freedom*, 330.

72. Glymph, "Black Women and Children," 126–27.

73. Takagi, *Rearing Wolves*, 141.

74. Fields, *Slavery and Freedom*, 138; Statement of Harriet Ann Maria Banks, November 14, 1864, in Berlin et al., *Freedom*, 518–19.

75. Fields, *Slavery and Freedom*, 69.

76. Captain Andrew Stafford to General H. H. Lockwood, November 4, 1864, in Berlin et al., *Freedom*, 511; Farmer-Kaiser, *Freedwomen*, 58; Zip, *Labor of Innocents*, 91.

77. Fields, *Slavery and Freedom*, 35–36.

78. Statement of Jane Kamper, November 14, 1864, Letters Received, in Berlin et al., *Freedom*, 519.

79. Masur, *Example*, 60.

80. John Eaton to William F. Spurgin letter, June n.d. 1865, Records of the Assistant Commissioner for the District of Columbia, Bureau of Refugees, Freedmen, and Abandoned Lands, 1865–1869, Microfilm M1055, roll 1, NARA.

81. "Summary Report of the Destitute," February 6, 1866, Records of the Assistant Commissioner for the District of Columbia, Bureau of Refugees, Freedmen, and Abandoned Lands, 1865–1869, Microfilm M1055, roll 1, NARA.

82. Amy Murrell Taylor, *Embattled Freedom*, 193–96.

83. Manning, "Emancipation as State Building," 60–61.

84. Harrison, *Washington during Civil War*, 85; Masur, *Example*, 51, 68.

85. Amy Murrell Taylor, *Embattled Freedom*, 115.

86. Harriet Jacobs, "Life among the Contrabands," *Liberator*, Boston, MA, September 5, 1862.

87. Jean Fagan Yellin, *The Harriet Jacobs Family Papers* (Chapel Hill: The University of North Carolina Press, 2015), 639.

88. "Life among the Contrabands."

89. Keckly, *Behind the Scenes*, 62. For a nuanced reading of "dependence," see Downs, *Declarations of Dependence*, 216–18.

90. Yellin, *Harriet Jacobs*, 184; Louisa Managed to Finish, "Jacobs School," Harriet Jacobs, Alexandria, January 13, 1865, *Freedmen's Record*, Boston, MA, March 1865, 41.

91. Heather Andrea Williams, *Help Me*, 13, 153–59.

92. John Eaton to Mrs. E. Thomas, July 8, 1865, Records of the Assistant Commissioner for the District of Columbia, Bureau of Refugees, Freedmen, and Abandoned Lands, 1865–1869, Microfilm M1055, roll 1, NARA.

93. John Eaton to Andrew Lallad Esq., July 8, 1865, Records of the Assistant Commissioner for the District of Columbia, Bureau of Refugees, Freedmen, and Abandoned Lands, 1865–1869, Microfilm M1055, roll 1, NARA.

94. Harrison, *Washington during Civil War*, 94.

95. Masur, *Example*, 65.

96. John Eaton on behalf of Mrs. Catherine Green, addressed to an unnamed colonel, August 24, 1865, Records of the Assistant Commissioner for the District of Columbia, Bureau of Refugees, Freedmen, and Abandoned Lands, 1865–1869, Microfilm M1055, roll 1, NARA.

97. John Eaton to Mrs. Betty DeVaughn, August 25, 1865, Records of the Assistant Commissioner for the District of Columbia, Bureau of Refugees, Freedmen, and Abandoned Lands, 1865–1869, Microfilm M1055, roll 21, NARA.

98. John Eaton to Mrs. Betty DeVaughan, August 31, 1865, Records of the Assistant Commissioner for the District of Columbia, Bureau of Refugees, Freedmen, and Abandoned Lands, 1865–1869, Microfilm M1055, roll 21, NARA.

99. Glymph, *Out of the House*, 190–91.

100. Letter to Capt. W.F. Spurgin requesting another letter to Betty DeVaughn, September 1, 1865, Records of the Assistant Commissioner for the District of Columbia, Bureau of Refugees, Freedmen, and Abandoned Lands, 1865–1869, Microfilm M1055, roll 1, NARA.

101. Letter concerning Patsey Berlin, July 8, 1865, Records of the Assistant Commissioner for the District of Columbia, Bureau of Refugees, Freedmen, and Abandoned Lands, 1865–1869, Microfilm M1055, roll 1, NARA.

102. Letter concerning Patsey Berlin.

103. John Eaton on behalf of Mrs. Mary Marshall (no designated recipient listed), July 11, 1865, Records of the Assistant Commissioner for the District of Columbia, Bureau of Refugees, Freedmen, and Abandoned Lands, 1865–1869, Microfilm M1055, roll 1, NARA.

104. John Eaton on behalf of Amelia Hanson, August 31, 1865 (addressed to "Sir" no name), Records of the Assistant Commissioner for the District of Columbia, Bureau of Refugees, Freedmen, and Abandoned Lands, 1865–1869, Microfilm M1055, roll 1, NARA.

105. John Eaton to Mrs. Lucinda Dodson, September 14, 1865, Records of the Assistant Commissioner for the District of Columbia, Bureau of Refugees, Freedmen, and Abandoned Lands, 1865–1869, Microfilm M1055, roll 1, NARA.

106. John Eaton to Charles Mills, September 8, 1865, Records of the Assistant Commissioner for the District of Columbia, Bureau of Refugees, Freedmen, and Abandoned Lands, 1865–1869, Microfilm M1055, roll 1, NARA.

107. Harrison, *Washington during Civil War*, 10–11, 39–40.

108. Dola Ann Jones to John Eaton, August 16, 1865, Records of the Assistant Commissioner for the District of Columbia, Bureau of Refugees, Freedmen, and Abandoned Lands, 1865–1869, Microfilm M1055, roll 21, NARA.

109. John Eaton to the governor of Maryland, September 1, 1865, Records of the Assistant Commissioner for the District of Columbia, Bureau of Refugees, Freedmen, and Abandoned Lands, 1865–1869, Microfilm M1055, roll 1, NARA.

110. John Eaton to President Andrew Johnson, September 12, 1865, Records of the Assistant Commissioner for the District of Columbia, Bureau of Refugees, Freedmen, and Abandoned Lands, 1865–1869, Microfilm M1055, roll 1, NARA.

111. Order from C. H. Howard, February 15, 1866, Records of the Assistant Commissioner for the District of Columbia, Bureau of Refugees, Freedmen, and Abandoned Lands, 1865–1869, Microfilm M1055, roll 1, NARA.

112. Order of Col. John Eaton, September 12, 1865, Records of the Assistant Commissioner for the District of Columbia, Bureau of Refugees, Freedmen, and Abandoned Lands, 1865–1869, Microfilm M1055, roll 1, NARA.

113. Letter from S. N. Clark, August 21, 1865, Records of the Assistant Commissioner for the District of Columbia, Bureau of Refugees, Freedmen, and Abandoned Lands, 1865–1869, Microfilm M1055, roll 1, NARA.

114. Orders from Gen. Howard, February 17, 1866, Records of the Assistant Commissioner for the District of Columbia, Bureau of Refugees, Freedmen, and Abandoned Lands, 1865–1869, Microfilm M1055, roll 1, NARA.

115. Order of John Eaton, November 1, 1865, Records of the Assistant Commissioner for the District of Columbia, Bureau of Refugees, Freedmen, and Abandoned Lands, 1865–1869, Microfilm M1055, roll 1, NARA.

116. Order of S. N. Clark, December 28, 1865, Records of the Assistant Commissioner for the District of Columbia, Bureau of Refugees, Freedmen, and Abandoned Lands, 1865–1869, Microfilm M1055, roll 1, NARA.

117. *Christian Recorder*, August 29, 1863.

118. Letter to Gen. Howard from S.N. Clark, February 6, 1866, Records of the Assistant Commissioner for the District of Columbia, Bureau of Refugees, Freedmen, and Abandoned Lands, 1865–1869, Microfilm M1055, roll 1, NARA.

119. Elizabeth Keckly, "Societies for the Benefit of Contraband," *Christian Recorder*, November 1, 1862.

120. *Christian Recorder*, March 14, 1863.

121. John Eaton to Gen. Howard, June n.d. 1865, Records of the Assistant Commissioner for the District of Columbia, Bureau of Refugees, Freedmen, and Abandoned Lands, 1865–1869, Microfilm M1055, roll 1, NARA.

122. For more on late nineteenth- and early twentieth-century black women's activism, see Lindsey, *Colored No More*.

123. Manning, "Working for Citizenship."

Conclusion

1. Hartman, *Scenes of Subjection*, 176.

2. Mary Brent to Myrtilla Miner, May 12, 1853, Papers of Myrtilla Miner, 1825–1950, Manuscript Division, Library of Congress, Reel 2.

3. Thomas Jefferson to Isaac Tiffany, April 4, 1819, in *Papers of Thomas Jefferson*, 201.

4. Thavolia Glymph, "Black Women and Children in the Civil War," in Blight and Downs, *Beyond Freedom*, 129.

5. Keckly, *Behind the Scenes*.

Bibliography

Archives

Historical Society of Washington, D.C.
  City of Washington Maps
  City of Washington Records
  Letters of Alexandria, D.C., and Alexandria, VA, Officials, 1812–1856
Howard University, Moorland-Spingarn Research Center
  Cook Family Papers
  Fifteenth Street Presbyterian Church
  Israel Metropolitan A.M.E. Church Papers
  Metropolitan A.M.E. Church Papers
  Simms Family Papers
Library of Congress
  American Colonization Society Papers
  Myrtilla Miner Papers
  Michael Shiner Papers
Maryland State Archives
  Newspapers
  Historical and Biographical Series
National Archives and Records Administration
  Records of the Board of Commissioners for the Emancipation of Slaves in
    the District of Columbia, 1862–1863 (Microfilm M520)
  Records of the Bureau of Refugees, Freedmen, and Abandoned Lands
    (Record Group 105)
  Records of the Government of the District of Columbia, Records of
    the Metropolitan Police (Record Group 351)
  Records of the United States House of Representatives (Record Group 233)
  Records of the U.S. District and Other Courts in the District of Columbia
    (Record Group 21)
  Records of the U.S. District Court for the District of Columbia Relating
    to Slaves, 1851–1863 (Microfilm M433)

Digital Sources

National Endowment for the Humanities, National Digital Newspaper Program (U.S.),
  and Library of Congress. Chronicling America: Historic American Newspapers.
  Accessed June 2019. http://chroniclingamerica.loc.gov.

Thomas, William G., III, Kaci Nash, Laura Weakly, Karin Dalziel, and Jessica Dussault. O Say Can You See: Early Washington, D.C., Law & Family. University of Nebraska–Lincoln. Accessed June 2019. http://earlywashingtondc.org.

Periodicals

Baltimore Sun	*National Republican*
Christian Recorder	*New National Era* (Washington, DC)
Constitutional Union	*North Star* (Rochester, NY)
Daily Union	*Washington Evening Star*
Frank Leslie's Illustrated Newspaper	*Washington National Intelligencer*
National Era (Washington, DC)	*Washington National Republican*

Primary Sources

Abdy, Edward Strutt. *Journal of a Residence and Tour in the United States of North America, from April, 1833, to October, 1834.* London: J. Murray, 1835.

Andrews, E. A. *Slavery and the Domestic Slave-Trade in the United States in a Series of Letters Addressed to the Executive Committee of the American Union for the Relief and Improvement of the Colored Race.* Boston: Light and Stearns, 1836.

"Appropriations and Expenditures in the District of Columbia." In *Congressional Serial Set*, 185–212 Washington, DC: U.S. Government Printing Office, 1877.

Berlin, Ira, Barbara J. Fields, Steven F. Miller, Joseph P. Reidy, and Leslie S. Rowland, eds. *Free at Last: A Documentary History of Slavery, Freedom, and the Civil War.* Publications of the Freedmen and Southern Society Project. New York: New Press, 1992.

Berlin, Ira, Thavolia Glymph, Stephen Hahn, Rene Hayden, Steven F. Miller, Joseph P. Reidy, Leslie S. Rowland, and Julie Saville, eds. *Freedom: A Documentary History of Emancipation, 1861–1867.* Ser. 1, vol. 2, *The Wartime Genesis of Free Labor: The Upper South.* New York: Cambridge University Press, 1993.

Boyd's Directory of the District of Columbia for . . . Washington, D.C. Washington, DC: R. L. Polk, 1858.

Boyd's Washington and Georgetown Directory. Washington, DC: Taylor and Maury, 1860.

Bruch, Samuel. *A Digest of the Laws of the Corporation of the City of Washington, to the First of June, 1823.* Washington, DC: James Wilson, 1823.

Cranch, William. *Code of Laws for the District of Columbia.* Washington, DC: Davis and Force, 1819.

———. *Reports of Cases Civil and Criminal in the United States Circuit Court of the District of Columbia, from 1801 to 1841.* 6 vols. New York: Voorhies, 1852–53.

Curtis, B. R. *Reports of the Decisions in the Supreme Court of the United States: With Notes, and a Digest.* Vol. 2. Boston: Little, Brown, 1855.

Da Costa, John Chalmers. *A Manual of Modern Surgery.* Philadelphia: W. B. Saunders, 1894.

Department of Education. *Special Report of the Commissioner of Education on the Condition and Improvement of Public Schools in the District of Columbia, Submitted to the Senate*

June, 1868, and the House, with Additions, June 13, 1870. Washington, DC: Government Printing Office, 1871.

Dickens, Charles. *American Notes for General Circulation.* 2 vols. Boston: Ticknor and Fields, 1867.

District of Columbia, Maryland, Virginia, and the United States. *The Slavery Code of the District of Columbia, Together with Notes and Judicial Decisions Explanatory of the Same.* Washington, DC: L. Towers, 1862.

Douglass, Frederick. *Narrative Life of Frederick Douglass, an American Slave.* Boston: Antislavery Office, 1849.

Jefferson, Thomas. *The Papers of Thomas Jefferson: Retirement Series.* Edited by J. Jefferson Looney. Vol. 14. Princeton, NJ: Princeton University Press, 2018.

Jennings, Paul. *A Colored Man's Reminiscences of James Madison.* Brooklyn: G. C. Beadle, 1865.

Keckly, Elizabeth. *Behind the Scenes; or, Thirty Years a Slave, and Four Years in the White House.* New York: G. W. Carleton, 1868.

Lewis, Enoch, ed. *Friends' Review: A Religious, Literary and Miscellaneous Journal.* Vol. 2. Philadelphia: Tatum, 1849.

Lincoln, Abraham. *Collected Works of Abraham Lincoln.* Edited by Roy P. Basler. Vol. 5. New Brunswick, NJ: Rutgers University Press, 1953.

Madison, Dolley Payne. *The Selected Letters of Dolley Payne Madison.* Edited by David B. Mattern and Holly C. Shulman. Charlottesville: University of Virginia Press, 2003.

Miner, Myrtilla. *School for Colored Girls, Washington, D.C.* Philadelphia: Merihew and Thompson's, 1854.

Provine, Dorothy S. *District of Columbia Free Negro Registers, 1821–1861.* Westminster, MD: Heritage Books, 1996.

Rogers, Helen Hoban, comp. *Freedom and Slavery Documents in the District of Columbia.* District of Columbia Office of the Recorder of Deeds. Baltimore: Gateway, 2007.

Shepherd, Samuel. *The Statutes at Large of Virginia: From October Session 1792 to December Session 1806, Inclusive, in Three Volumes, Being a Continuation of Hening.* Richmond, VA: printed by S. Shepherd, 1835.

Smallwood, Thomas. *A Narrative of Thomas Smallwood, (Colored Man): Giving an Account of His Birth—the Period He Was Held in Slavery—His Release—and Removal to Canada, Etc: Together with an Account of the Underground Railroad.* Toronto: printed by James Stephens, 1851.

Smith, Margaret Bayard. *The First Forty Years of Washington Society: Portrayed by the Family Letters of Mrs. Samuel Harrison Smith (Margaret Bayard) from the Collection of Her Grandson, J. Henley Smith.* New York: Scribner, 1909.

Still, William. *The Underground Rail Road: A Record of Facts, Authentic Narratives, Letters, Etc.* Philadelphia: Porter and Coates, 1872.

Torrey, Jesse. *A Portraiture of Domestic Slavery, in the United States* [. . .]. Philadelphia: published by the author; John Bioren, printer, 1817.

United States. Bureau of the Census. *Population schedules of the second census of the United States, 1800.* District of Columbia. National Archives, 1959.

Webb, William Benning. *The Laws of the Corporation of the City of Washington: Digested and Arranged under Appropriate Heads in Accordance with a Joint Resolution of the City*

Councils, Together with an Appendix, Containing a Digest of the Charter and Other Acts of Congress Concerning the City. Washington, DC: R. A. Waters, 1868.

Weld, Theodore Dwight. *The Power of Congress over the District of Columbia.* New York: American Anti-slavery Society, 1838.

Williamson, Passmore. *Case of Passmore Williamson.* Philadelphia: U. Hunt and Son, 1856.

Secondary Sources

Abbott, Carl. *Political Terrain: Washington, D.C., from Tidewater Town to Global Metropolis.* Chapel Hill: University of North Carolina Press, 1999.

Albert, Alexa. *Brothel: Mustang Ranch and Its Women.* New York: Random House, 2001.

Alexander, Adele Logan. *Ambiguous Lives: Free Women of Color in Rural Georgia, 1789–1879.* Fayetteville: University of Arkansas Press, 1991.

Alfers, Kenneth G. Law and order in the capital city: A history of the Washington Police, 1800–1886. No. 5 George Washington University, 1976.

Allgor, Catherine. *Parlor Politics: In Which the Ladies of Washington Help Build a City and a Government.* Charlottesville: University Press of Virginia, 2000.

———. *A Perfect Union: Dolley Madison and the Creation of the American Nation.* New York: Henry Holt, 2007.

Ames, Williams E. *A History of the National Intelligencer.* Chapel Hill: University of North Carolina Press, 1972.

———. "The National Intelligencer: Washington's Leading Political Newspaper." *Records of the Columbia Historical Society* 66/68 (1966/1968): 71–83.

Arnebeck, Bob. *Slave Labor in the Capital: Building Washington's Iconic Federal Landmarks.* Charleston: History Press, 2014.

Asch, Chris Myers, and George Derek Musgrove. *Chocolate City: A History of Race and Democracy in the Nation's Capital.* Chapel Hill: University of North Carolina Press, 2017.

Ayers, Edward. *In the Presence of Mine Enemies: The Civil War in the Heart of America, 1859–1864.* New York: W. W. Norton, 2004.

Ball, Erica L. *To Live an Antislavery Life: Personal Politics and the Antebellum Black Middle Class.* Athens: University of Georgia Press, 2012.

Bancroft, Frederic. "New Orleans: The Mistress of the Slave Trade." In *The Slavery Experience in the United States,* edited by Irwin Unger and David Reimers. New York: Holt, Rinehart and Winston, 1970.

———. *Slave-Trading in the Old South.* Baltimore: J. H. Furst, 1931.

Baptist, Edward. "'Cuffy,' 'Fancy Maids,' and 'One-Eyed Men': Rape, Commodification, and the Domestic Slave Trade in the United States." *American Historical Review* 106, no. 5 (December 2001): 1619–50.

———. *The Half Has Never Been Told: Slavery and the Making of American Capitalism.* New York: Basic Books, 2014.

Barber, E. Susan. "Depraved and Abandoned Women: Prostitution in Richmond, Virginia, across the Civil War." In *Neither Lady nor Slave: Working Women of the Old South,* edited by Susanna Delfino and Michele Gillespie, 155–73. Chapel Hill: University of North Carolina Press, 2002.

Barth, Gunther. *City People: The Rise of Modern City Culture in Nineteenth-Century America*. New York: Oxford University Press, 1980.

Baumgartner, Kabria. "Love and Justice: African American Women, Education, and Protest in Antebellum New England." *Journal of Social History* 52, no. 3 (Spring 2019): 652–76.

Bay, Mia. *The White Image in the Black Mind: African-American Ideas about White People, 1830–1925*. New York: Oxford University Press, 2000.

Beckert, Sven. *Empire of Cotton: A Global History*. New York: Alfred A. Knopf, 2014.

Beckert, Sven, and Seth Rockman, eds. *Slavery's Capitalism: A New History of American Economic Development*. Philadelphia: University of Pennsylvania Press, 2016.

Bederman, Gail. *Manliness and Civilization: A Cultural History of Gender and Race in the United States, 1880–1917*. Chicago: University of Chicago Press, 1995.

Berlin, Ira. *Many Thousands Gone: The First Two Centuries of Slavery in North America*. Cambridge, MA: Harvard University Press, 2000.

———. *Slaves without Masters: The Free Negro in the Antebellum South*. New York: New Press, 2007.

Bernheimer, Charles. *Figures of Ill Repute: Representing Prostitution in Nineteenth-Century France*. Cambridge, MA: Harvard University Press, 1989.

Bernier, Julia. "'Never Be Free without Trustin' Some Person': Networking and Buying Freedom in the Nineteenth-Century United States." *Slavery and Abolition* 40, no. 2 (2019): 341–60.

Berry, Daina Ramey. *The Price for Their Pound of Flesh: The Value of the Enslaved, from Womb to Grave, in the Building of a Nation*. Boston: Beacon, 2017.

———. *"Swing the Sickle for the Harvest Is Ripe": Gender and Slavery in Antebellum Georgia*. Urbana: University of Illinois Press, 2007.

Berry, Mary Frances. *Military Necessity and Civil Rights Policy: Black Citizenship and the Constitution, 1861–1868*. LaJolla, CA: National University, 1977.

Beul, James William. *Mysteries and Miseries of America's Great Cities: Embracing New York, Washington City, San Francisco, Salt Lake City, and New Orleans*. Saint Louis: Historical Publishing, 1883.

Blackett, Richard J. M. *The Captive's Quest for Freedom: Fugitive Slaves, the 1850 Fugitive Slave Law, and the Politics of Slavery*. Cambridge: Cambridge University Press, 2018.

Blair, Cynthia M. *I've Got to Make My Livin': Black Women's Sex Work in Turn-of-the Century Chicago*. Chicago: University of Chicago Press, 2010.

Bledsoe, Adam, LaToya Eaves, Brian Williams, and Willie Jamaal Wright. Introduction to "II. Black Geographies." Special issue, *Southeastern Geographer* 900 (2018): 1–18.

Blight, David W. *A Slave No More: Two Men Who Escaped to Freedom, Including Their Own Narratives of Emancipation*. Orlando: First Mariner Books, 2007.

———. *The Underground Railroad in History and Memory: Passages to Freedom*. Washington, DC: Smithsonian Books, 2004.

Blight, David W., and Jim Downs, eds. *Beyond Freedom: Disrupting the History of Emancipation*. Athens: University of Georgia Press, 2017.

Borchert, James. *Alley Life in Washington: Family, Community, Religion and Folklife in the City, 1850–1970*. Urbana: University of Illinois Press, 1980.

Bowling, Kenneth. *The Creation of Washington, D.C.: The Idea and Location of the American Capital.* Fairfax, VA: George Mason University Press, 1991.

Boyer, Paul. *Urban Masses and Moral Order in America, 1820–1920.* Cambridge, MA: Harvard University Press, 1978.

Brana-Shute, Rosemary, and Randy J. Sparks, eds. *Paths to Freedom: Manumission in the Atlantic.* Columbia: University of South Carolina Press, 2009.

Brandt, Nat, and Yanna Kroyt Brandt. *In the Shadow of the Civil War: Passmore Williamson and the Rescue of Jane Johnson.* Columbia: University of South Carolina Press, 2007.

Brier, Jennifer, Jim Downs, and Jennifer L. Morgan, eds. *Connexions: Histories of Race and Sex in North America.* Urbana: University of Illinois Press, 2016.

Brown, Elsa Barkley. "Negotiating and Transforming the Public Sphere: African American Political Life in the Transition from Slavery to Freedom." *Public Culture* 7 (Fall 1994): 107–46.

Brown, Elsa Barkley, and Gregg D. Kimball. "Mapping the Terrain of Black Richmond." In *The New African American Urban History*, edited by Kenneth W. Goings and Raymond A. Mohl, 66–115. Thousand Oaks, CA: Sage, 1996.

Brown, Kathleen. *Good Wives, Nasty Wenches, and Anxious Patriarchs: Gender, Race, and Power in Colonial Virginia.* Chapel Hill: University of North Carolina Press, 1996.

Brown, Letitia Woods. *Free Negroes in the District of Columbia, 1790–1846.* New York: Oxford University Press, 1972.

Browne, Simone. *Dark Matters: On the Surveillance of Blackness.* Durham, NC: Duke University Press, 2015.

Bryan, Wilhelmus B. "Hotels of Washington Prior to 1814." *Columbia Historical Society* 7 (1904): 71–106.

Bynum, Victoria E. *Unruly Women: The Politics of Social and Sexual Control in the Old South.* Chapel Hill: University of North Carolina Press, 1992.

Calderhead, William. "Slavery in Maryland in the Age of Revolution, 1775–1790." *Maryland Historical Magazine* 98, no. 3 (Fall 2003): 302–34.

Camp, Stephanie M. H. *Closer to Freedom: Enslaved Women and Everyday Resistance in the Plantation South.* Chapel Hill: University of North Carolina Press, 2004.

———. "Making Racial Beauty in the United States: Toward a History of Black Beauty." In *Connexions: Histories of Race and Sex in North America*, edited by Jennifer Brier, Jim Downs, Jennifer L. Morgan, 113–24. Urbana: University of Illinois Press, 2016.

Carby, Hazel. "Policing the Black Woman's Body in an Urban Context." *Critical Inquiry* 18 (Summer 1992): 738–55.

Castells, Manuel, and Alejandro Portes. "World Underneath: The Origins, Dynamics, and Effects of the Informal Economy." In *The Informal Economy: Studies in Advanced and Less Developed Countries*, edited by Alejandro Portes, Manuel Castells, and Lauren A. Benton, 11–37. Baltimore: Johns Hopkins University Press, 1989.

Clark-Lewis, Elizabeth. *First Freed: Washington, D.C. in the Emancipation Era.* Washington, DC: Howard University Press, 2002.

———. *Living In, Living Out: African American Domestics in Washington, D.C., 1910–1940.* New York: Kodansha International, 1996.

Clephane, Walter C. "The Local Aspects of Slavery in the District of Columbia." *Records of the Columbia Historical Society* 3 (1900): 224–56.

Clinton, Catherine. *Public Women and the Confederacy*. Frank L. Klement Lectures, No. 8. Milwaukee: Marquette University Press, 1999.

Coates, Ta-Nehisi. *We Were Eight Years in Power: An American Tragedy*. New York: Random House, 2018.

Condon, Sean. "The Significance of Group Manumissions in Post-revolutionary Rural Maryland." *Slavery and Abolition* 32, no. 1 (March 2011): 75–89.

Cooper, Brittney C. *Beyond Respectability: The Intellectual Thought of Race Women*. Urbana: University of Illinois Press, 2017.

Corbin, Alain. *Women for Hire: Prostitution and Sexuality in France after 1850*. Cambridge, MA: Harvard University Press, 1996.

Cornelius, Janet Duitsman. *When I Can Read My Title Clear: Literacy, Slavery, and Religion in the Antebellum South*. Columbia: University of South Carolina Press, 1991.

Corrigan, Mary Beth. "Imaginary Cruelties? A History of the Slave Trade in Washington, D.C." *Washington History* 13, no. 2 (Fall/Winter 2001/2002): 4–27.

———. "Making the Most of an Opportunity: Slaves and the Catholic Church in Early Washington." *Washington History* 12, no. 1 (Spring/Summer 2000): 90–101.

———. "'Whether They Be Ours or No, They May Be Heirs of the Kingdom': The Pursuit of Family Ties among Enslaved People in the District of Columbia." In *In the Shadow of Freedom: The Politics of Slavery in the National Capital*, edited by Paul Finkelman and Donald R. Kennon, 169–94. Athens: Ohio University Press, 2011.

Costanzo, Adam. *George Washington's Washington: Visions for the National Capital in the Early American Republic*. Athens: University of Georgia Press, 2018.

Cott, Nancy F. *The Bonds of Womanhood: "Woman's Sphere" in New England, 1780–1835*. New Haven, CT: Yale University Press, 1997.

Cromwell, John W. "The First Negro Churches in the District of Columbia." *Journal of Negro History* 7, no. 1 (January 1922): 64–106.

Curry, Leonard P. *The Free Black in Urban America, 1800–1850: The Shadow of the Dream*. Chicago: University of Chicago Press, 1981.

Daniel, Sadie. "Myrtilla Miner: Pioneer in Teacher Education for Negro Women." *Journal of Negro History* 34, no. 1 (January 1949): 30–45.

Davis, Adrienne. "'Don't Let Nobody Bother Yo' Principle': The Sexual Economy of American Slavery." In *Sister Circle: Black Women and Work*, edited by Sharon Harley and the Black Women and Work Collective, 103–27. New Brunswick, NJ: Rutgers University Press, 2003.

Davis, Angela. "Reflections on the Black Woman's Role in the Community of Slaves." *Black Scholar* 12, no. 6 (November 1981): 2–15.

Davis, Cyprian. "Black Catholics in Nineteenth Century America." *U.S. Catholic Historian* 5, no. 1 (1986): 1–17.

Davis, Madison. *A History of the Washington City Post-Office, from 1795 to 1903*. Lancaster, PA: New Era, 1902.

Delbanco, Andrew. *The War before the War: Fugitive Slaves and the Struggle for America's Soul from the Revolution to the Civil War*. New York: Penguin Books, 2018.

Deyle, Steven. *Carry Me Back: The Domestic Slave Trade in American Life*. New York: Oxford University Press, 2005.

Dillon, Merton L. *Slavery Attacked: Southern Slaves and Their Allies, 1619–1865*. Baton Rouge: Louisiana State University Press, 1990.

Dorsey, Bruce. "A Gendered History of African Colonization in the Antebellum United States." *Journal of Social History* 34, no. 1 (Autumn 2000): 77–103.

Downs, Gregory P. *Declarations of Dependence: The Long Reconstruction of Popular Politics in the South, 1861–1908*. Chapel Hill: University of North Carolina Press, 2011.

Downs, Jim. *Sick from Freedom: African-American Illness and Suffering during the Civil War and Reconstruction*. New York: Oxford University Press, 2012.

Du Bois, W. E. B. "How Negroes Have Taken Advantage of Educational Opportunities Offered by Friends." *Journal of Negro Education* 7, no. 2 (April 1938): 124–31.

Dunaway, Wilma A. *The African-American Family in Slavery and Emancipation*. New York: Cambridge University Press, 2003.

Dunbar, Erica Armstrong. *A Fragile Freedom: African American Women and Emancipation in the Antebellum City*. New Haven, CT: Yale University Press, 2008.

———. *Never Caught: The Washingtons' Relentless Pursuit of Their Runaway Slave, Ona Judge*. New York: Atria Books, 2017.

Edwards, Laura F. *Gendered Strife and Confusion: The Political Culture of Reconstruction*. Urbana: University of Illinois Press, 1997.

———. *A Legal History of the Civil War and Reconstruction: A Nation of Rights*. New York: Cambridge University Press, 2015.

———. *The People and Their Peace: Legal Culture and the Transformation of Inequality in the Post-revolutionary South*. Chapel Hill: University of North Carolina Press, 2008.

Eltis, David. *Economic Growth and the Ending of the Transatlantic Slave Trade*. New York: Oxford University Press, 1987.

Fabian, Ann. *Card Sharps, Dream Books, and Bucket Shops: Gambling in Nineteenth-Century America*. Ithaca, NY: Cornell University Press, 1990.

Farmer-Kaiser, Mary. *Freedwomen and the Freedmen's Bureau: Race, Gender, and Public Policy in the Age of Emancipation*. New York: Fordham University Press, 2010.

Farnham, Christie Anne. *The Education of the Southern Belle: Higher Education and Student Socialization in the Antebellum South*. New York: New York University Press, 1994.

Field, Corrine. *The Struggle for Equal Adulthood: Gender, Race, Age, and the Fight for Citizenship in Antebellum America*. Chapel Hill: University of North Carolina Press, 2014.

Fields, Barbara Jeanne. *Slavery and Freedom on the Middle Ground: Maryland during the Nineteenth Century*. New Haven, CT: Yale University Press, 1985.

Finkelman, Paul. "*Prigg v. Pennsylvania* and Northern State Courts: Anti-slavery Use of a Pro-slavery Decision." *Civil War History* 25 (1979): 5–35.

———. "Sorting Out *Prigg v. Pennsylvania*." *Rutgers Law Journal* 24 (1993): 605–65.

"The Civil War, Emancipation, and the Thirteenth Amendment: Understanding Who Freed the Slaves." In *The Promises of Liberty: The History and Contemporary Relevance of the Thirteenth Amendment*, edited by Alexander Tsesis, 36–57. New York: Columbia University Press, 2010.

———. *Supreme Injustice: Slavery in the Nation's Highest Court*. Cambridge, MA: Harvard University Press, 2018.

Finkelman, Paul, and Donald R. Kennon, eds. *In the Shadow of Freedom: The Politics of Slavery in the National Capital*. Athens: Ohio University Press, 2011.

Fleischner, Jennifer. *Mrs. Lincoln and Mrs. Keckly: The Remarkable Story of the Friendship between a First Lady and a Former Slave*. New York: Broadway Books, 2003.

Fletcher, Robert Samuel. *A History of Oberlin College: From Its Foundation to the Civil War*. Vols. 1–2. New York: Arno, 1971.

Follett, Richard. *The Sugar Masters: Planters and Slaves in Louisiana's Cane World, 1820–1860*. Baton Rouge: Louisiana State University Press, 2005.

Foner, Eric. *Gateway to Freedom: The Hidden History of the Underground Railroad*. New York: W. W. Norton, 2015.

Foner, Philip Sheldon, and Josephine F. Pacheco. *Three Who Dared: Prudence Crandall, Margaret Douglass, Myrtilla Miner: Champions of Antebellum Black Education*. Westport, CT: Greenwood, 1984.

Forret, Jeff. *Williams' Gang: A Notorious Slave Trader and His Cargo of Black Convicts*. New York: Cambridge University Press, 2020.

Fox-Genovese, Elizabeth. *Within the Plantation Household: Black and White Women of the Old South*. Chapel Hill: University of North Carolina Press, 1988.

Frankel, Noralee. *Freedom's Women: Black Women and Families in Civil War Era Mississippi*. Bloomington: Indiana University Press, 1999.

Franklin, John Hope, and Loren Schweninger. *Runaway Slaves: Rebels on the Plantation*. New York: Oxford University Press, 1999.

Frederickson, George M. *The Black Image in the White Mind: The Debate on Afro-American Character and Destiny, 1817–1914*. Middletown, CT: Wesleyan University Press, 1971.

Frederickson, Mary E., and Delores M. Walters. *Gendered Resistance: Women, Slavery, and the Legacy of Margaret Garner*. Urbana: University of Illinois Press, 2013.

Fuentes, Marisa. *Dispossessed Lives: Enslaved Women, Violence, and the Archive*. Philadelphia: University of Pennsylvania Press, 2016.

Furgurson, Ernest. *Freedom Rising: Washington in the Civil War*. New York: Alfred P. Knopf, 2004.

Gaspar, D. Barry, and Darlene Clark Hine, eds. *More Than Chattel: Black Women and Slavery in the Americas*. Bloomington: Indiana University Press, 1996.

Gates, Henry Louis, Jr., Claude Steel, Lawrence D. Bobo, Michael Dawson, Gerald Jaynes, Lisa Crooms-Robinson, and Linda Darling-Hammond, eds. *The Oxford Handbook of African American Citizenship, 1865–Present*. New York: Oxford University Press, 2012.

Genovese, Eugene. *Roll, Jordan, Roll: The World the Slaves Made*. New York: Vintage Books, 1976.

Giesberg, Judith. *Sex and the Civil War: Soldiers, Pornography, and the Making of American Morality*. Chapel Hill: University of North Carolina Press, 2017.

Gilfoyle, Timothy J. *City of Eros: New York City, Prostitution, and the Commercialization of Sex, 1790–1920*. New York: W. W. Norton, 1992.

———. "Prostitutes in History: From Parables of Pornography to Metaphors of Modernity." *American Historical Review* 104, no. 1 (February 1999): 117–41.

Gillette, Howard, Jr. *Between Justice and Beauty: Race, Planning, and the Failure of Urban Policy in Washington, D.C.* Baltimore: Johns Hopkins University Press, 1995.

Gillmer, Jason. "Suing for Freedom: Interracial Sex, Slave Law, and Racial Identity in the Post-revolutionary and Antebellum South." *North Carolina Law Review* 82, no. 2 (January 2004): 535–619.

Glenn, Evelyn Nakano. *Unequal Freedom: How Race and Gender Shaped American Citizenship and Labor.* Cambridge, MA: Harvard University Press, 2000.

Glymph, Thavolia. *Out of the House of Bondage: The Transformation of the Plantation Household.* New York: Cambridge University Press, 2008.

———. "Rose's War and the Gendered Politics of a Slave Insurgency in the Civil War." *Journal of the Civil War Era* 3, no. 4 (December 2013): 501–532.

———. "'This Species of Property': Female Slave Contrabands in the Civil War." In *A Woman's War: Southern Women, Civil War, and the Confederate Legacy,* edited by Edward D. C. Campbell and Kym S. Rice, 55–71. Richmond: Museum of the Confederacy, 1996.

———. *The Women's Fight: The Civil War's Battles for Home, Freedom, and Nation.* Chapel Hill: University of North Carolina Press, 2020.

Gordon-Reed, Annette. *The Hemingses of Monticello: An American Family.* New York: W. W. Norton, 2008.

Graves, Kelisha B. *Nannie Helen Burroughs: A Documentary Portrait of an Early Civil Rights Pioneer, 1900–1959.* South Bend: University of Notre Dame Press, 2019.

Green, Constance McLaughlin. *Secret City: A History of Race Relations in the Nation's Capital.* Princeton, NJ: Princeton University Press, 1962.

———. *Washington: Capital City, 1879–1950.* Princeton, NJ: Princeton University Press, 1962.

———. *Washington: Village and Capital, 1800–1862.* Princeton, NJ: Princeton University Press, 1962.

Green, Elna C. *This Business of Relief: Confronting Poverty in a Southern City, 1740–1940.* Athens: University of Georgia Press, 2003.

Green, Sharony. *Remember Me to Miss Louisa: Hidden Black-White Intimacies in Antebellum America.* DeKalb: Northern Illinois University Press, 2015.

Greene, Dolores Dunmore. "Mount Zion, Washington's Oldest Black Church, Turns 200." *Washington History* 28, no. 2 (Fall 2016): 65–66.

Griffith, Ernest S., and Charles R. Adrian. *A History of American City Government: The Conspicuous Failure, 1870–1900.* New York: Praeger, 1973.

Grivno, Max. *Gleanings of Freedom: Free and Slave Labor along the Mason-Dixon Line, 1790–1860.* Urbana: University of Illinois Press, 2011.

Gross, Ariela J. *Double Character: Slavery and Mastery in Antebellum Southern Courtroom.* Athens: University of Georgia Press, 2006.

Gross, Kali. *Colored Amazons: Crime, Violence, and Black Women in the City of Brotherly Love, 1880–1910.* Durham, NC: Duke University Press, 2006.

Gudmestad, Robert H. *A Troublesome Commerce: The Transformation of the Interstate Slave Trade.* Baton Rouge: Louisiana State University Press, 2003.

Hahn, Steven. *A Nation under Our Feet: Black Political Struggles in the Rural South from Slavery to the Great Migration.* Cambridge, MA: Harvard University Press, 2003.

Halttunen, Karen. *Confidence Men and Painted Women: A Study of Middle-Class Culture in America, 1830–1870.* New Haven, CT: Yale University Press, 1986.

————. "Grounded Histories of Land and Landscape in Early America." *William and Mary Quarterly* 68, no. 4 (October 2011): 513–32.

Harley, Sharon, and the Black Women and Work Collective, eds. *Sister Circle: Black Women and Work.* New Brunswick, NJ: Rutgers University Press, 2003.

Harper, Judith E. *Women during the Civil War: An Encyclopedia.* New York: Taylor and Francis, 2004.

Harris, Cheryl. "Whiteness as Property." *Harvard Law Review* 106, no. 8 (June 1993): 1701–91.

Harris, Leslie M. *In the Shadow of Slavery: African Americans in New York City, 1626–1863.* Chicago: University of Chicago Press, 2003.

Harrison, Robert. *Washington during Civil War and Reconstruction: Race and Radicalism.* New York: Cambridge University Press, 2011.

Harrold, Stanley. "On the Borders of Slavery and Race: Charles T. Torrey and the Underground Railroad." *Journal of the Early Republic* 20, no. 2 (Summer 2000): 273–92.

————. *Subversives: Antislavery Community in Washington, D.C., 1828–1865.* Baton Rouge: Louisiana State University Press, 2003.

Hartman, Saidiya. *Scenes of Subjection: Terror, Slavery, and Self-Making in Nineteenth-Century America.* London: Oxford University Press, 1997.

————. "Seduction and the Ruses of Power." *Callaloo* 19, no. 2 (Spring 1996): 537–60.

————. "Venus in Two Acts." *Small Axe* 26 (2003): 1–14.

Haynes, April R. *Riotous Flesh: Women, Physiology, and the Solitary Vice in Nineteenth-Century American.* Chicago: University of Chicago Press, 2015.

Higginbotham, Evelyn Brooks. "African-American Women's History and the Metalanguage of Race." *Signs* 17, no. 2 (Winter 1992): 251–74.

————. *Righteous Discontent: The Women's Movement in the Black Baptist Church.* Cambridge, MA: Harvard University Press, 1993.

Hine, Darlene Clark. *Hine Sight: Black Women and the Re-construction of American History.* Bloomington: Indiana University Press, 1994.

Hobson, Barbara Meil. *Uneasy Virtue: The Politics of Prostitution and the American Reform Tradition.* New York: Basic Books, 1987.

Hodes, Martha, ed. *Sex, Love, Race: Crossing Boundaries in North American History.* New York: New York University Press, 1999.

————. *White Women, Black Men: Illicit Sex in the Nineteenth-Century South.* New Haven, CT: Yale University Press, 1997.

Holland, Jesse. *Black Men Built the Capitol: Discovering African-American History in and around Washington.* Guilford, CT: Rowman and Littlefield, 2007.

Holmes, Oliver W. "The City Tavern: A Century of Georgetown History, 1796–1898." *Columbia Historical Society* 50 (1980): 1–29.

Hunter, Tera. *Bound in Wedlock: Slave and Free Black Marriage in the Nineteenth Century.* Cambridge: Harvard University Press, 2017.

————. *To 'Joy My Freedom: Southern Women's Lives and Labors after the Civil War.* Cambridge, MA: Harvard University Press, 1991.

Hutton, Frankie. "Social Morality in the Antebellum Black Press." *Journal of Popular Culture* 26, no. 2 (Fall 1992): 71–84.

Isenberg, Nancy. *Sex and Citizenship in Antebellum America*. Chapel Hill: University of North Carolina Press, 1998.

Jabour, Anya. "'Grown Girls, Highly Cultivated': Female Education in an Antebellum Southern Family." *Journal of Southern History* 64, no. 1 (February 1998): 23–64.

Jackson, Kellie Carter. *Force and Freedom: Black Abolitionists and the Politics of Violence*. Philadelphia: University of Pennsylvania Press, 2019.

Jasanoff, Maya. *Liberty's Exiles: American Loyalists in the Revolutionary World*. New York: Knopf, 2011.

Johnson, Claudia D. "That Guilty Third Tier: Prostitution in Nineteenth-Century Theaters." *American Quarterly* 27, no. 5 (December 1975): 575–84.

Johnson, Jessica Marie. "Death Rites as Birthrights in Atlantic New Orleans: Kinship and Race in the Case of *Maria Teresa v. Perine Dauphine*." *Slavery and Abolition* 36 (2015): 233–56.

Johnson, Jessica Marie, and Treva B. Lindsey. "Searching for Climax: Black Erotic Lives in Slavery and Freedom." *Meridians* 12 (2014): 169–95.

Johnson, Karen A. *Uplifting the Women and the Race: The Educational Philosophies and Social Activism of Anna Julia Cooper and Nannie Helen Burroughs*. New York: Routledge, 2013.

Johnson, Rashauna. *Slavery's Metropolis: Unfree Labor in New Orleans during the Age of Revolutions*. New York: Cambridge University Press, 2016.

Johnson, Walter, ed. *The Chattel Principle: Internal Slave Trades in the Americas, 1808–1888*. New Haven, CT: Yale University Press, 2004.

———. "On Agency." *Journal of Social History* 37, no. 1 (Fall 2003): 113–24.

———. *Soul by Soul: Life in the Antebellum Slave Market*. Cambridge, MA: Harvard University Press, 1999.

Johnston, Allan. *Surviving Freedom: The Black Community in Washington, D.C., 1860–1880*. New York: Garland, 1993.

Jones, Jacqueline. *American Work: Four Centuries of Black and White Labor*. New York: W. W. Norton, 1998.

———. *Labor of Love, Labor of Sorrow: Black Women, Work, and the Family from Slavery to Present*. New York: Basic Books, 1985.

Jones, Martha S. *All Bound Up Together: The Woman Question in African American Public Culture, 1830–1900*. Chapel Hill: University of North Carolina Press, 2007.

———. *Birthright Citizens: A History of Race and Rights in Antebellum America*. New York: Cambridge University Press, 2018.

Jones-Rogers, Stephanie E. "'[S]he Could . . . Spare One Ample Breast for the Profit of Her Owner': White Mothers and Enslaved Wet Nurses' Invisible Labor in American Slave Markets." *Slavery and Abolition* 38, no. 2 (2017): 337–55.

———. *They Were Her Property: White Women as Slave Owners in the American South*. New Haven, CT: Yale University Press, 2019.

Kammerer, Elise. "Uplift in Schools and the Church: Abolitionist Approaches to Free Black Education in Early National Philadelphia." *Historical Social Research* 42, no. 1 (2017): 299–319.

Kantrowitz, Stephen. *More Than Freedom: Fighting for Black Citizenship in a White Republic, 1829–1889*. New York: Penguin Books, 2013.

Kapsch, Robert J. *The Potomac Canal: George Washington and the Waterway West.* Morgantown: West Virginia University Press, 2007.

Kaye, Anthony E. *Joining Places: Slave Neighborhoods in the Old South.* Chapel Hill: University of North Carolina Press, 2007.

Kelley, Mary. *Learning to Stand and Speak: Women, Education, and Public Life in America's Republic.* Chapel Hill: University of North Carolina Press, 2006.

Kelley, Robin D. G. *Race Rebels: Culture, Politics, and the Black Working Class.* New York: Free Press, 1994.

Kilbourne, Richard Holcombe. *Debt, Investment, Slaves: Credit Relations in East Feliciana Parish, Louisiana, 1825–1885.* Tuscaloosa: University of Alabama Press, 2014.

King, Julia. *George Hadfield: Architect of the Federal City.* New York: Routledge, 2017.

King, Wilma. *The Essence of Liberty: Free Black Women during the Slave Era.* Columbia: University of Missouri Press, 2006.

———. *Stolen Childhood: Slave Youth in Nineteenth-Century America.* Bloomington: Indiana University Press, 1995.

Kurtz, Michael J. "Emancipation in the Federal City." *Civil War History* 24, no. 3 (1978): 250–67.

Lasser, Carol. "Gender, Ideology, and Class in the Early Republic." *Journal of the Early Republic* 10, no. 3 (Autumn 1990): 331–37.

Lebsock, Suzanne. *The Free Women of Petersburg: Status and Culture in a Southern Town, 1784–1860.* New York: W. W. Norton, 1984.

Lawson, Kate Clifford. *Bound for the Promised Land: Harriet Tubman, Portrait of an American Hero.* New York: Ballantine, 2004.

Leech, Margaret. *Reveille in Washington, 1860–1865.* New York: Harper, 1941.

Leepson, Marc. *What So Proudly We Hailed: Francis Scott Key, a Life.* New York: Palgrave Macmillan, 2014.

Lessoff, Alan. *The Nation and Its City: Politics, "Corruption," and Progress in Washington, D.C., 1861–1902.* Baltimore: Johns Hopkins University Press, 1994.

Lightner, David L. *Slavery and the Commerce Power: How the Struggle against the Interstate Slave Trade Led to the Civil War.* New Haven, CT: Yale University Press, 2006.

Lindsey, Treva. *Colored No More: Reinventing Black Womanhood in Washington, D.C.* Urbana: University of Illinois Press, 2017.

Link, William A., and James J. Broomall, eds. *Rethinking American Emancipation: Legacies of Slavery and the Quest for Black Freedom.* New York: Cambridge University Press, 2016.

Lowry, Thomas P. *Sexual Misbehavior in the Civil War: A Compendium.* Bloomington: Xlibris, 2006.

———. *The Story the Soldiers Wouldn't Tell: Sex in the Civil War.* Mechanicsburg, PA: Stackpole Books, 1994.

Lubet, Steven. *Fugitive Justice: Runaways, Rescuers, and Slavery on Trial.* Cambridge, MA: Harvard University Press, 2010.

Lusane, Clarence. *The Black History of the White House.* San Francisco: City Light Books, 2011.

Lyons, Clare. *Sex among the Rabble: An Intimate History of Gender and Power in the Age of Revolution, Philadelphia, 1730–1830.* Chapel Hill: University of North Carolina Press, 2006.

Malone, Christopher. *Between Freedom and Bondage: Race, Party, and Voting Rights in the Antebellum North.* New York: Routledge, 2008.

Manion, Jen. *Liberty's Prisoners: Carceral Culture in Early America.* Philadelphia: University of Pennsylvania Press, 2015.

Mann, Alison T. "'Horrible Barbarity': The 1837 Murder Trial of Dorcas Allen, a Georgetown Slave." *Washington History* 22, no. 1 (Spring 2015): 3–14.

Manning, Chandra. *Troubled Refuge: Struggling for Freedom in the Civil War.* New York: Alfred A. Knopf, 2016.

———. "Working for Citizenship in Civil War Contraband Camps." *Journal of the Civil War Era* 4, no. 2 (June 2014): 172–204.

Marshall, Amani T. "'They Are Supposed to Be Lurking about the City': Enslaved Women Runaways in Antebellum Charleston." *South Carolina Historical Magazine* 115, no. 3 (July 2014): 188–212.

Mason, Matthew. "Slavery Overshadowed: Congress Debates Prohibiting the Atlantic Slave Trade to the United States, 1806–1807." *Journal of the Early Republic* 20, no. 1 (Spring 2000): 59–81.

Massey, Mary. *Women in the Civil War.* Lincoln: University of Nebraska Press, 1966.

Masur, Kate. "The African American Delegation to Abraham Lincoln: A Reappraisal." *Civil War History* 56, no. 2 (June 2010): 117–44.

———. *An Example for All the Land: Emancipation and the Struggle over Equality in Washington, D.C.* Chapel Hill: University of North Carolina Press, 2010.

———. "'A Rare Phenomenon of Philological Vegetation': The Word 'Contraband' and the Meanings of Emancipation in the United States." *Journal of American History* 93, no. 4 (March 2007): 1050–84.

May, Vivian M. "Under-theorized and Under-taught: Re-examining Harriet Tubman's Place in Women's Studies." *Meridians* 12, no. 2 (2014): 28–49.

McCaskill, Barbara. *Love, Liberation, and Escaping Slavery: William and Ellen Craft in Cultural Memory.* Athens: University of Georgia Press, 2015.

McCluskey, Audrey Tomas. *A Forgotten Sisterhood: Pioneering Black Women Educators and Activists in the Jim Crow South.* Lanham, MD: Rowman and Littlefield, 2014.

McCurry, Stephanie. *Confederate Reckoning: Power and Politics in the Civil War South.* Cambridge, MA: Harvard University Press, 2012.

McGraw, Marie Tyler. *An African Republic: Black and White Virginians in the Making of Liberia.* Chapel Hill: University of North Carolina Press, 2009.

McInnis, Maurie D. "Mapping the Slave Trade in Richmond and New Orleans." *Buildings and Landscapes: Journal of the Vernacular Architecture Forum* 20, no. 2 (Fall 2013): 102–25.

———. *Slaves Waiting for Sale: Abolitionist Art and the American Slave Trade.* Chicago: University of Chicago Press, 2011.

McKittrick, Katherine. *Demonic Grounds: Black Women and the Cartographies of Struggle.* Minneapolis: University of Minnesota Pres, 2006.

McLaurin, Melton Alonza. *Celia, a Slave.* Athens: University of Georgia Press, 1991.

Meaders, Daniel. *Advertisements for Runaway Slaves in Virginia, 1801–1820.* Studies in American History and Culture. London: Routledge, 1997.

Melosh, Barbara, ed. *Gender and American History since 1890.* New York: Routledge, 1993.

Miller-Sommerville, Diane. "Moonlight, Magnolias, and Brigadoon; or 'Almost like Being in Love': Mastery and Sexual Exploitation in Eugene D. Genovese's Plantation South." *Radical History Review* 88 (Winter 2004): 68–82.

Millward, Jessica. *Finding Charity's Folk: Enslaved and Free Black Women in Maryland.* Athens: University of Georgia Press, 2015.

———. "'That All Her Increase Shall Be Free': Enslaved Women's Bodies and the Maryland 1809 Law of Manumission." *Women's History Review* 21, no. 3 (July 2012): 363–78.

Morgan, Edmund S. *American Slavery, American Freedom: The Ordeal of Colonial Virginia.* New York: W. W. Norton, 1975.

Morgan, Jennifer L. *Laboring Women: Reproduction and Gender in the New World Slavery.* Philadelphia: University of Pennsylvania Press, 2004.

———. "Partus sequitur ventrem: Law, Race, and Reproduction in Colonial Slavery." *Small Axe* 22, no. 1 (2018): 1–17.

Morgan, Philip D. *Slave Counterpoint: Black Culture in the Eighteenth-Century Chesapeake and Lowcountry.* Chapel Hill: University of North Carolina Press, 1998.

Morley, Jefferson. *Snow-Storm in August: The Crime That Sparked Washington City's First Race Riot in the Violent Summer of 1835.* New York: Random House, 2012.

Morrison, Michael A., and James Brewer Stewart, eds. *Race and the Early Republic: Racial Consciousness and Nation-Building in the Early Republic.* Lanham, MD: Rowman and Littlefield, 2002.

Moss, Hilary J. *Schooling Citizens: The Struggle for African American Education in Antebellum America.* Chicago: University of Chicago Press, 2009.

"Education's Inequity: Opposition to Black Higher Education in Antebellum Connecticut." *History of Education Quarterly* 46 no. 1 (2006): 16–35.

Moulton, Amber D. *The Fight for Interracial Marriage Rights in Antebellum Massachusetts.* Cambridge, MA: Harvard University Press, 2015.

Myers, Amrita Chakrabarti. *Forging Freedom: Black Women and the Pursuit of Liberty in Antebellum Charleston.* Chapel Hill: University of North Carolina Press, 2011.

Myers, John L. *Senator Henry Wilson and the Civil War.* Lanham, MD: University Press of America, 2008.

Myers, Mildred. *Miss Emily: Emily Howland, Teacher of Freed Slaves, Suffragist and Friend of Susan B. Anthony and Harriet Tubman: With Excerpts from Her Diaries and Letters.* Charlotte Harbor, FL: Tabby House, 1998.

Newman, Richard, and James Mueller, eds. *Antislavery and Abolition in Philadelphia: Emancipation and the Long Struggle for Racial Justice in the City of Brotherly Love.* Baton Rouge: Louisiana State University Press, 2011.

Newmyer, R. Kent. *John Marshall and the Heroic Age of the Supreme Court.* Baton Rouge: Louisiana State University Press, 2007.

Nicholls, Michael. "'The Squint of Freedom': African-American Freedom Suits in Post-revolutionary Virginia." *Slavery and Abolition* 20, no. 2 (1999): 47–62.

Nieves, Angela David. *Architecture of Education: African American Women Design the New South.* Rochester, NY: University of Rochester Press, 2018.

Null, Druscilla J. "Myrtilla Miner's 'School for Colored Girls': A Mirror on Antebellum Washington." *Records of the Columbia Historical Society* 52 (1989): 254–68.

Oakes, James. *Freedom National: The Destruction of Slavery in the United States, 1861–1865.* New York: W. W. Norton, 2013.

O'Connor, Ellen M. *Myrtilla Miner: A Memoir.* Boston: Houghton, Mifflin, 1885.

Onuf, Peter. *Jefferson's Empire: The Language of American Nationhood.* Charlottesville: University of Virginia Press, 2000.

Owens, Deirdre Cooper. *Medical Bondage: Race, Gender, and the Origins of American Gynecology.* Athens: University of Georgia Press, 2017.

Pacheco, Josephine. *The Pearl: A Failed Slave Escape on the Potomac.* Chapel Hill: University of North Carolina Press, 2005.

Pargas, Damian Alan. *Slavery and Forced Migration in the Antebellum South.* New York: Cambridge University Press, 2015.

———. *The Quarters and the Fields: Slave Families in the Non-cotton South.* Gainesville: University Press of Florida, 2010.

Partridge, William T. "L'Enfant's Methods and Features of His Plan for the Federal City." In *Reports and Plans, Washington Region: Supplementary and Technical Data to Accompany Annual Report,* by National Capital Park and Planning Commission, 21–38. Washington, DC: Government Printing Office, 1930.

Paynter, John H. "The Fugitives of the Pearl." *Journal of Negro History* 1, no. 3 (1916): 243–64.

Pease, Jane H., and William H. Pease. *They Who Would Be Free: Blacks' Search for Freedom, 1830–1861.* New York: Atheneum, 1974.

Penningroth, Dylan. *The Claims of Kinfolk: African American Property and Community in the Nineteenth-Century South.* Chapel Hill: University of North Carolina Press, 2003.

Petrik, Paula. "Capitalists with Rooms: Prostitution in Helena, Montana, 1865–1900." *Montana* 21, no. 2 (Spring 1991): 28–40.

Porter, Dorothy. "The Organized Educational Activities of Negro Literary Societies, 1828–1846." *Journal of Negro Education* 5, no. 4 (October 1936): 555–76.

Powell, Frances J. "A Statistical Profile of the Black Family in Washington, D.C., 1850–1880." *Records of the Columbia Historical Society* 52 (1989): 269–88.

Preston, Emmet D., Jr. "The Development of Negro Education in the District of Columbia, 1800–1860." *Journal of Negro Education* 12, no. 2 (Spring 1943): 189–98.

Primus, Richard A. *The American Language of Rights.* New York: Cambridge University Press, 1999.

Provine, Dorothy. "The Economic Position of the Free Blacks in the District of Columbia, 1800–1860." *Journal of Negro History* 58, no. 1 (1973): 61–72.

Pryor, Elizabeth Stordeur. *Colored Travelers: Mobility and the Fight for Citizenship before the Civil War.* Chapel Hill: University of North Carolina Press, 2016.

Radburn, Nicholas. "Keeping 'the Wheel in Motion': Trans-Atlantic Credit Terms, Slave Prices, and the Geography of Slavery in the British Americas, 1755–1807." *Journal of Economic History* 75, no. 3 (September 2015): 660–89.

Rael, Patrick. *Black Identity and Black Protest in the Antebellum North.* Chapel Hill: University of North Carolina Press, 2002.

Ransom, Roger L. *Conflict and Compromise: The Political Economy of Slavery, Emancipation, and the American Civil War.* Cambridge: Cambridge University Press, 1989.

Rhodes, Jane. *Mary Ann Shad Cary: The Black Press and Protest in the Nineteenth Century.* Bloomington: Indiana University Press, 1998.

Richards, Leonard L. *"Gentlemen of Property and Standing": Anti-abolition Mobs in Jacksonian America.* New York: Oxford University Press, 1970.

Ricks, Mary Kay. *Escape on the Pearl: The Heroic Bid for Freedom on the Underground Railroad.* New York: HarperCollins , 2007.

Risley, Ford. *Abolition and the Press: The Moral Struggle against Slavery.* Evanston, IL: Northwestern University Press, 2008.

Robinson, Cedric J. *Black Marxism: The Making of the Black Radical Tradition.* Chapel Hill: University of North Carolina Press, 2000.

Rockman, Seth. *Scraping By: Wage, Labor, Slavery, and Survival in Early Baltimore.* Baltimore: Johns Hopkins University Press, 2009.

Rothman, Adam. *Beyond Freedom's Reach: A Kidnapping in the Twilight of Slavery.* Cambridge, MA: Harvard University Press, 2015.

Rothman, Joshua D. *Flush Times and Fever Dreams: A Story of Capitalism and Slavery in the Age of Jackson.* Athens: University of Georgia Press, 2012.

Russell, Hilary. Final Research Report: The Operation of the Underground Railroad in Washington, D.C., c. 1800–1860. United States: n.p., 2001.

Sadiq, Nazera. *Black Girlhood in the Nineteenth Century.* Urbana: University of Illinois Press, 2016.

Saville, Julie. *The Work of Reconstruction: From Slave to Wage Laborer in South Carolina, 1860–1870.* Cambridge: Cambridge University Press, 1994.

Schaefer, Kelleher Judith. *Becoming Free, Remaining Free: Manumission and Enslavement in New Orleans, 1846–1962.* Baton Rouge: Louisiana State University Press, 2003.

———. *Brothels, Depravity, and Abandoned Women: Illegal Sex in Antebellum New Orleans.* Baton Rouge: Louisiana State University Press, 2009.

Schermerhorn, Calvin. *The Business of Slavery and the Rise of American Capitalism, 1815–1860.* New Haven, CT: Yale University, 2015.

———. *Unrequited Toil: A History of United States Slavery.* Cambridge: Cambridge University Press, 2018.

Schwalm, Leslie A. *A Hard Fight for We: Women's Transition from Slavery to Freedom in South Carolina.* Urbana: University of Illinois Press, 1997.

Schwartz, Marie Jenkins. *Birthing a Slave: Motherhood and Medicine in the Antebellum South.* Cambridge, MA: Harvard University Press, 2009.

———. *Ties That Bound: Founding First Ladies and Slaves.* Chicago: University of Chicago Press, 2017.

Schweninger, Loren. *Appealing for Liberty: Freedom Suits in the South.* New York: Oxford University Press, 2018.

———. "Freedom Suits: African American Women, and the Genealogy of Slavery." *William and Mary Quarterly* 71, no. 1 (January 2014): 35–62.

———. *Weapons of the Weak: Everyday Forms of Peasant Resistance.* New Haven, CT: Yale University Press, 1987.

Scott, James C. *Domination and the Arts of Resistance: Hidden Transcripts.* New Haven, CT: Yale University Press, 1990.

Scott, Pamela. "L'Enfant's Washington Described: The City in the Public Press, 1791–1795." *Washington History* 3, no. 1 (1991): 96–111.

Seifert, Donna J., and Joseph Balicki. "Mary Ann Hall's House." *Historical Archaeology* 39, no. 1 (2005): 59–73.

Sernett, Milton C. *Harriet Tubman: Myth, Memory, and History.* Durham, NC: Duke University Press, 2007.

Sharpe, Christina Elizabeth. *In the Wake: On Blackness and Being.* Durham, NC: Duke University Press, 2016.

Shelden, Rachel A. *Washington Brotherhood: Politics, Social Life, and the Coming of the Civil War.* Chapel Hill: University of North Carolina Press, 2015.

Shklar, Judith. *American Citizenship: The Quest for Inclusion.* Cambridge, MA: Harvard University Press, 1991.

Siddali, Silvana R. *From Property to Person: Slavery and the Confiscation Acts, 1861–1862.* Baton Rouge: Louisiana State University Press, 2005.

Siebert, Wilbert H. "Light on the Underground Railroad." *American Historical Review* 1, no. 3 (April 1896): 455–63.

Sinha, Manisha. *The Slave's Case: A History of Abolition.* New Haven, CT: Yale University Press, 2016.

Smith, Jessie Carney, ed. *Notable Black American Women.* Bk. 2. New York: Gale Research, 1996.

Snethen, Worthington Garrettson. *The Black Code of the District of Columbia, in Force September 1st 1848.* New York: published for the A. and F. Anti-slavery Society by W. Harned, 1848.

Snyder, Terri L. *The Power to Die: Slavery and Suicide in British North America.* Chicago: University of Chicago Press, 2015.

Stanley, Amy Dru. *From Bondage to Contract: Wage Labor, Marriage, and the Market in the Age of Slave Emancipation.* New York: Cambridge University Press, 1998.

———. "Instead of Waiting for the Thirteenth Amendment: The War Power, Slave Marriage, and Inviolate Human Rights." *American Historical Review* 115, no. 3 (June 2010): 732–65.

Stansell, Christine. *City of Women: Sex and Class in New York, 1789–1860.* Urbana: University of Illinois Press, 1987.

Staudenraus, Philip J. *The African Colonization Movement.* New York: Columbia University Press, 1961.

———. *Life in Black and White: Family and Community in the Slave South.* New York: Oxford University Press, 1997.

Stevenson, Brenda. "Gender Conventions, Ideals, and Identity among Antebellum Virginia Slave Women." In *More than Chattel: Black Women and Slavery in the Americas,* edited by David Barry Gaspar and Darlene Clark Hine, 169–190. Bloomington: Indiana University Press, 1996.

Stewart, James Brewer. *Holy Warriors: The Abolitionists and American Slavery.* 2nd ed. New York: Hill and Wang, 1997.

Sylvester, Richard. *District of Columbia Police: A Retrospect of the Police Organizations of the Cities of Washington and Georgetown and the District of Columbia, with Biographical Sketches, Illustrations, and Historic Cases.* Washington, DC: Gibson Bros., 1894.

Tadman, Michael. *Speculators and Slaves: Masters, Traders, and Slaves in the Old South.* Madison: University of Wisconsin Press, 1996.

Takagi, Midori. *Rearing Wolves to Our Own Destruction: Slavery in Richmond Virginia, 1782–1865.* Charlottesville: University of Virginia, 2000.

Tate, Gayle T. *Unknown Tongues: Black Women's Political Activism in the Antebellum Era, 1830–1860.* East Lansing: Michigan State University Press, 2003.

Taylor, Alan. *The Internal Enemy: Slavery and War in Virginia, 1772–1832.* New York: W. W. Norton, 2013.

Taylor, Amy Murrell. *Embattled Freedom: Journeys through the Civil War's Slave Refugee Camps.* Chapel Hill: University of North Carolina Press, 2018.

Taylor, Elizabeth Downing. *A Slave in the White House: Paul Jennings and the Madisons.* New York: Palgrave Macmillan, 2012.

Taylor, Nikki Marie. *Driven toward Madness: The Fugitive Slave Margaret Garner and Tragedy on the Ohio.* Athens: Ohio University Press, 2016.

Thomas, William, III. *Out of the Vineyard: The Freedom Suits and the Families That Challenged American Slavery.* New Haven, CT: Yale University Press, 2020.

Tomlins, Christopher. *The Cambridge History of Law in America.* Vol. 2. New York: Cambridge University Press, 2008.

Tong, Benson. *Unsubmissive Women: Chinese Prostitutes in Nineteenth-Century San Francisco.* Norman: University of Oklahoma Press, 1994.

Torrey, E. Fuller. *The Martyrdom of Abolitionist Charles Torrey.* Baton Rouge: Louisiana State University Press, 2013.

Twitty, Anne. *Before Dred Scott: Slavery and Legal Culture in the American Confluence, 1787–1857.* New York: Cambridge University Press, 2016.

Unger, Irwin, and David Reimers, eds. *The Slavery Experience in the United States.* New York: Holt, Rinehart and Winston, 1970.

Varon, Elizabeth R. *Armies of Deliverance: A New History of the Civil War.* London: Oxford University Press, 2019.

———. *Disunion! The Coming of the American Civil War, 1789–1859.* Chapel Hill: University of North Carolina Press, 2008.

Venaktesh, Sudhir Alladi. *Off the Books: The Underground Economy of the Urban Poor.* Cambridge, MA: Harvard University Press, 2006.

Vinovskis, Maris A., and Richard M. Bernard. "Beyond Catharine Beecher: Female Education in the Antebellum Period." *Signs* 3, no. 4 (Summer 1978): 856–69.

von Daacke, Kirt. *Freedom Has a Face: Race, Identity, and Community.* Charlottesville: University of Virginia, 2012.

Vorenberg, Michael. *Final Freedom: The Civil War, the Abolition of Slavery and the Thirteenth Amendment.* New York: Cambridge University Press, 2001.

Wade, Richard C. *Slavery in the Cities: The South, 1820–1860.* New York: Oxford University Press, 1964.

Walsh, Lorena. "Rural African Americans in the Constitutional Era in Maryland, 1776–1810." *Maryland Historical Magazine* 84, no. 4 (Winter 1989): 327–41.

Wells, Lester Grosvenor. "Myrtilla Miner." *New York History* 24, no. 3 (July 1943): 358–75.

Welter, Barbara. "The Cult of True Womanhood: 1820–1860." *American Quarterly* 18, no. 2 (Summer 1966): 151–74.

West, Emily. *Family or Freedom: People of Color in the Antebellum South.* Lexington: University of Kentucky Press, 2012.

Wheatley, Phillis. *The Collected Works of Phillis Wheatley.* Edited by John C. Shields. New York: Oxford University Press, 1988.

White, Deborah Gray. *Ar'n't I a Woman? Female Slaves in the Plantation South.* New York: Norton, 1985.

Whitman, Stephen T. *The Price of Freedom: Slavery and Manumission in Baltimore and Early National Maryland.* Lexington: University Press of Kentucky, 1997.

Wiencek, Henry. *An Imperfect God: George Washington, His Slaves, and the Creation of America.* New York: Farrar, Straus and Giroux, 2003.

Williams, Eric Eustace. *Capitalism and Slavery.* London: Deutsch, 1964.

Williams, Heather Andrea. *Help Me to Find My People: The African American Search for Family Lost in Slavery.* Chapel Hill: University of North Carolina Press, 2012.

———. *Self-Taught: African American Education in Slavery and Freedom.* Chapel Hill: University of North Carolina Press, 2005.

Williams, Melvin R. "A Blueprint for Change: The Black Community in Washington, D.C. 1860–1870." *Records of the Columbia Historical Society* 71/72 (1971): 359–93.

Williams, William H. *Slavery and Freedom in Delaware, 1639–1865.* Wilmington: Rowman and Littlefield, 1999.

Wilson, Carol. *Freedom at Risk: The Kidnapping of Free Blacks in America, 1780–1865.* Lexington: University Press of Kentucky, 1994.

Winch, Julie. "Philadelphia and the Other Underground Railroad." *Pennsylvania Magazine of History and Biography* 111, no. 1 (January 1987): 3–25.

Winkle, Kenneth J. *Lincoln's Citadel: The Civil War in Washington, D.C.* New York: W. W. Norton, 2013.

Wolcott, Victoria W. "Bible, Bath, and Broom: Nannie Helen Burrough's National Training School and African-American Racial Uplift." *Journal of Women's History* 9, no. 1 (Spring): 88–110.

Wright, Gavin. *Old South, New South: Revolutions in the Southern Economy since the Civil War.* New York: Basic Books, 1986.

———. *Slavery and American Economic Development.* Baton Rouge: Louisiana State University Press, 2006.

———. *The Harriet Jacobs Family Papers.* Chapel Hill: University of North Carolina Press, 2015.

Yellin, Jean Fagan. *Harriet Jacobs: A Life.* New York: Basic Civitas Books, 2004.

Zip, Karin L. *Labor of Innocents: Forced Apprenticeship in North Carolina, 1715–1919.* Baton Rouge: Louisiana State University Press, 2005.

Ziparo, Jessica. *This Grand Experiment: When Women Entered the Federal Workforce in Civil War-Era Washington, D.C.* Chapel Hill: University of North Carolina Press, 2017.

Index

Note: Illustrations are indicated by page numbers in *italics*.